The Girl with the Sanpaku Eyes, vol. 1

Story and Art by Shunsuke Sorato

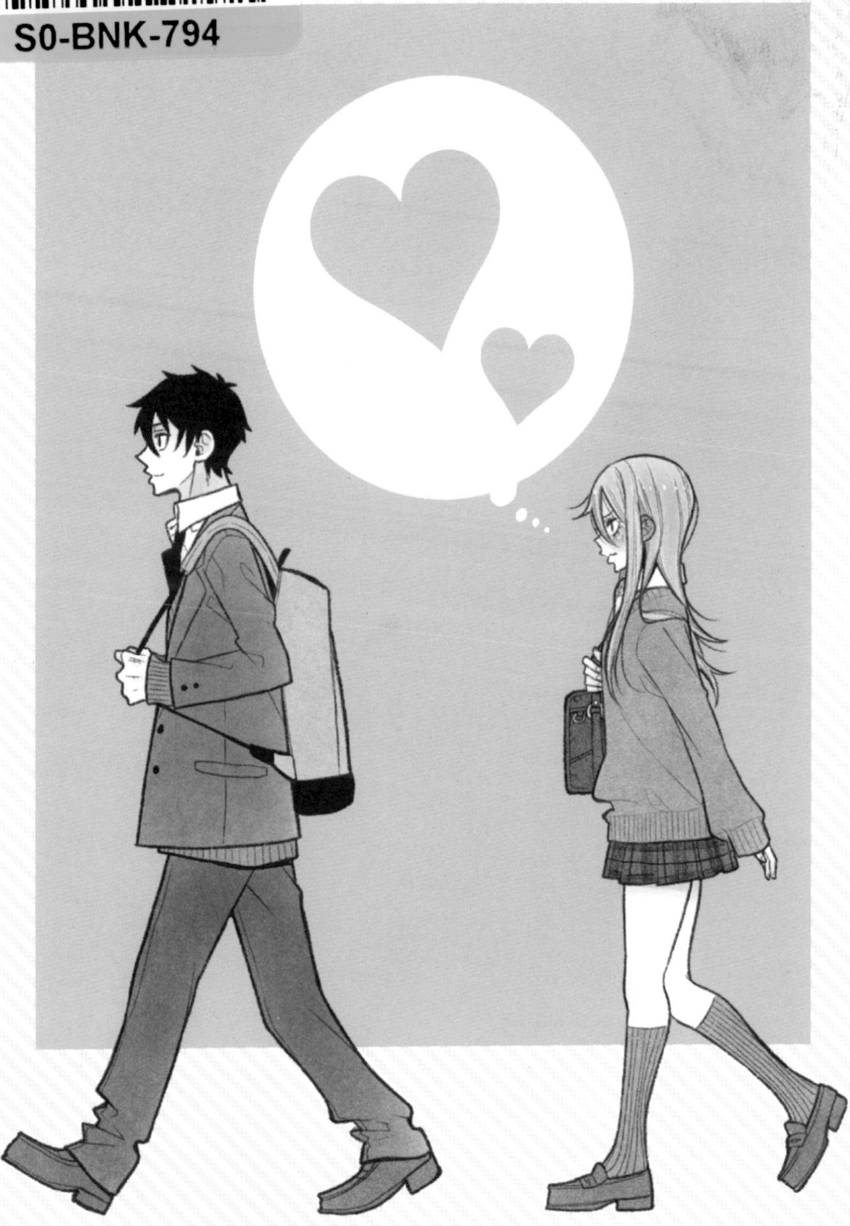

LOVE

Contents

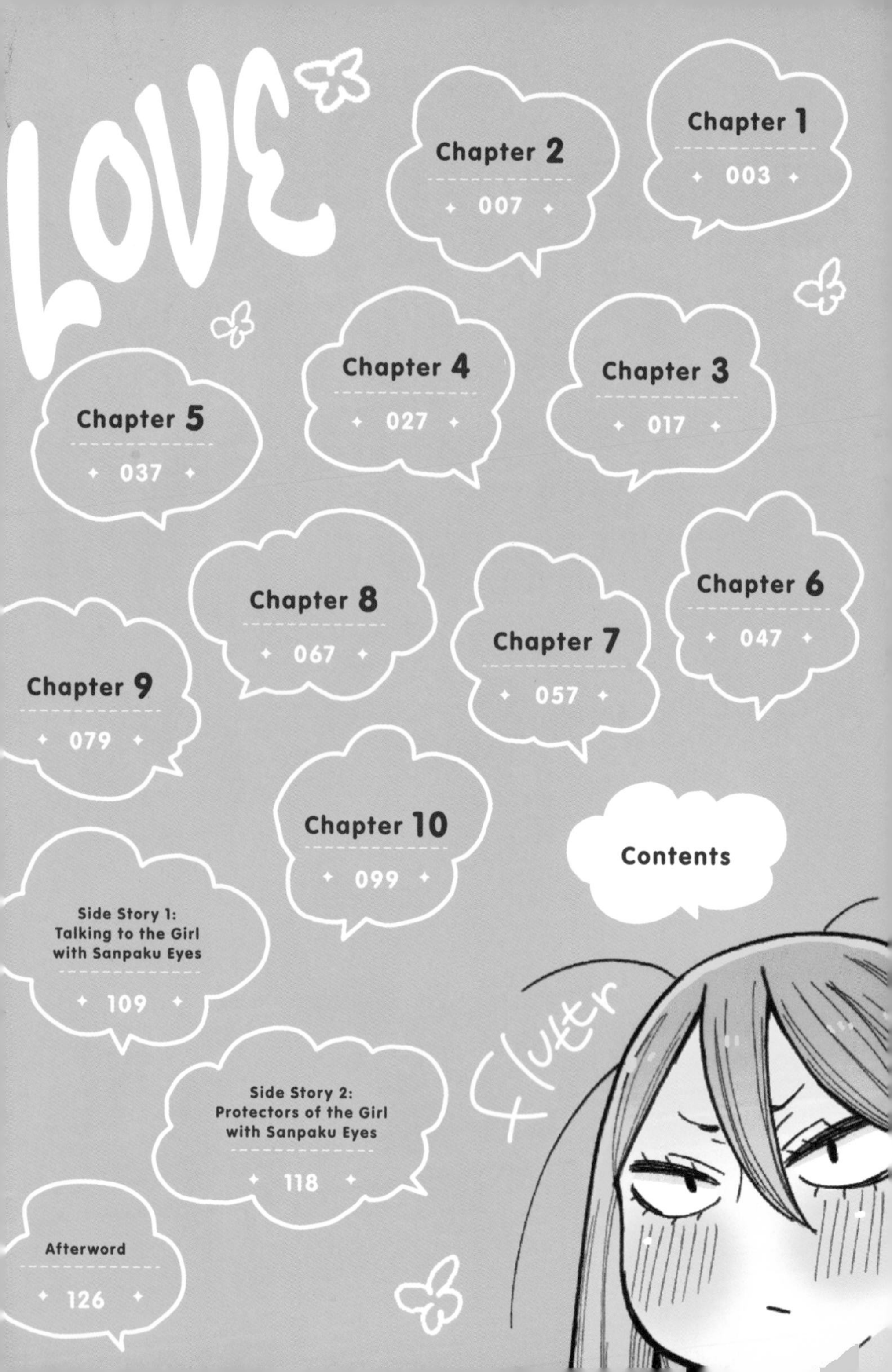

Flutter

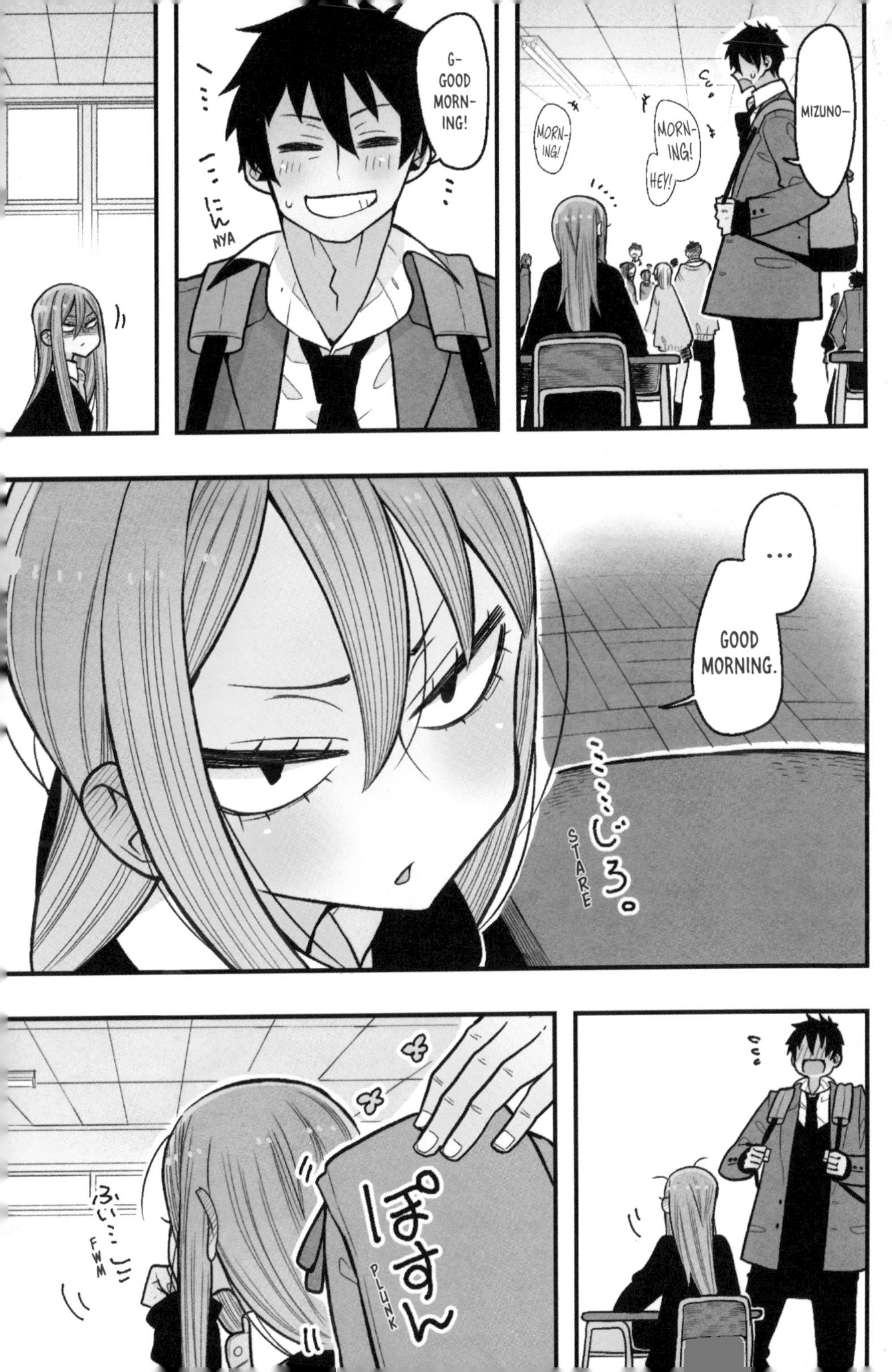
MIZUNO—
MORN-ING!
HEY!
MORN-ING!
G-GOOD MORNING!
にん
NYA
... GOOD MORNING.
じろ。
STARE
ぽすん
PLUNK
ふぃ…
FWM

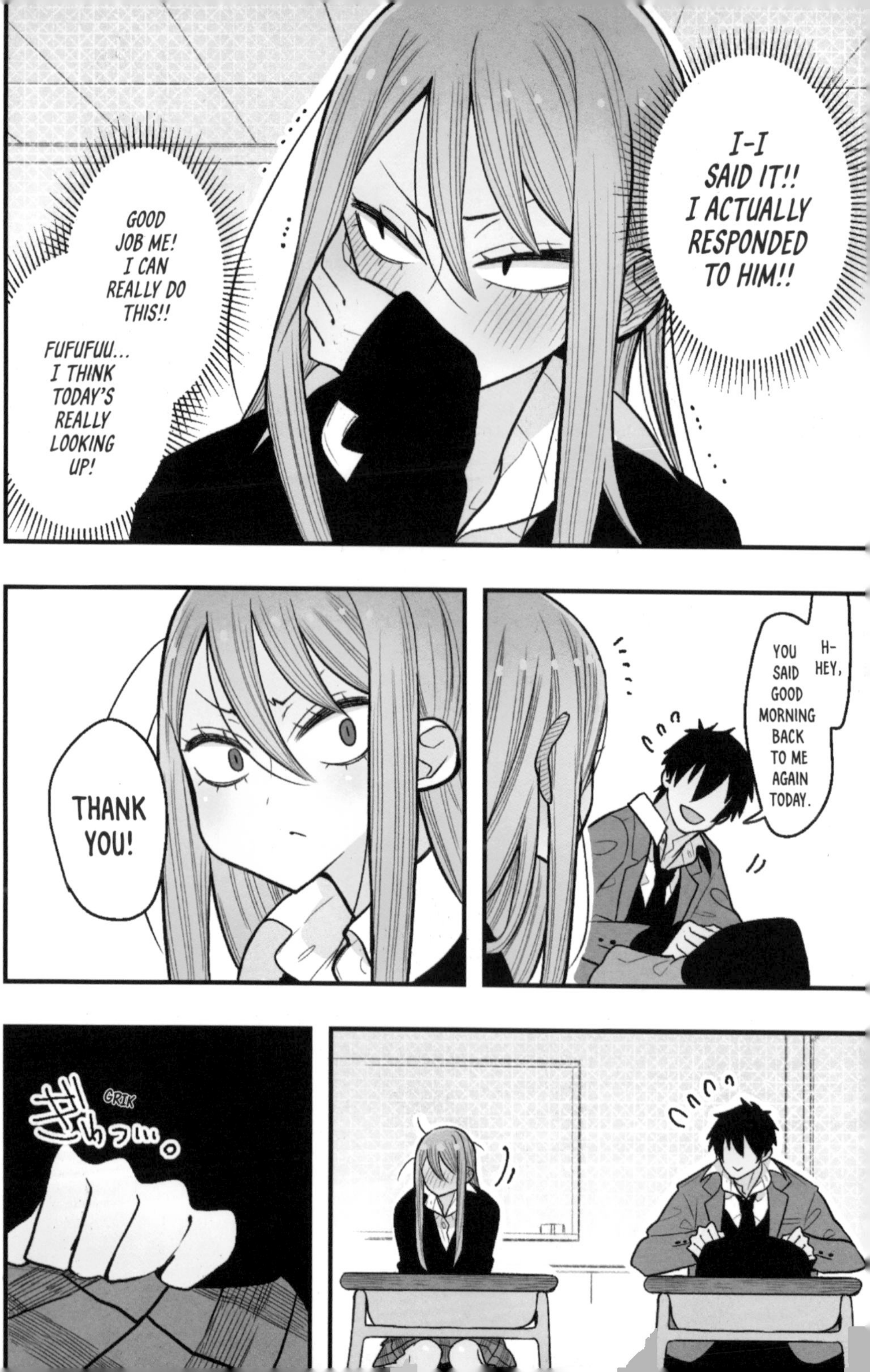
I-I SAID IT!! I ACTUALLY RESPONDED TO HIM!!
GOOD JOB ME! I CAN REALLY DO THIS!!
FUFUFUU... I THINK TODAY'S REALLY LOOKING UP!
H-HEY, YOU SAID GOOD MORNING BACK TO ME AGAIN TODAY.
THANK YOU!
GRIK

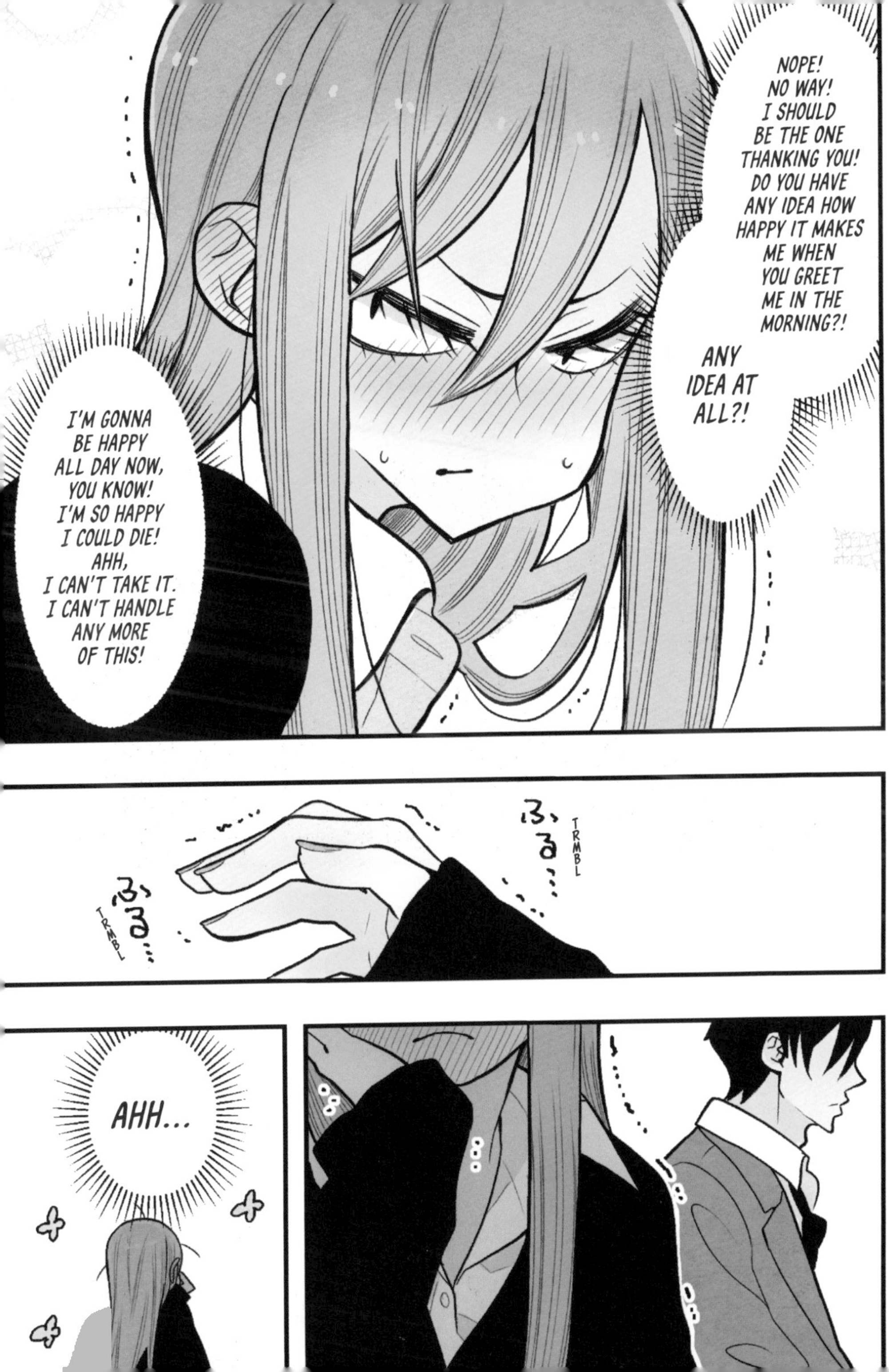
NOPE! NO WAY! I SHOULD BE THE ONE THANKING YOU! DO YOU HAVE ANY IDEA HOW HAPPY IT MAKES ME WHEN YOU GREET ME IN THE MORNING?!
ANY IDEA AT ALL?!
I'M GONNA BE HAPPY ALL DAY NOW, YOU KNOW! I'M SO HAPPY I COULD DIE! AHH, I CAN'T TAKE IT. I CAN'T HANDLE ANY MORE OF THIS!
ふる
TRMBL
ふる
TRMBL
AHH...

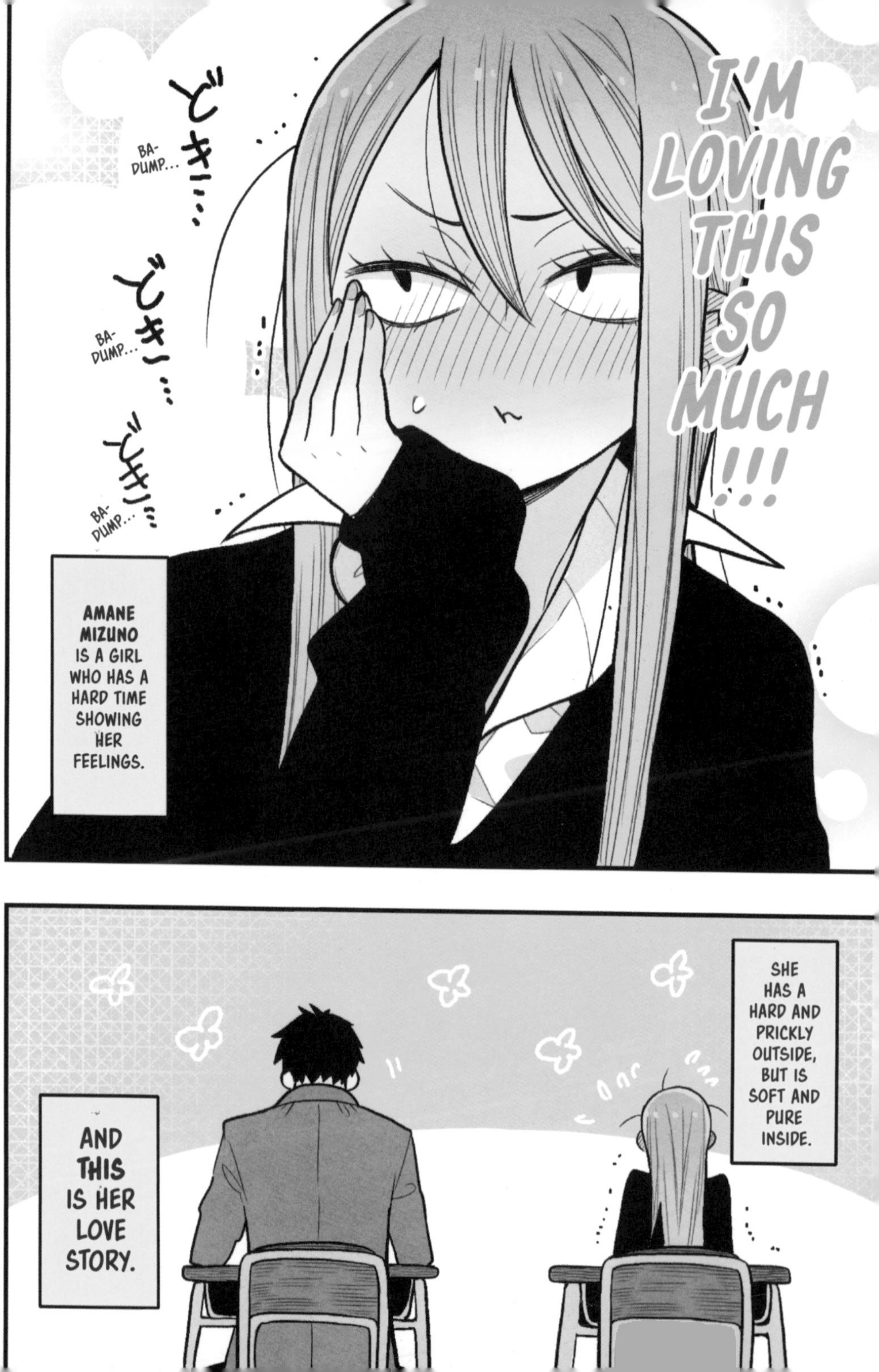
I'M LOVING THIS SO MUCH!!!
BA-DUMP...
BA-DUMP...
BA-DUMP...
AMANE MIZUNO IS A GIRL WHO HAS A HARD TIME SHOWING HER FEELINGS.
SHE HAS A HARD AND PRICKLY OUTSIDE, BUT IS SOFT AND PURE INSIDE.
AND THIS IS HER LOVE STORY.

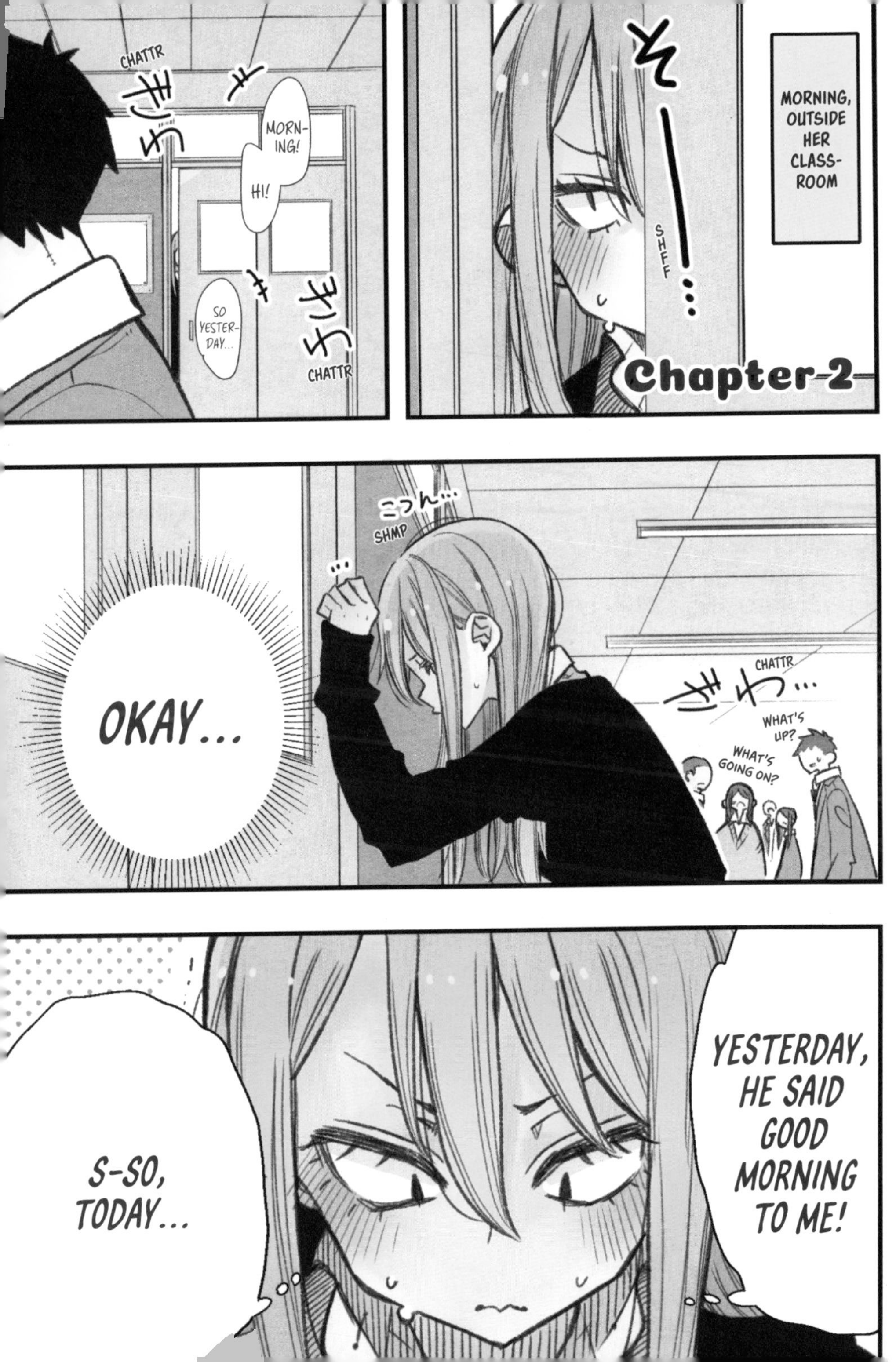
MORNING, OUTSIDE HER CLASSROOM
そー…
SHFF
Chapter 2
CHATTR
MORNING!
HI!
SO YESTERDAY...
CHATTR
こつん…
SHMP
...
OKAY...
CHATTR
WHAT'S UP?
WHAT'S GOING ON?
YESTERDAY, HE SAID GOOD MORNING TO ME!
S-SO, TODAY...

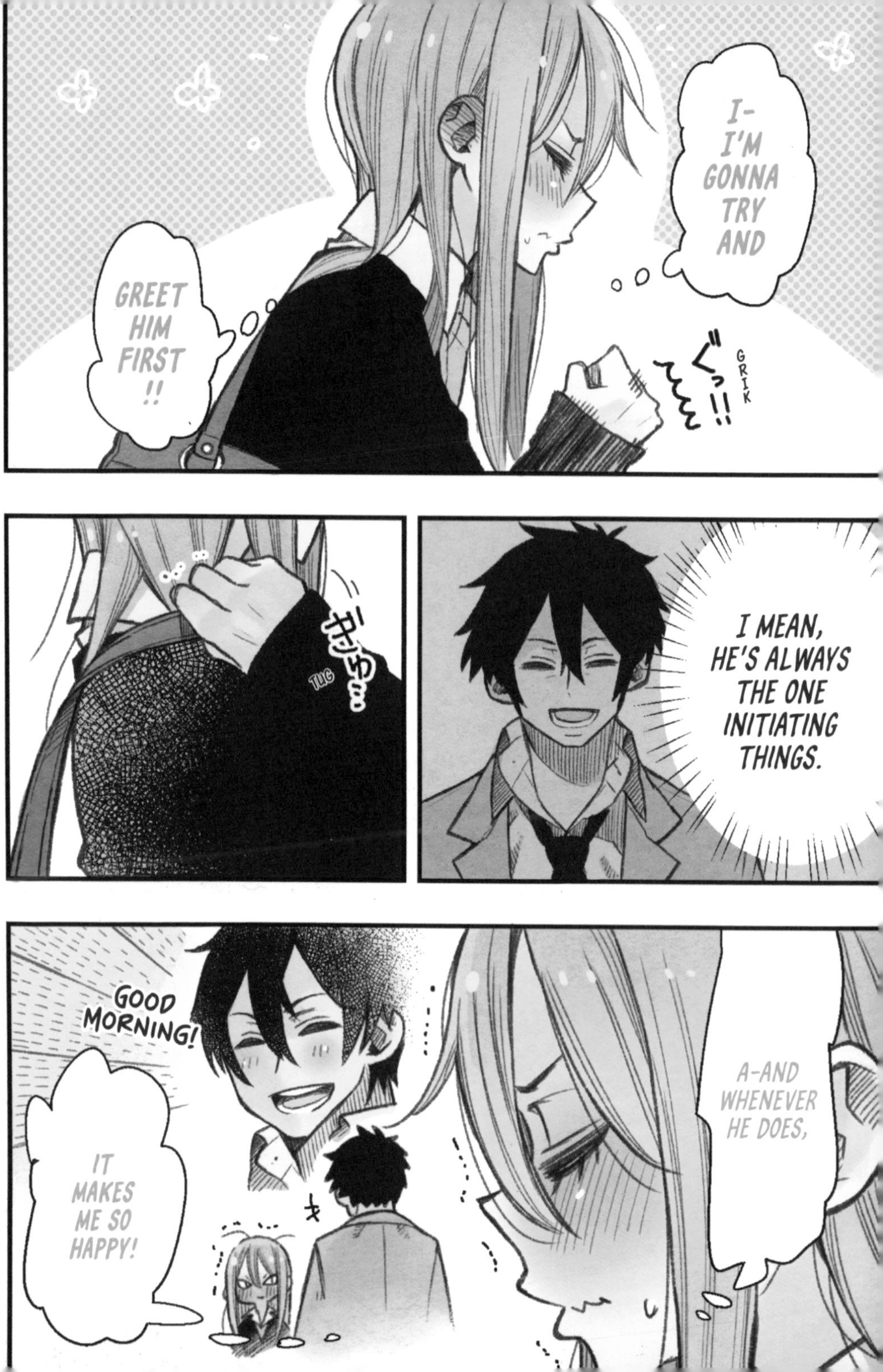
I- I'M GONNA TRY AND
GREET HIM FIRST !!
ぐっ!!
GRIK
I MEAN, HE'S ALWAYS THE ONE INITIATING THINGS.
ぎゅ…
TUG
A-AND WHENEVER HE DOES,
GOOD MORNING!
IT MAKES ME SO HAPPY!

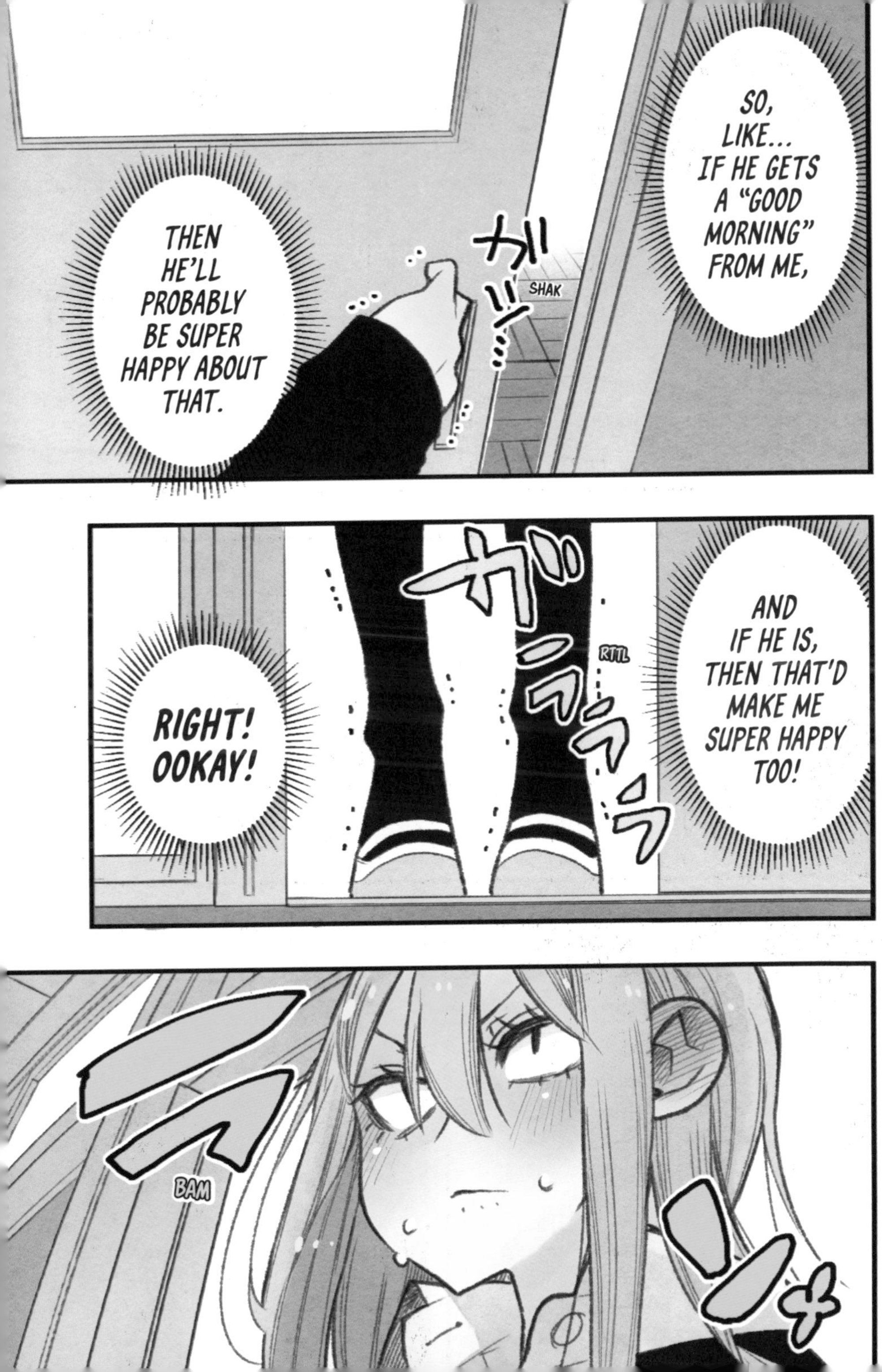
SO, LIKE... IF HE GETS A "GOOD MORNING" FROM ME,
SHAK
THEN HE'LL PROBABLY BE SUPER HAPPY ABOUT THAT.
AND IF HE IS, THEN THAT'D MAKE ME SUPER HAPPY TOO!
RTTL
RIGHT! OOKAY!
BAM

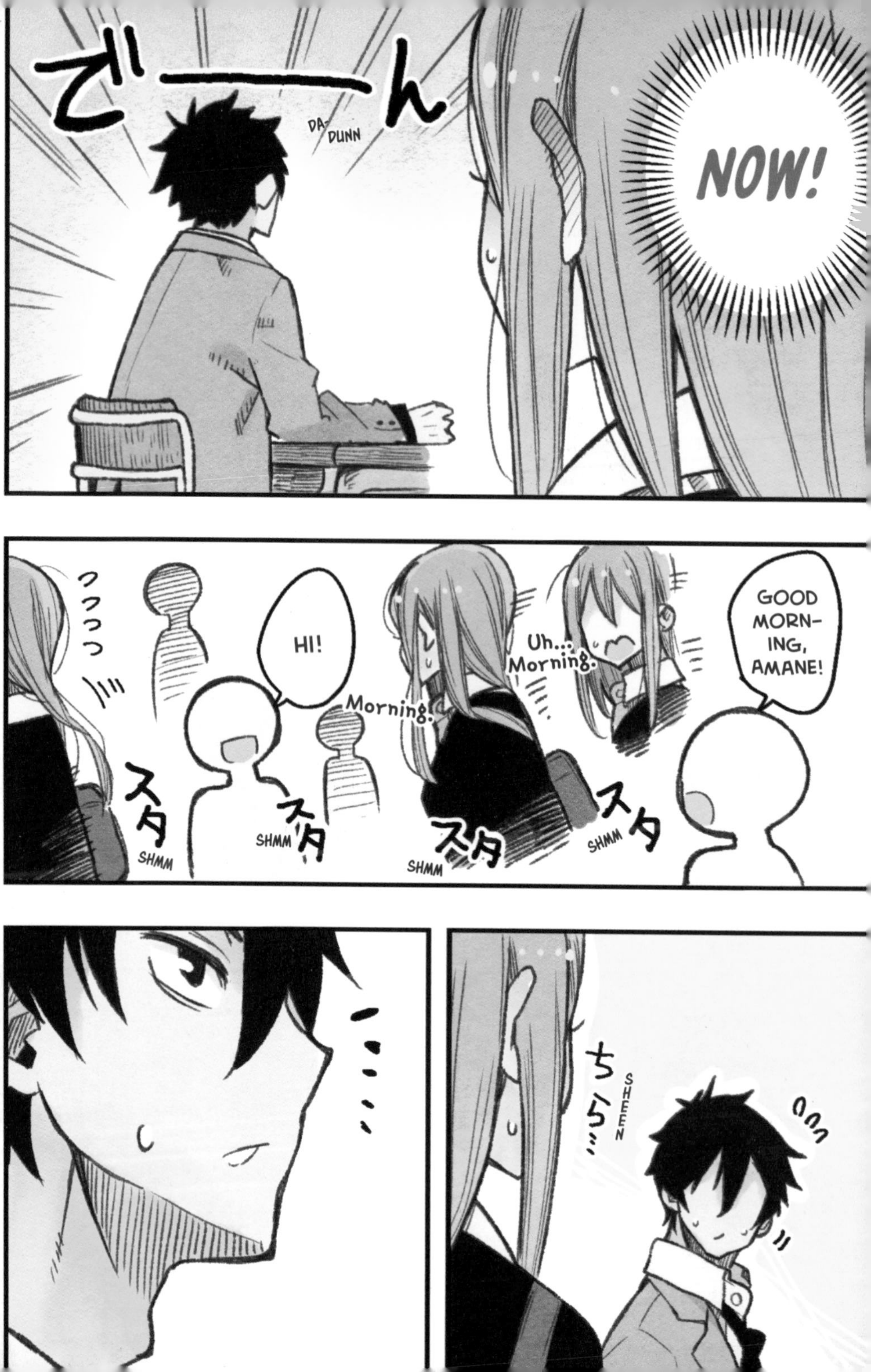
NOW!
でーーん
DA-DUNN
GOOD MORNING, AMANE!
Uh... Morning.
Morning.
HI!
スタ
SHMM
スタ
SHMM
スタ
SHMM
スタ
SHMM
ちら…
SHEEN
…

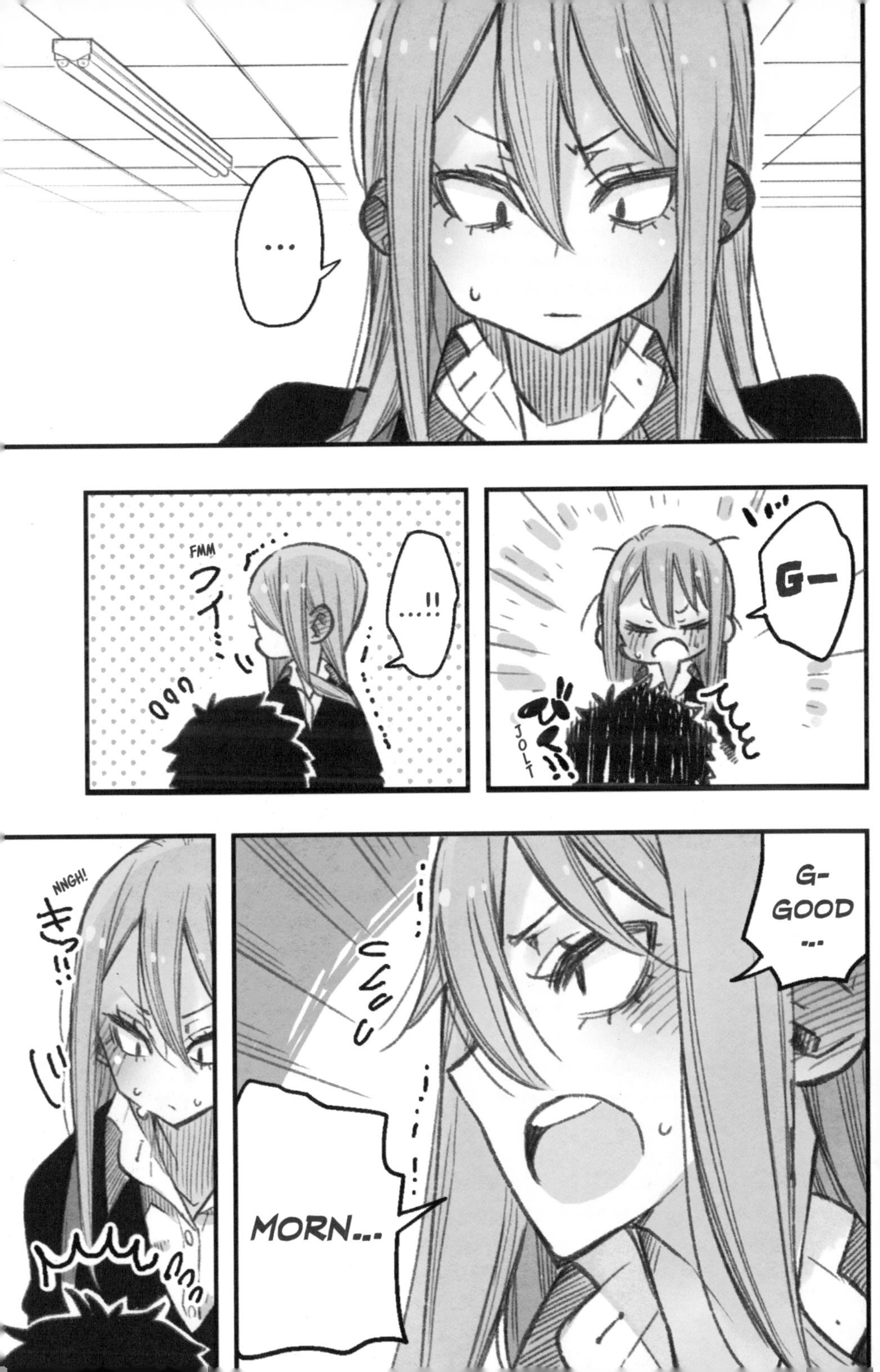
...
I...
G—
JOLT
...!!
FMM
G-GOOD...
MORN...
NNGH!

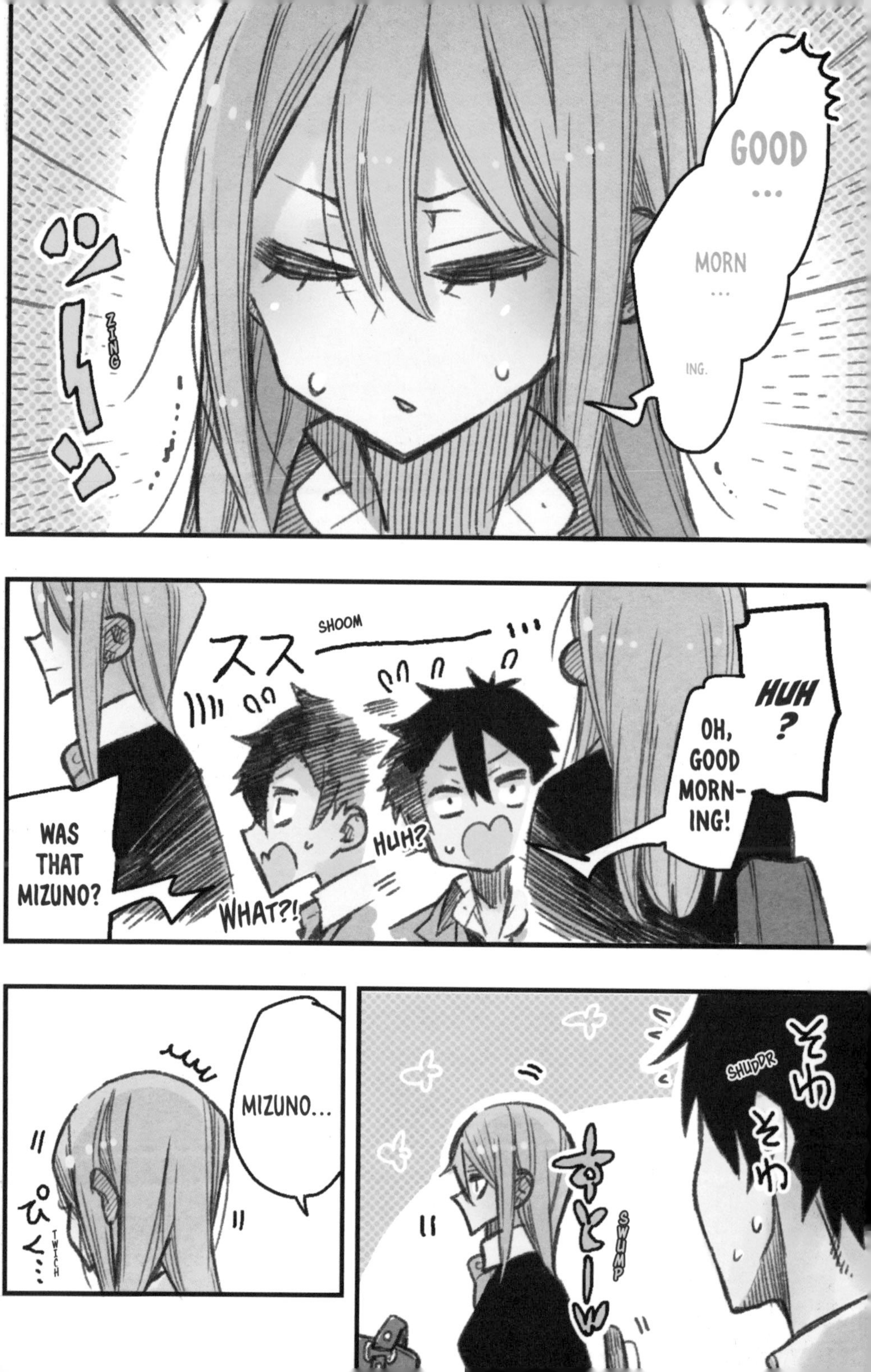
GOOD... MORN... ING.
ZING
HUH?
OH, GOOD MORNING!
SHOOM
スス—
HUH?
WHAT?!
WAS THAT MIZUNO?
そわそわ
SHUDDR
SWUMP
MIZUNO...
ぴく...
TWITCH

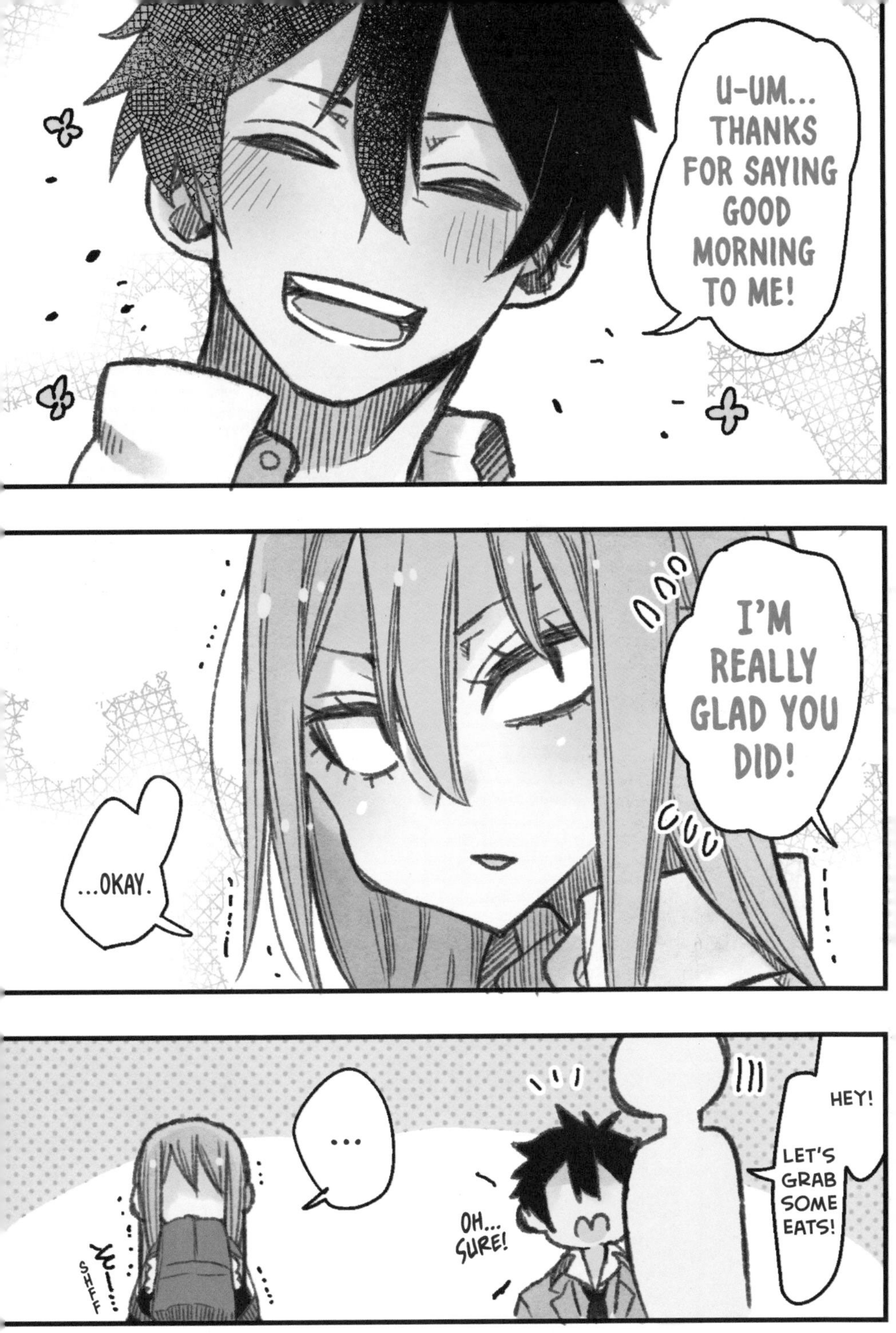
U-UM... THANKS FOR SAYING GOOD MORNING TO ME!
I'M REALLY GLAD YOU DID!
...OKAY.
HEY! LET'S GRAB SOME EATS!
OH... SURE!
...
SHFF

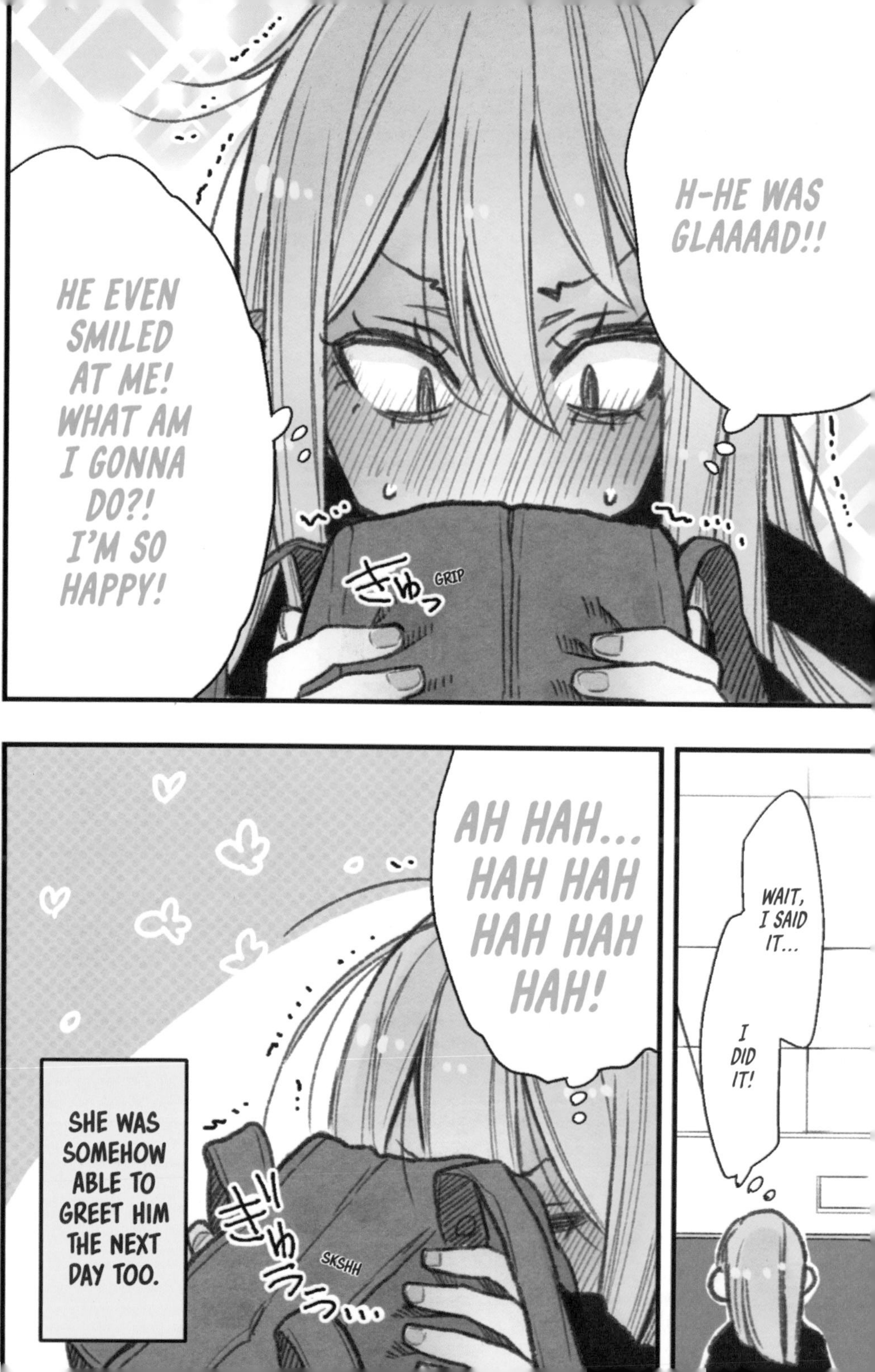
H-HE WAS GLAAAAD!!
HE EVEN SMILED AT ME! WHAT AM I GONNA DO?! I'M SO HAPPY!
GRIP
WAIT, I SAID IT...
I DID IT!
AH HAH... HAH HAH HAH HAH HAH!
SHE WAS SOMEHOW ABLE TO GREET HIM THE NEXT DAY TOO.
SKSHH

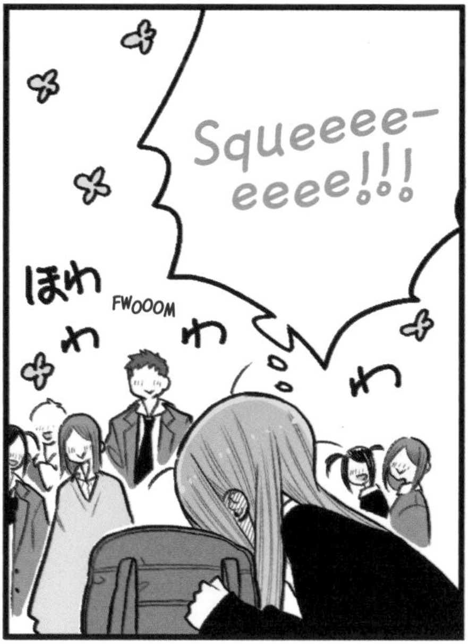
Squeeeee-eeee!!!
ほわ
FWOOOM
わ
わ
わ

THE GiRL
WiTH THE
SANPAKU
EYES

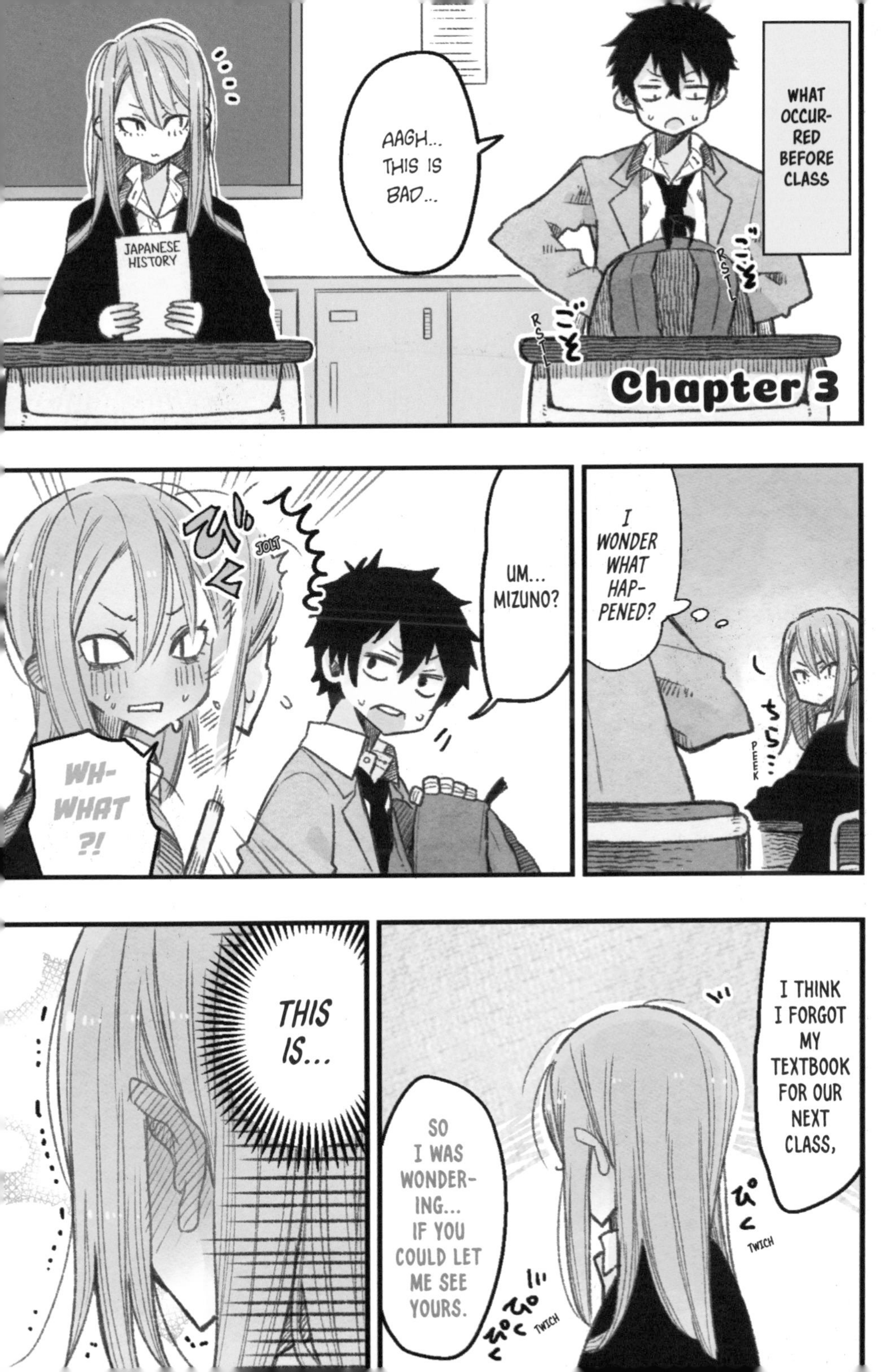
WHAT OCCURRED BEFORE CLASS
RSTL
RSTL
Chapter 3
AAGH... THIS IS BAD...
JAPANESE HISTORY
I WONDER WHAT HAPPENED?
PEEK
UM... MIZUNO?
JOLT
WH-WHAT?!
I THINK I FORGOT MY TEXTBOOK FOR OUR NEXT CLASS,
SO I WAS WONDERING... IF YOU COULD LET ME SEE YOURS.
TWICH
TWICH
THIS IS...

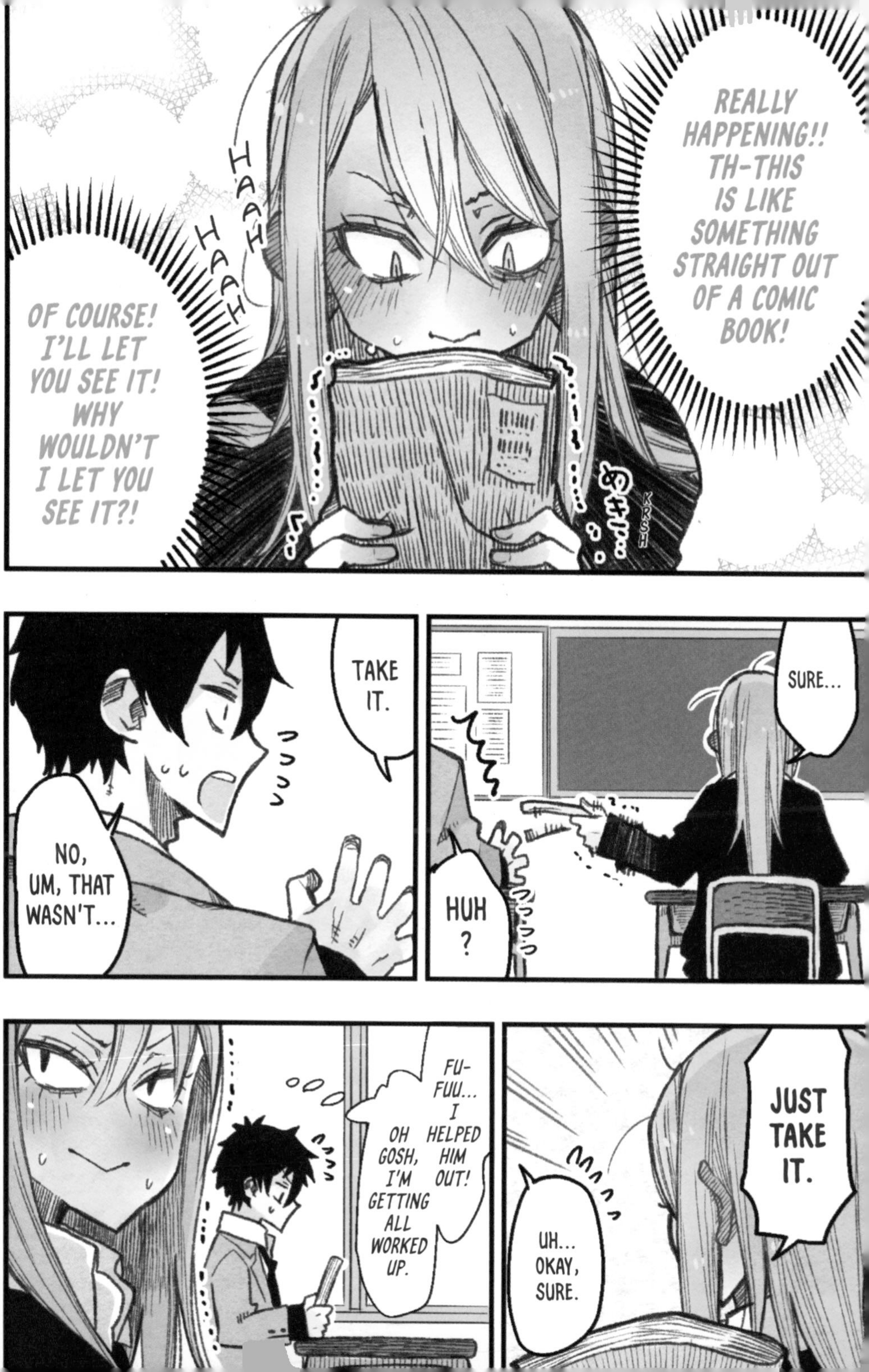
REALLY HAPPENING!! TH-THIS IS LIKE SOMETHING STRAIGHT OUT OF A COMIC BOOK!
HAAAH HAAAH
OF COURSE! I'LL LET YOU SEE IT! WHY WOULDN'T I LET YOU SEE IT?!
KRSH
SURE...
HUH?
TAKE IT.
NO, UM, THAT WASN'T...
JUST TAKE IT.
UH... OKAY, SURE.
FU-FUU... I HELPED HIM OUT!
OH GOSH, I'M GETTING ALL WORKED UP.

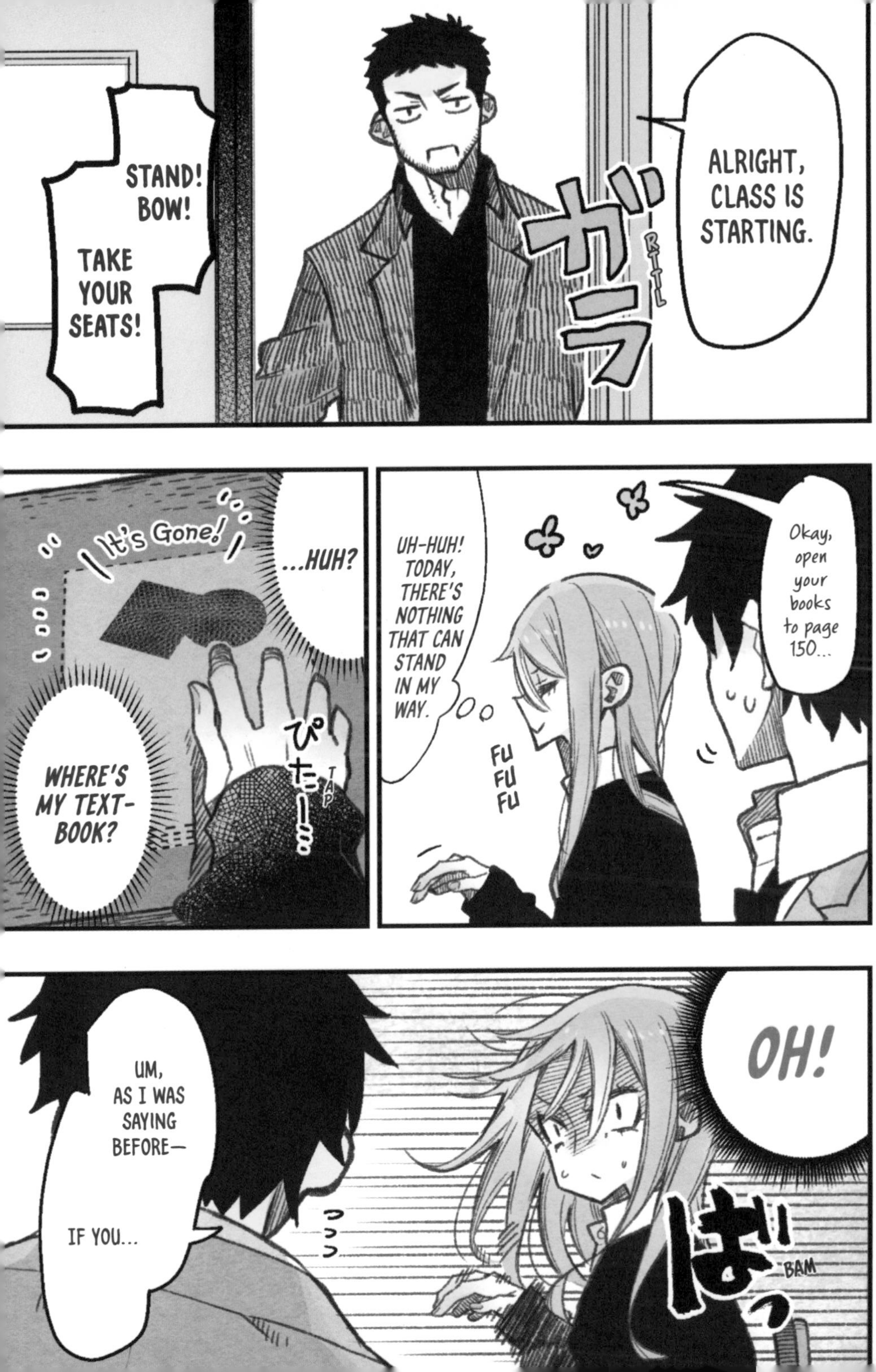
ALRIGHT, CLASS IS STARTING.
ガラ
RITL
STAND! BOW!
TAKE YOUR SEATS!
Okay, open your books to page 150...
UH-HUH! TODAY, THERE'S NOTHING THAT CAN STAND IN MY WAY.
FU FU FU
...HUH?
It's Gone!
ぴたー!!
TAP
WHERE'S MY TEXT-BOOK?
OH!
はっ
BAM
UM, AS I WAS SAYING BEFORE—
IF YOU...

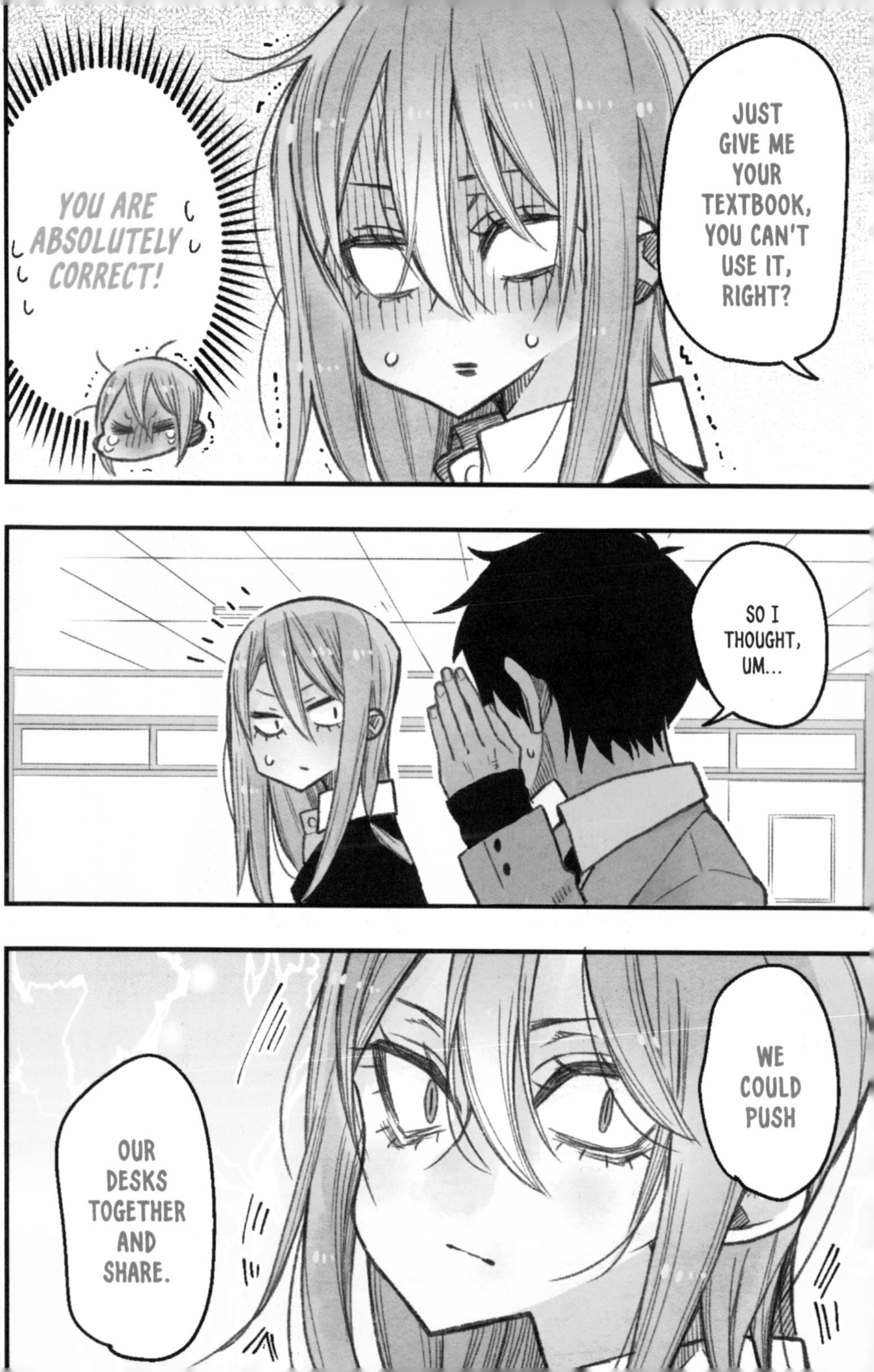
JUST GIVE ME YOUR TEXTBOOK, YOU CAN'T USE IT, RIGHT?
YOU ARE ABSOLUTELY CORRECT!
SO I THOUGHT, UM...
WE COULD PUSH
OUR DESKS TOGETHER AND SHARE.

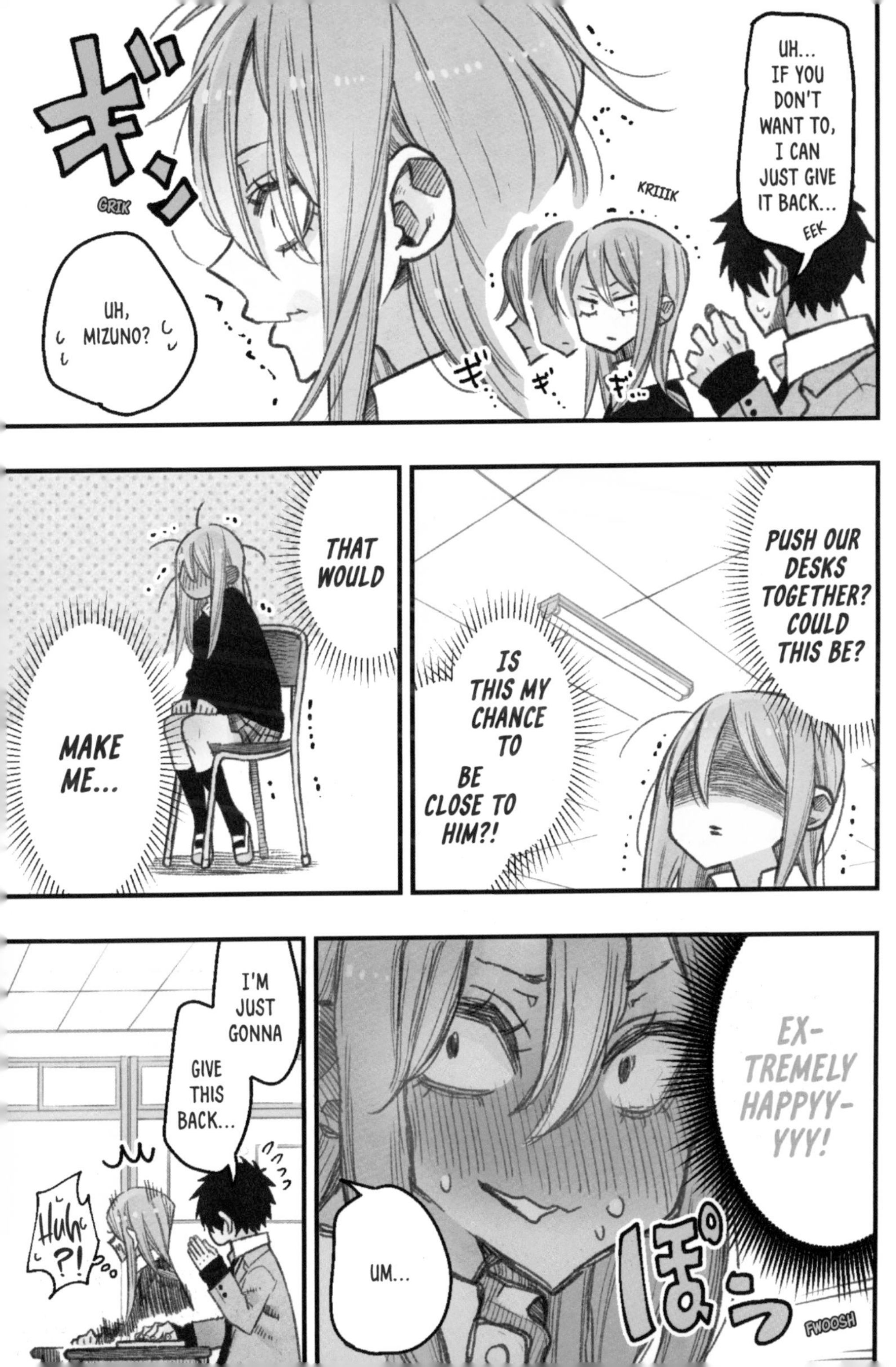
UH... IF YOU DON'T WANT TO, I CAN JUST GIVE IT BACK...
EEK
KRIIIK
ギ... ギ... ギ...
ギン
GRIK
UH, MIZUNO?
PUSH OUR DESKS TOGETHER? COULD THIS BE?
IS THIS MY CHANCE TO BE CLOSE TO HIM?!
THAT WOULD MAKE ME...
EX-TREMELY HAPPYY-YYY!
ぽっ
FWOOSH
UM...
I'M JUST GONNA GIVE THIS BACK...
HUH?!

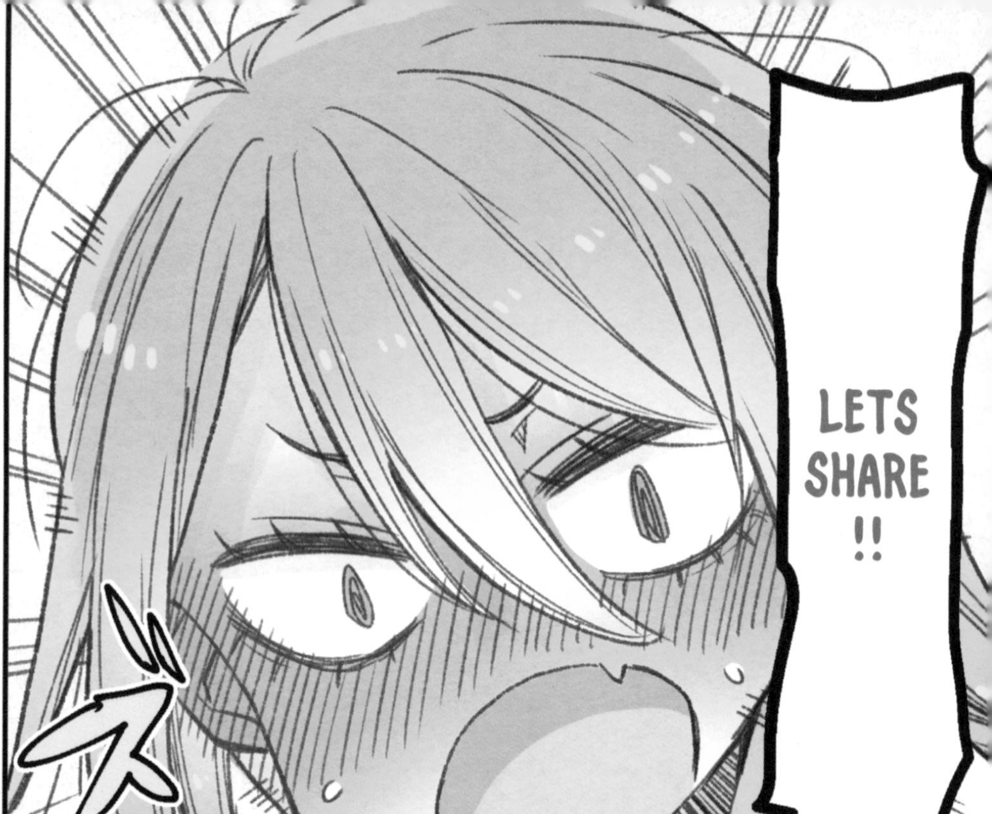
LETS SHARE !!
ZASH

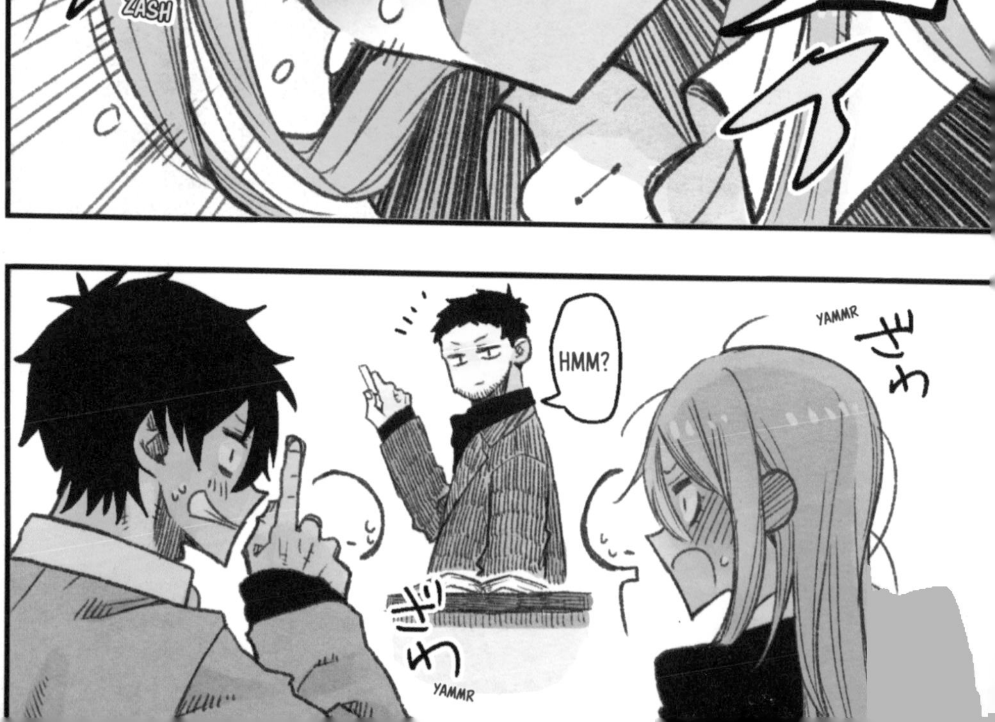
YAMMR
HMM?
YAMMR

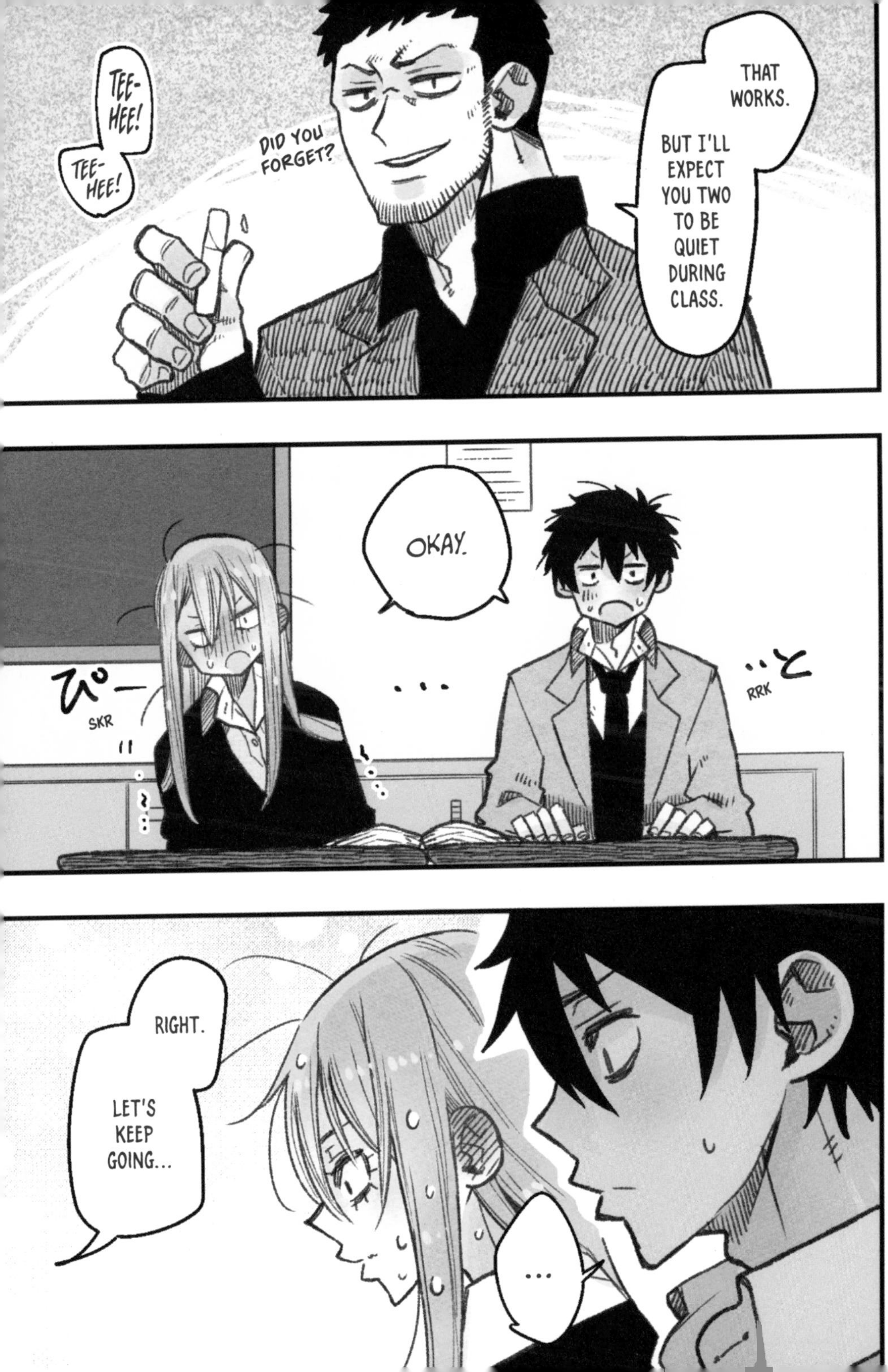
THAT WORKS.
BUT I'LL EXPECT YOU TWO TO BE QUIET DURING CLASS.
DID YOU FORGET?
TEE-HEE!
TEE-HEE!
…と
RRK
OKAY.
...
ぴー
SKR
...
RIGHT.
LET'S KEEP GOING...

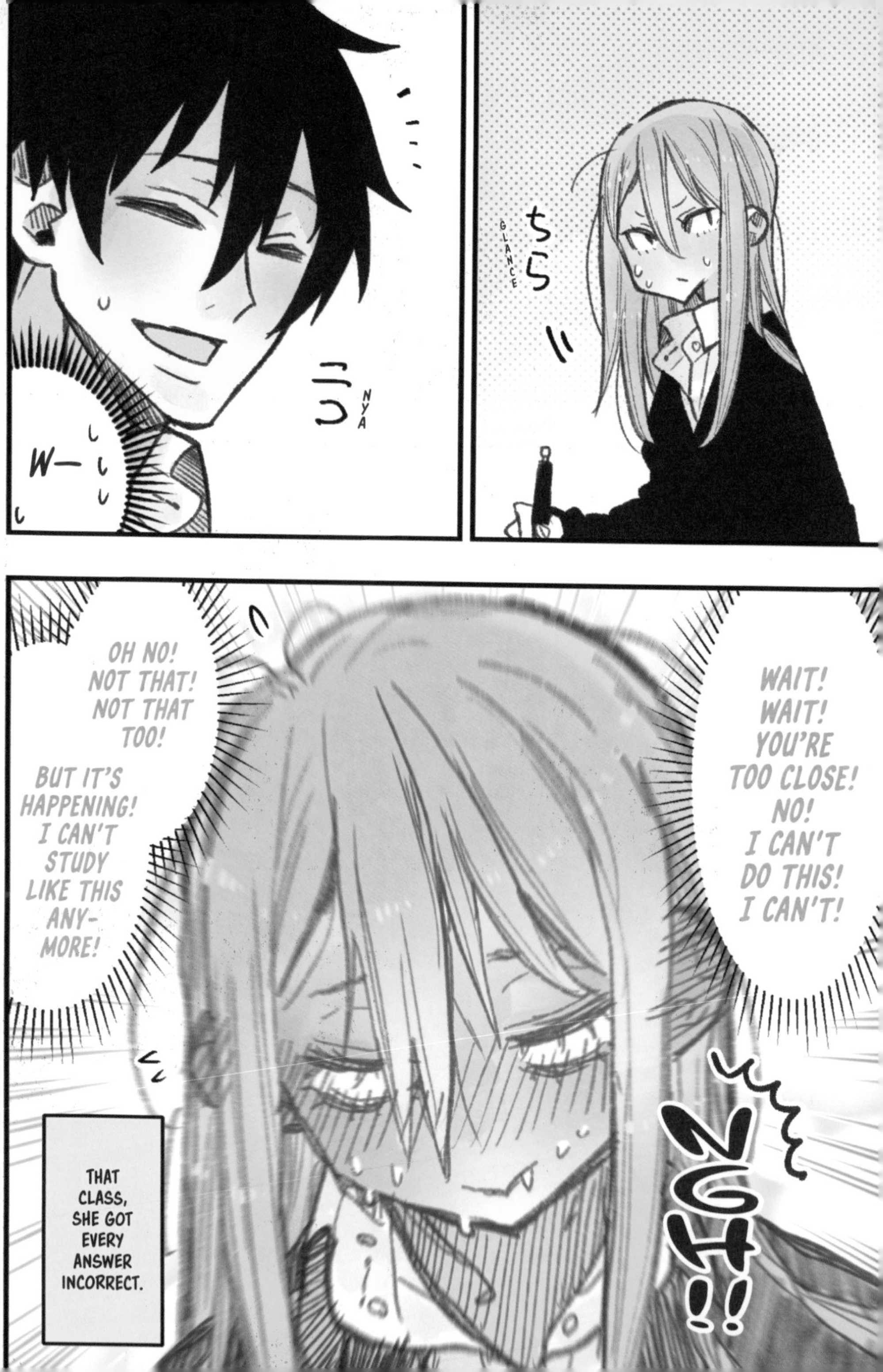
ちら
GLANCE
NYA
W—
WAIT! WAIT! YOU'RE TOO CLOSE! NO! I CAN'T DO THIS! I CAN'T!
OH NO! NOT THAT! NOT THAT TOO!
BUT IT'S HAPPENING! I CAN'T STUDY LIKE THIS ANY-MORE!
NGH!!
THAT CLASS, SHE GOT EVERY ANSWER INCORRECT.

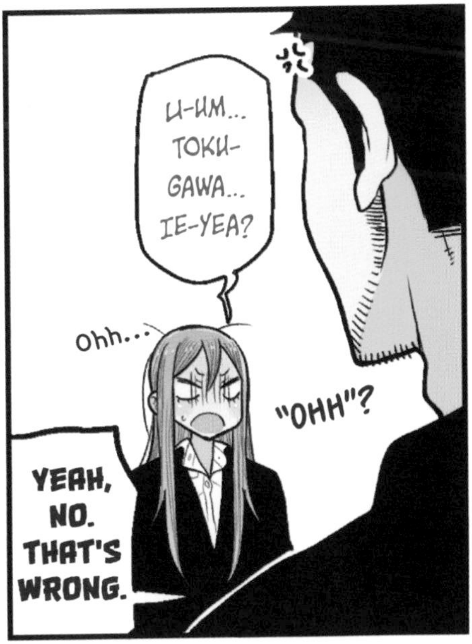
U-UM... TOKU-GAWA... IE-YEA?
Ohh...
"OHH"?
YEAH, NO. THAT'S WRONG.

THE GIRL
WITH THE
SANPAKU
EYES

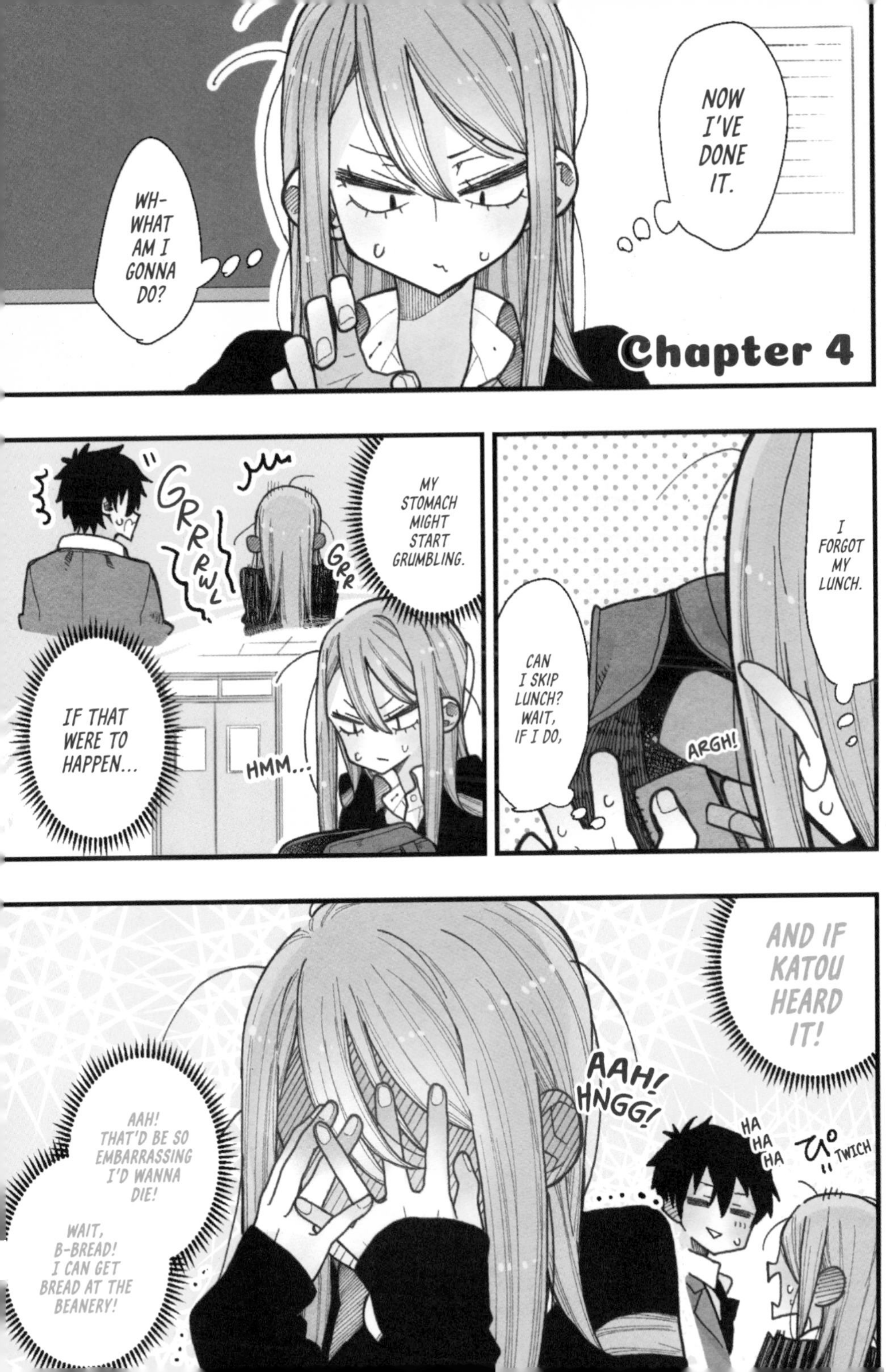
NOW I'VE DONE IT.
WH- WHAT AM I GONNA DO?
Chapter 4
I FORGOT MY LUNCH.
ARGH!
CAN I SKIP LUNCH? WAIT, IF I DO,
MY STOMACH MIGHT START GRUMBLING.
GRRRRWL
GRR
IF THAT WERE TO HAPPEN...
HMM...
AND IF KATOU HEARD IT!
AAH! HNGG!
HA HA HA
TWICH
AAH! THAT'D BE SO EMBARRASSING I'D WANNA DIE!
WAIT, B-BREAD! I CAN GET BREAD AT THE BEANERY!

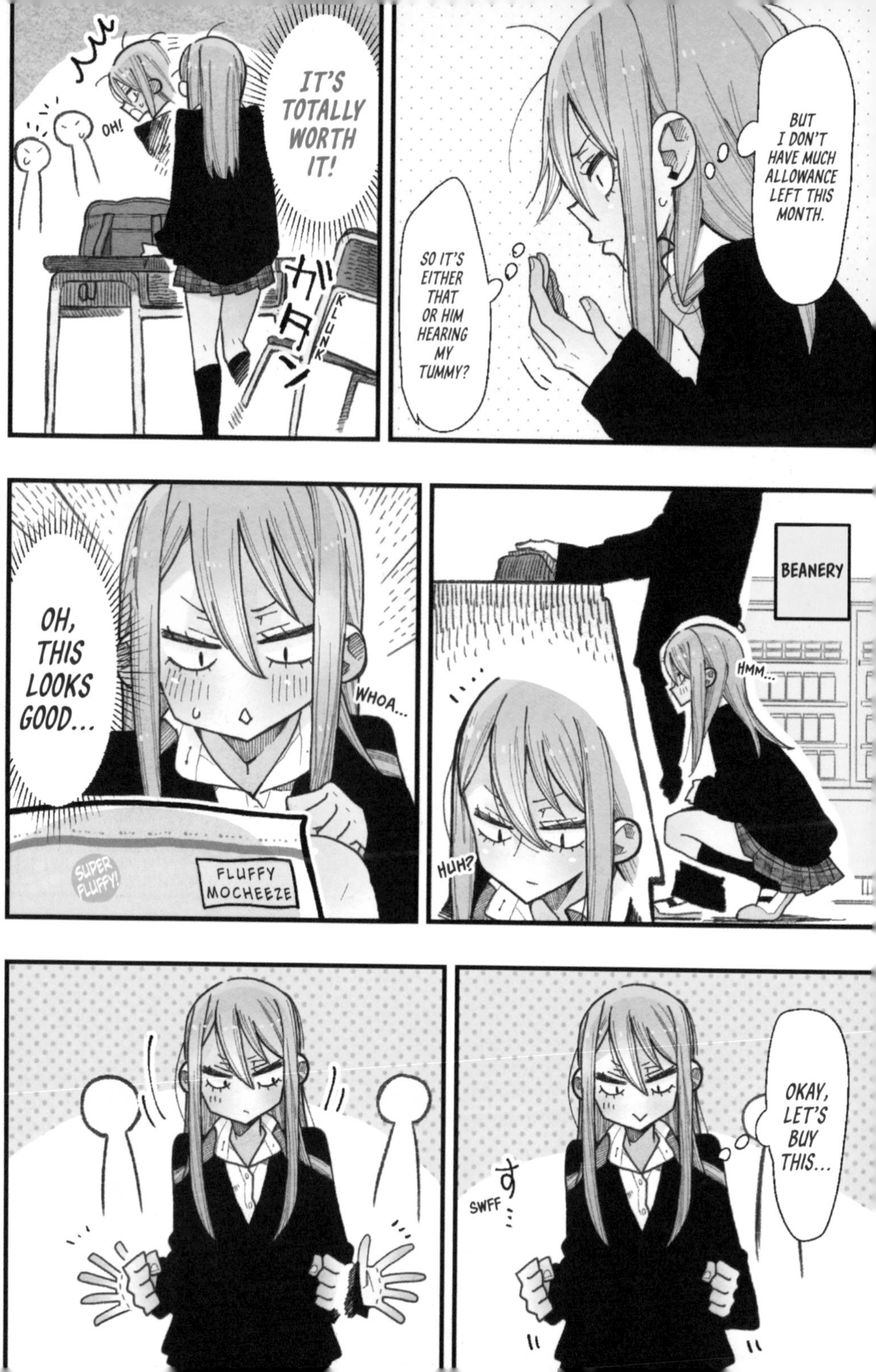

BUT I DON'T HAVE MUCH ALLOWANCE LEFT THIS MONTH.
SO IT'S EITHER THAT OR HIM HEARING MY TUMMY?
IT'S TOTALLY WORTH IT!
OH!
ガタン
KLUNK
BEANERY
HMM...
...
HUH?
OH, THIS LOOKS GOOD...
WHOA...
SUPER FLUFFY!
FLUFFY MOCHEEZE
OKAY, LET'S BUY THIS...
す
SWFF

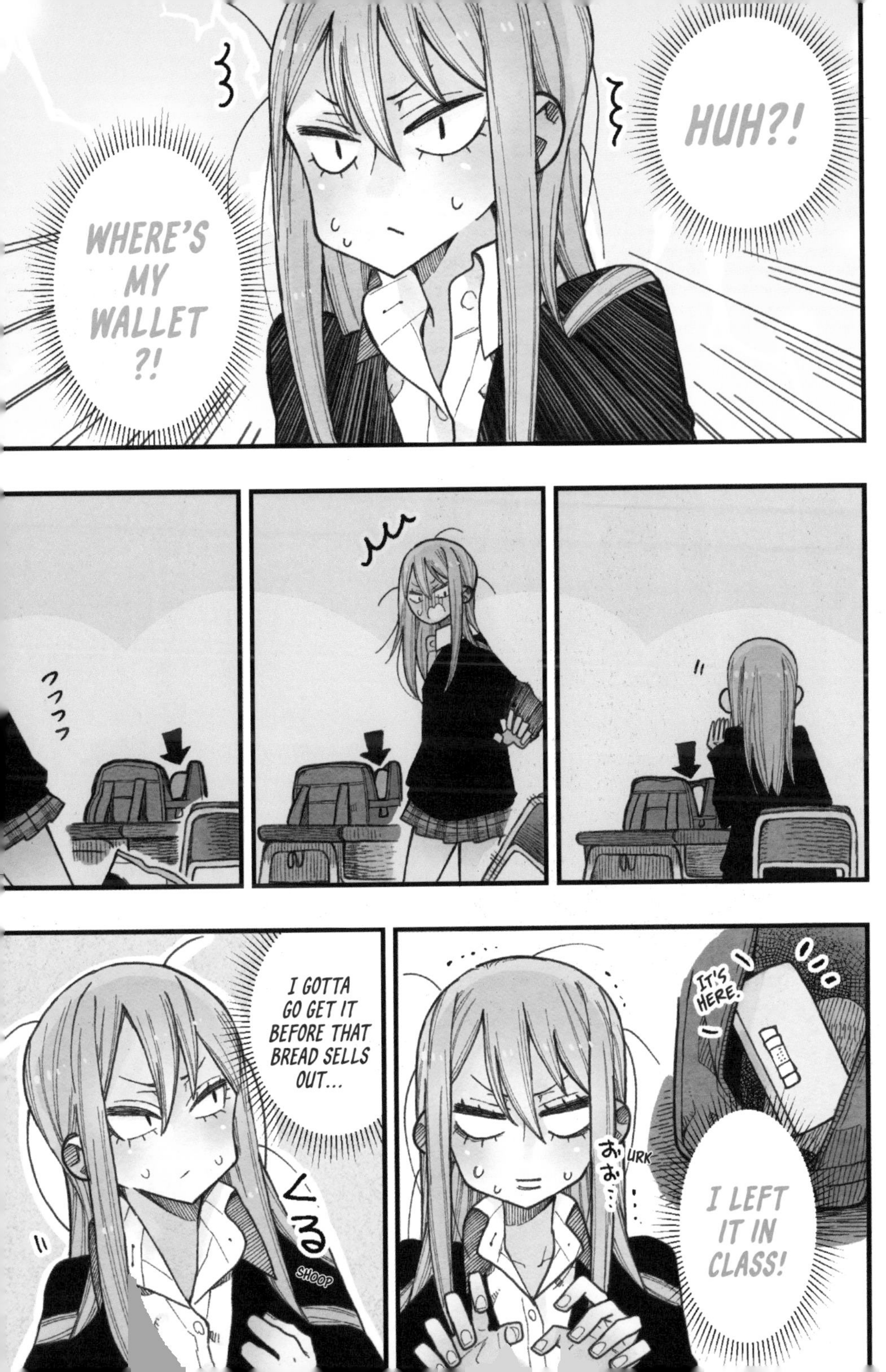
HUH?!
WHERE'S MY WALLET ?!
IT'S HERE.
I LEFT IT IN CLASS!
おお…
URK
I GOTTA GO GET IT BEFORE THAT BREAD SELLS OUT...
くる
SHOOP

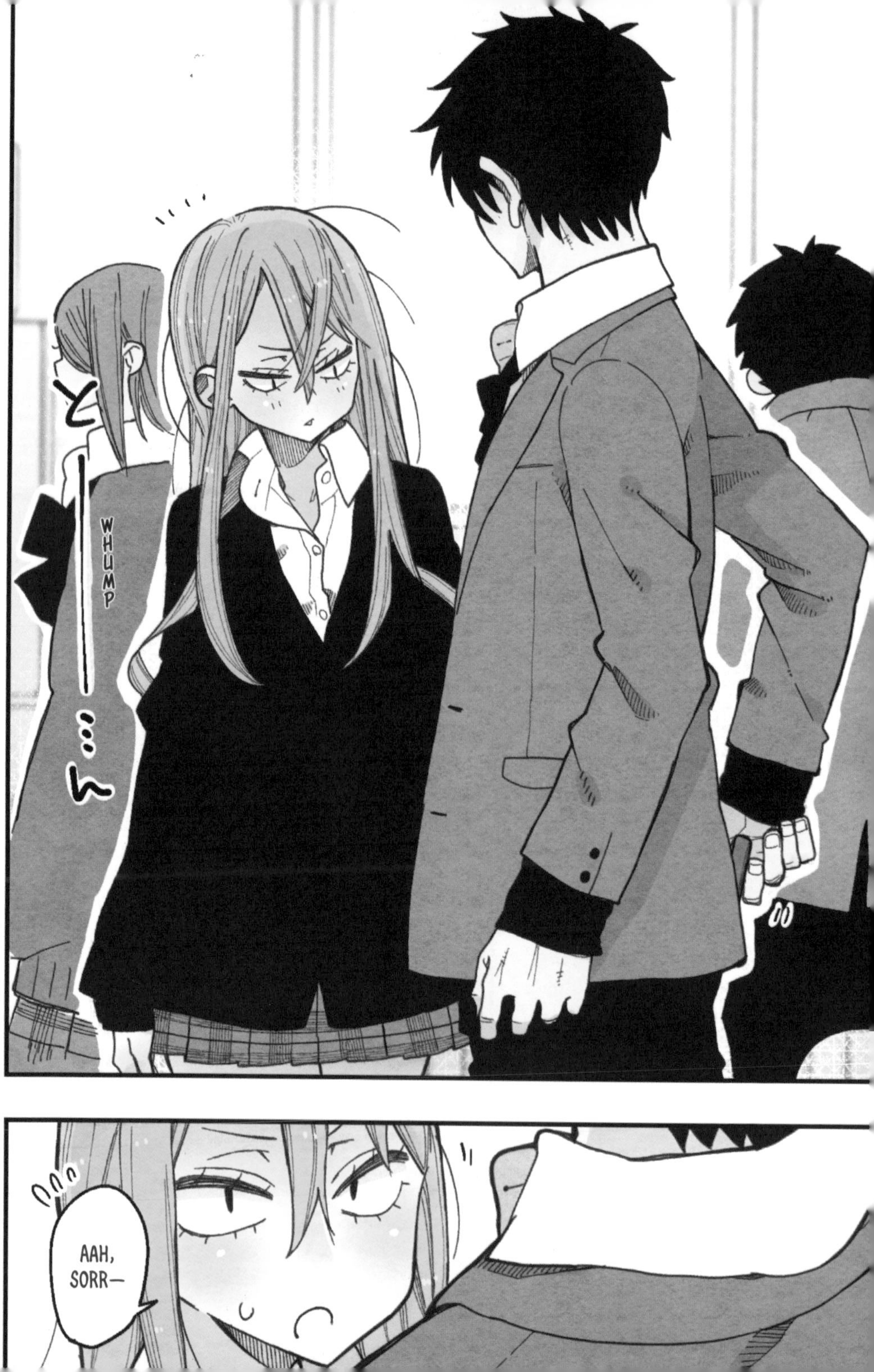
WHUMP
AAH, SORR—

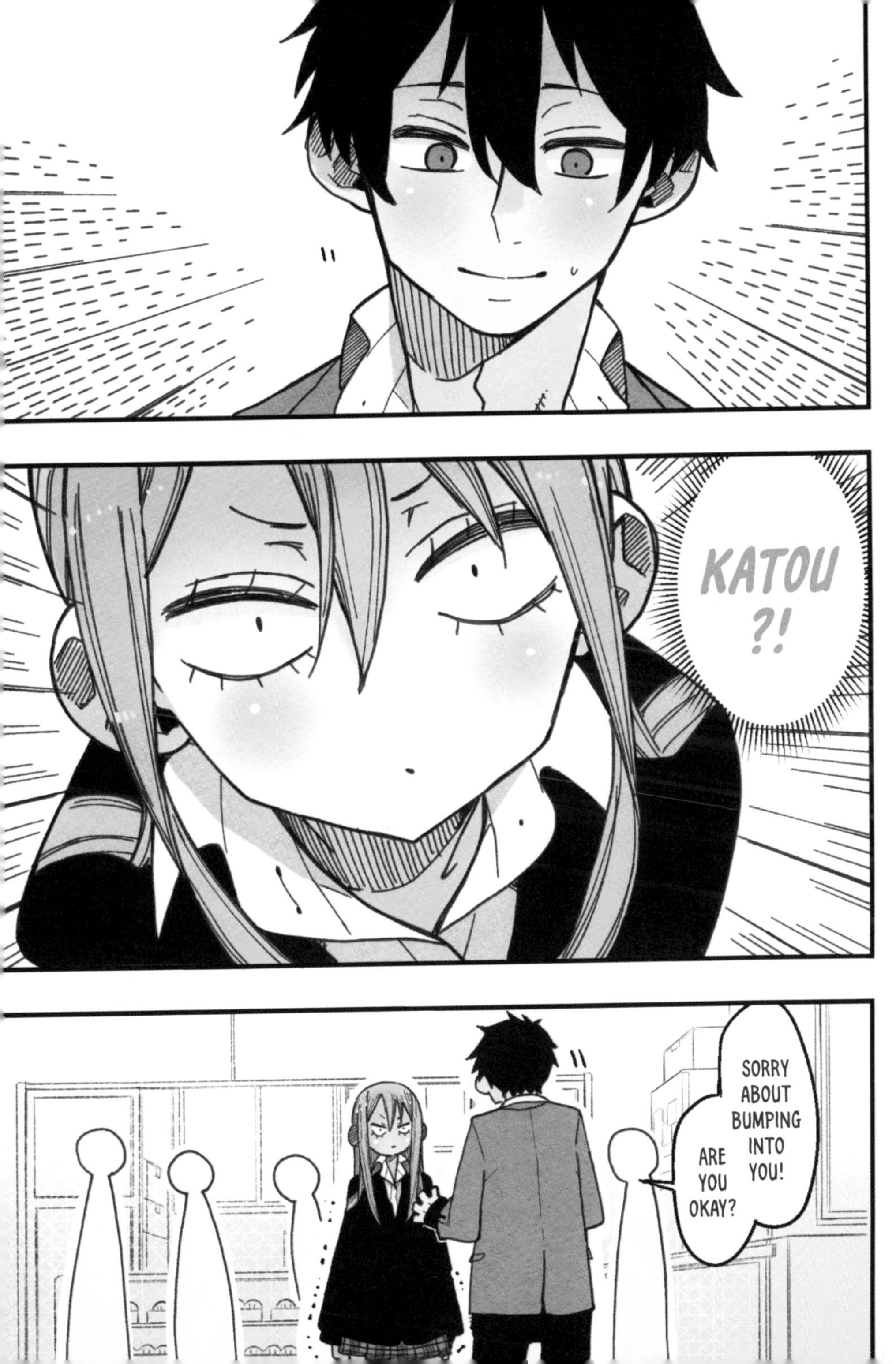
KATOU ?!
SORRY ABOUT BUMPING INTO YOU! ARE YOU OKAY?

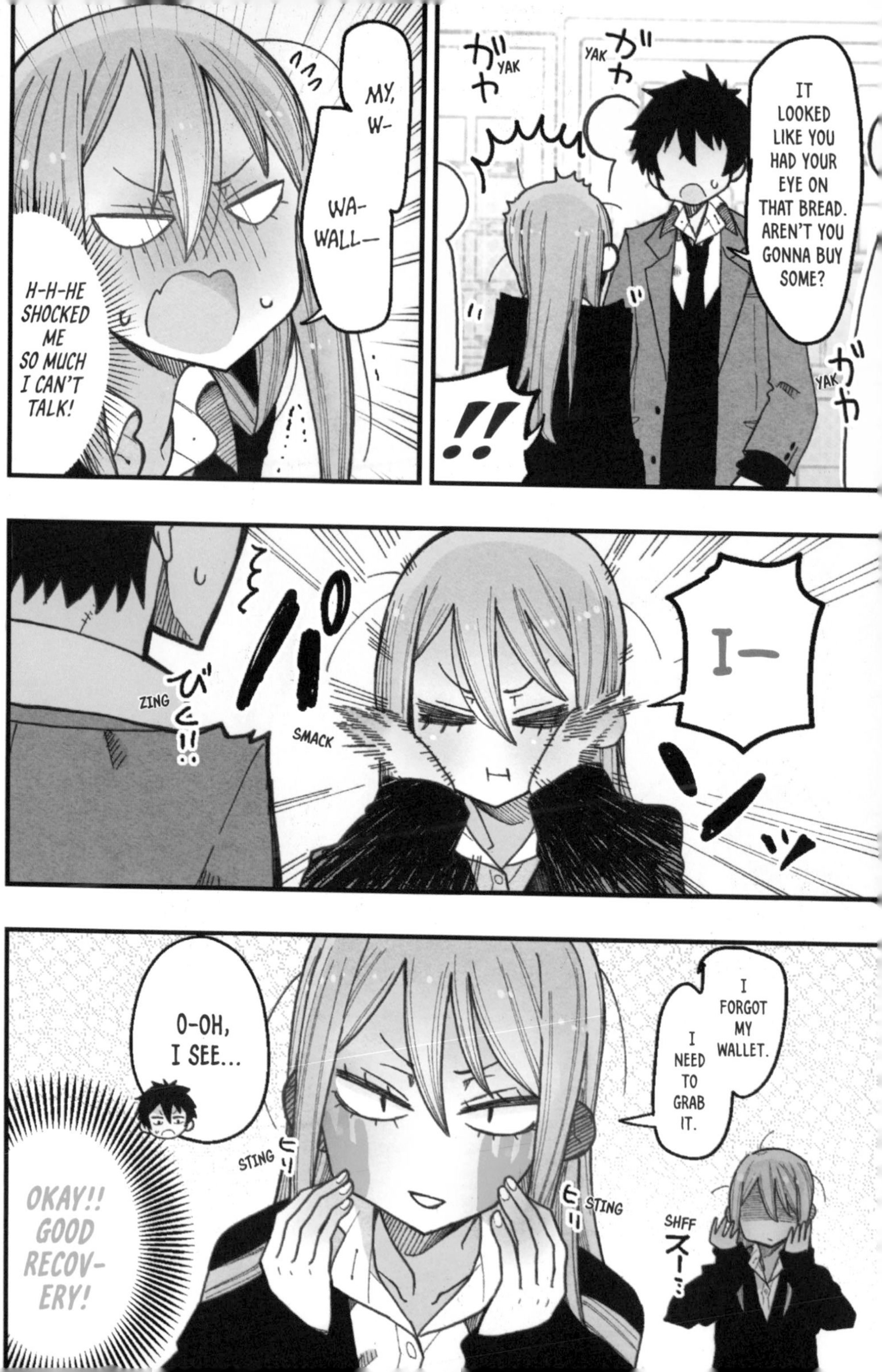
YAK
YAK
IT LOOKED LIKE YOU HAD YOUR EYE ON THAT BREAD. AREN'T YOU GONNA BUY SOME?
YAK
MY, W-
WA-WALL—
H-H-HE SHOCKED ME SO MUCH I CAN'T TALK!
I—
SMACK
ZING
I FORGOT MY WALLET.
I NEED TO GRAB IT.
SHFF
STING
STING
O-OH, I SEE...
OKAY!! GOOD RECOVERY!

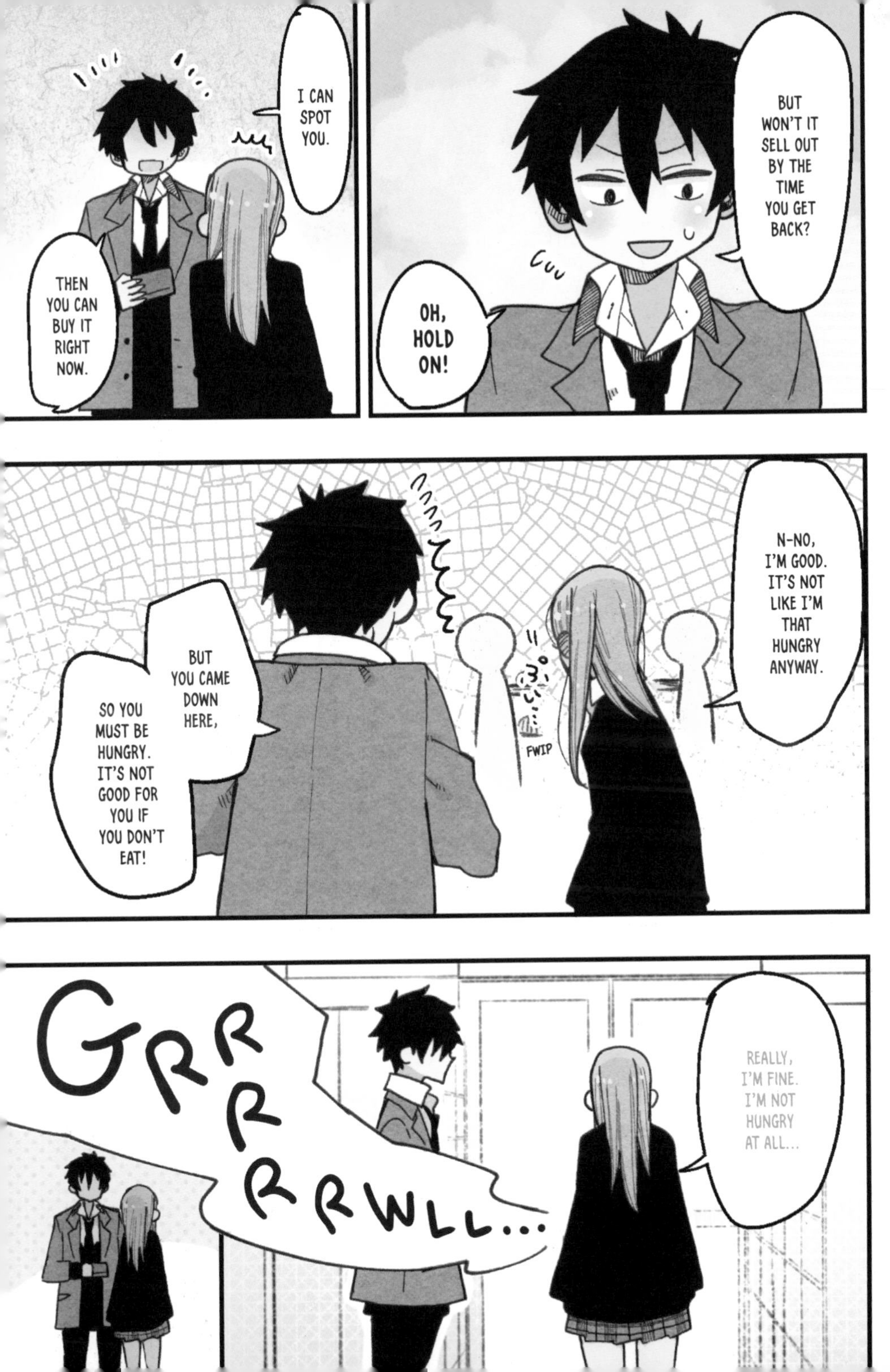
BUT WON'T IT SELL OUT BY THE TIME YOU GET BACK?
OH, HOLD ON!
I CAN SPOT YOU.
THEN YOU CAN BUY IT RIGHT NOW.
N-NO, I'M GOOD. IT'S NOT LIKE I'M THAT HUNGRY ANYWAY.
FWIP
BUT YOU CAME DOWN HERE,
SO YOU MUST BE HUNGRY. IT'S NOT GOOD FOR YOU IF YOU DON'T EAT!
REALLY, I'M FINE. I'M NOT HUNGRY AT ALL...
GRRRRRWLL...

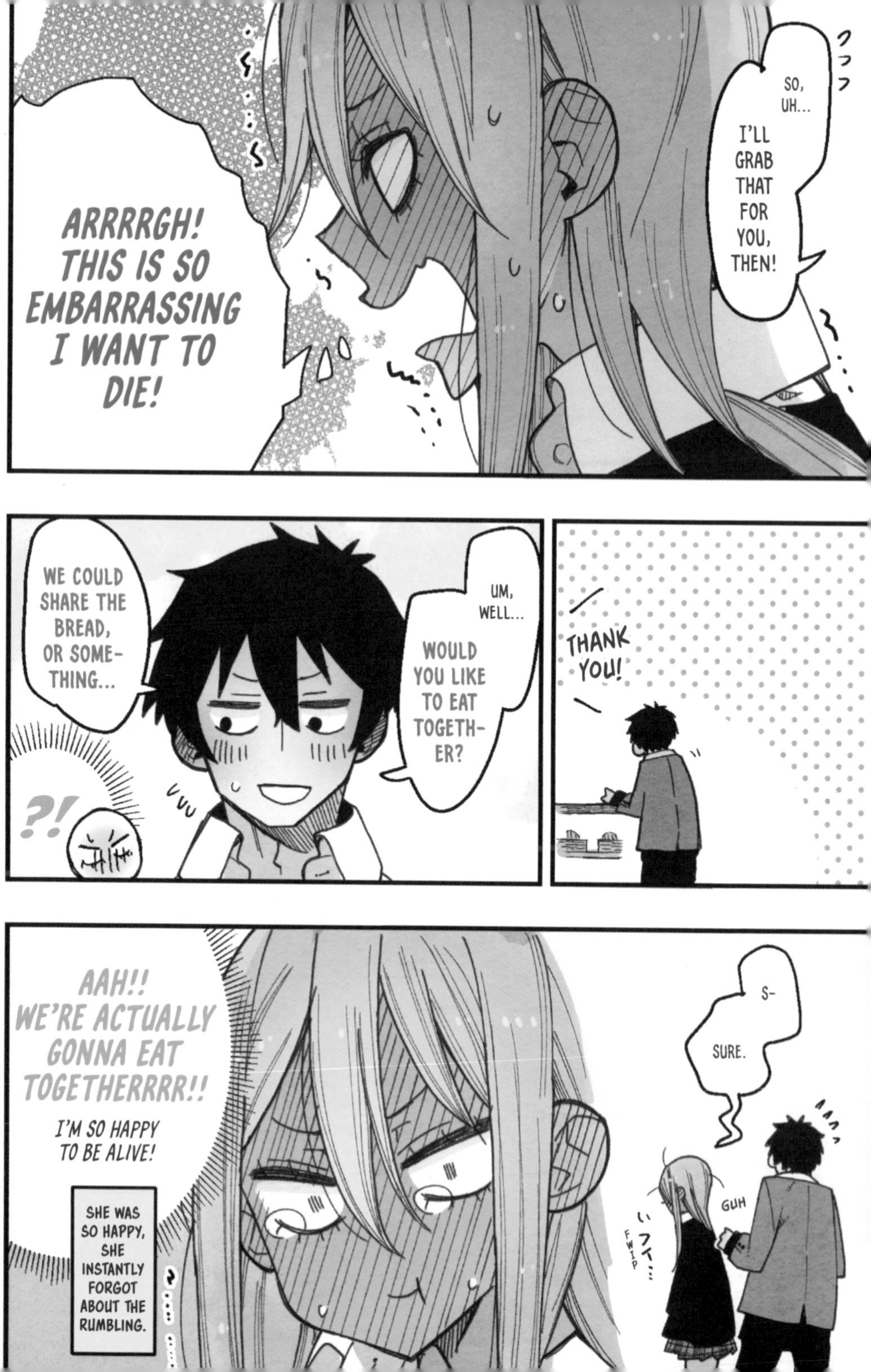
SO, UH... I'LL GRAB THAT FOR YOU, THEN!
ARRRRGH! THIS IS SO EMBARRASSING I WANT TO DIE!
THANK YOU!
UM, WELL... WOULD YOU LIKE TO EAT TOGETHER?
WE COULD SHARE THE BREAD, OR SOMETHING...
?!
S- SURE.
GUH
FWIP
AAH!! WE'RE ACTUALLY GONNA EAT TOGETHERRRR!!
I'M SO HAPPY TO BE ALIVE!
SHE WAS SO HAPPY, SHE INSTANTLY FORGOT ABOUT THE RUMBLING.

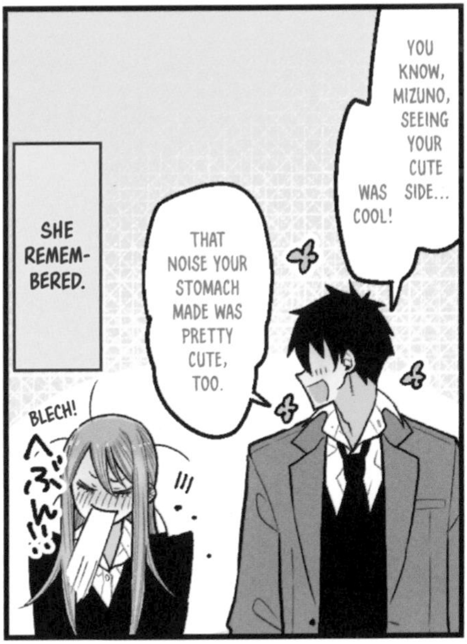
YOU KNOW, MIZUNO, SEEING YOUR CUTE SIDE... WAS COOL!
THAT NOISE YOUR STOMACH MADE WAS PRETTY CUTE, TOO.
SHE REMEMBERED.
BLECH!
へぶん!!

THE GIRL
WITH THE
SANPAKU
EYES

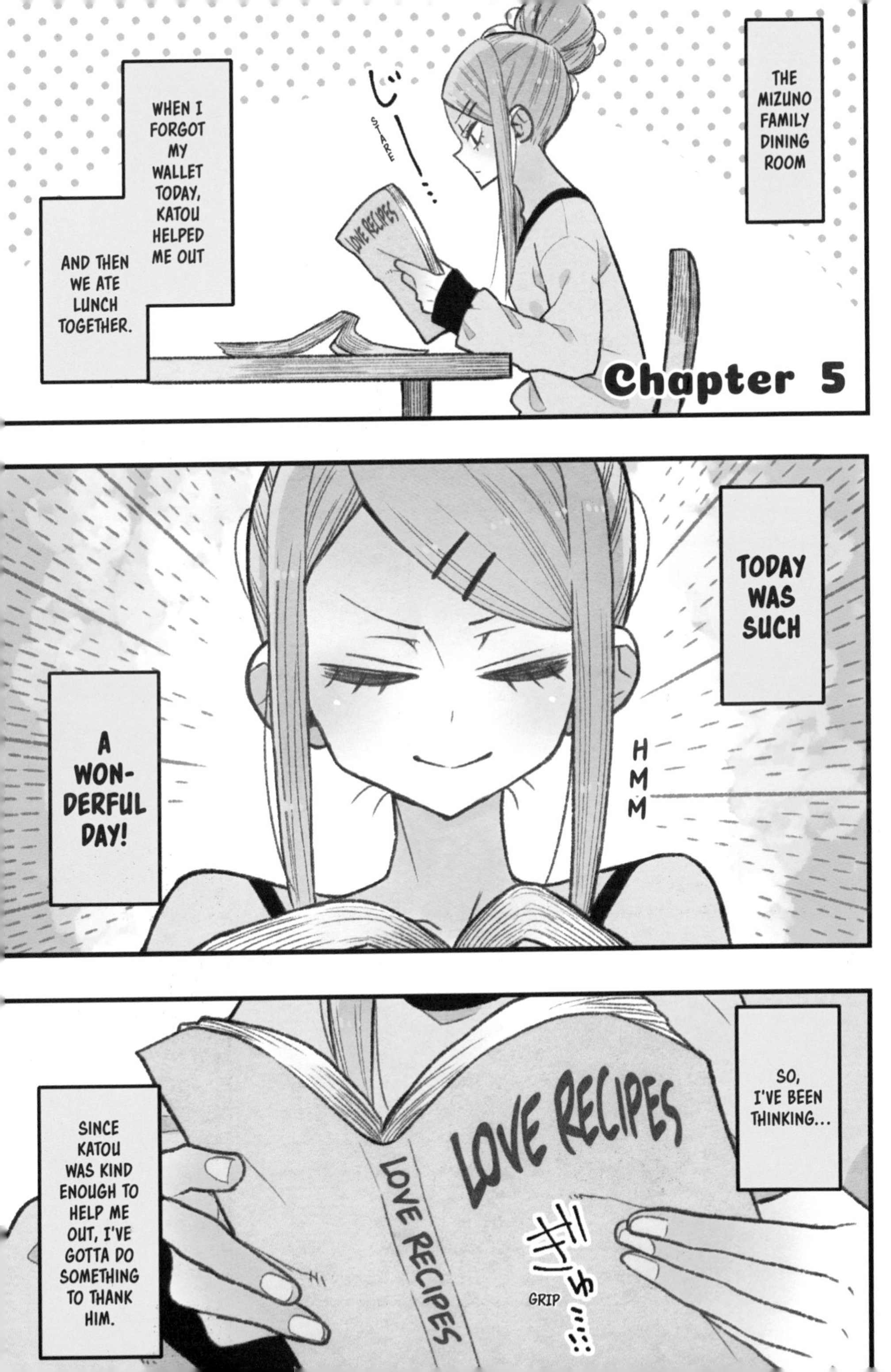
THE MIZUNO FAMILY DINING ROOM
じー…
STARE
LOVE RECIPES
WHEN I FORGOT MY WALLET TODAY, KATOU HELPED ME OUT
AND THEN WE ATE LUNCH TOGETHER.
Chapter 5
TODAY WAS SUCH
HMM
A WON-DERFUL DAY!
SO, I'VE BEEN THINKING...
LOVE RECIPES
LOVE RECIPES
GRIP
SINCE KATOU WAS KIND ENOUGH TO HELP ME OUT, I'VE GOTTA DO SOMETHING TO THANK HIM.

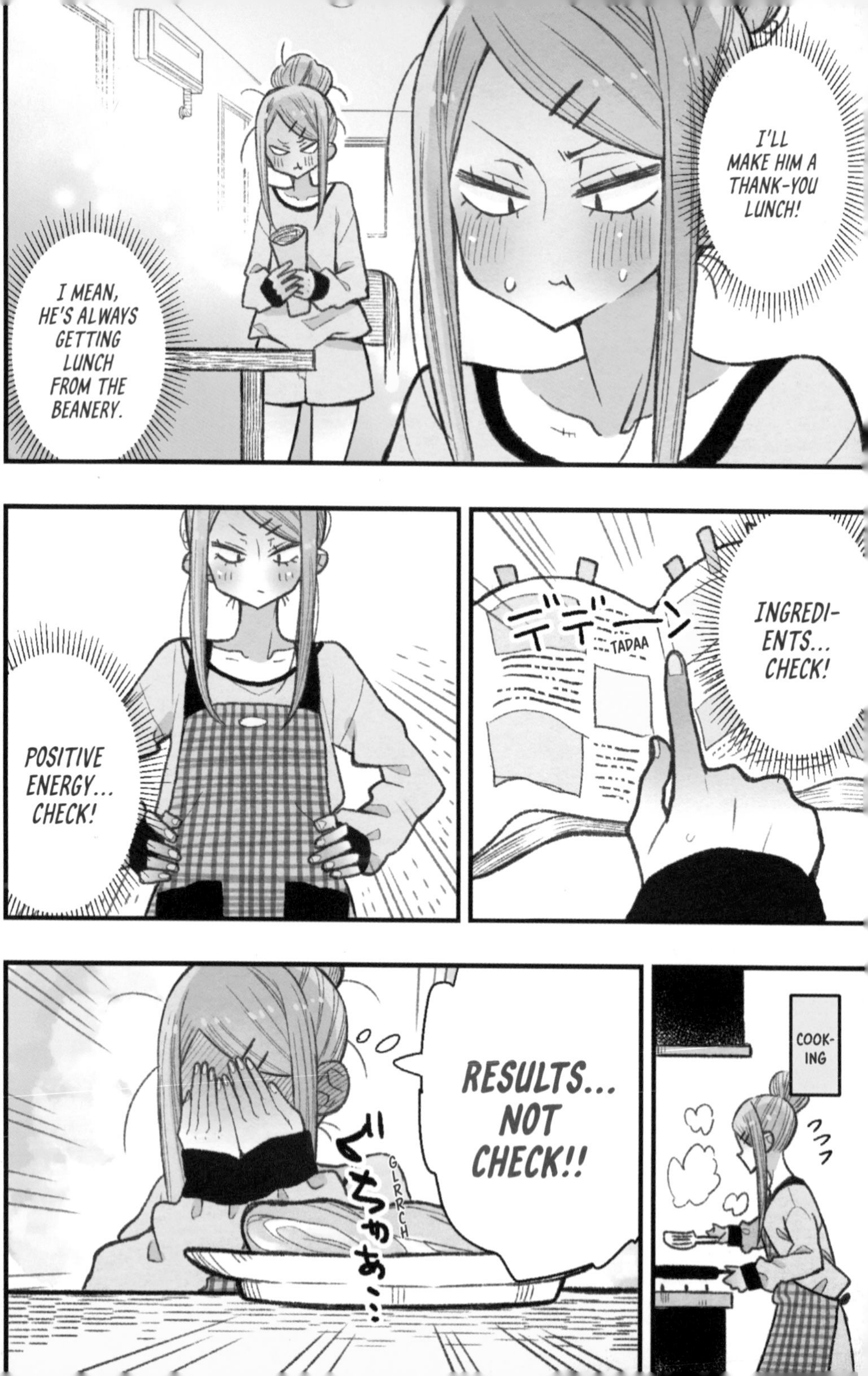
I'LL MAKE HIM A THANK-YOU LUNCH!
I MEAN, HE'S ALWAYS GETTING LUNCH FROM THE BEANERY.
デデーン
TADAA
INGREDI-ENTS... CHECK!
POSITIVE ENERGY... CHECK!
COOK-ING
RESULTS... NOT CHECK!!
ぐちゃあ…
GLRRCH

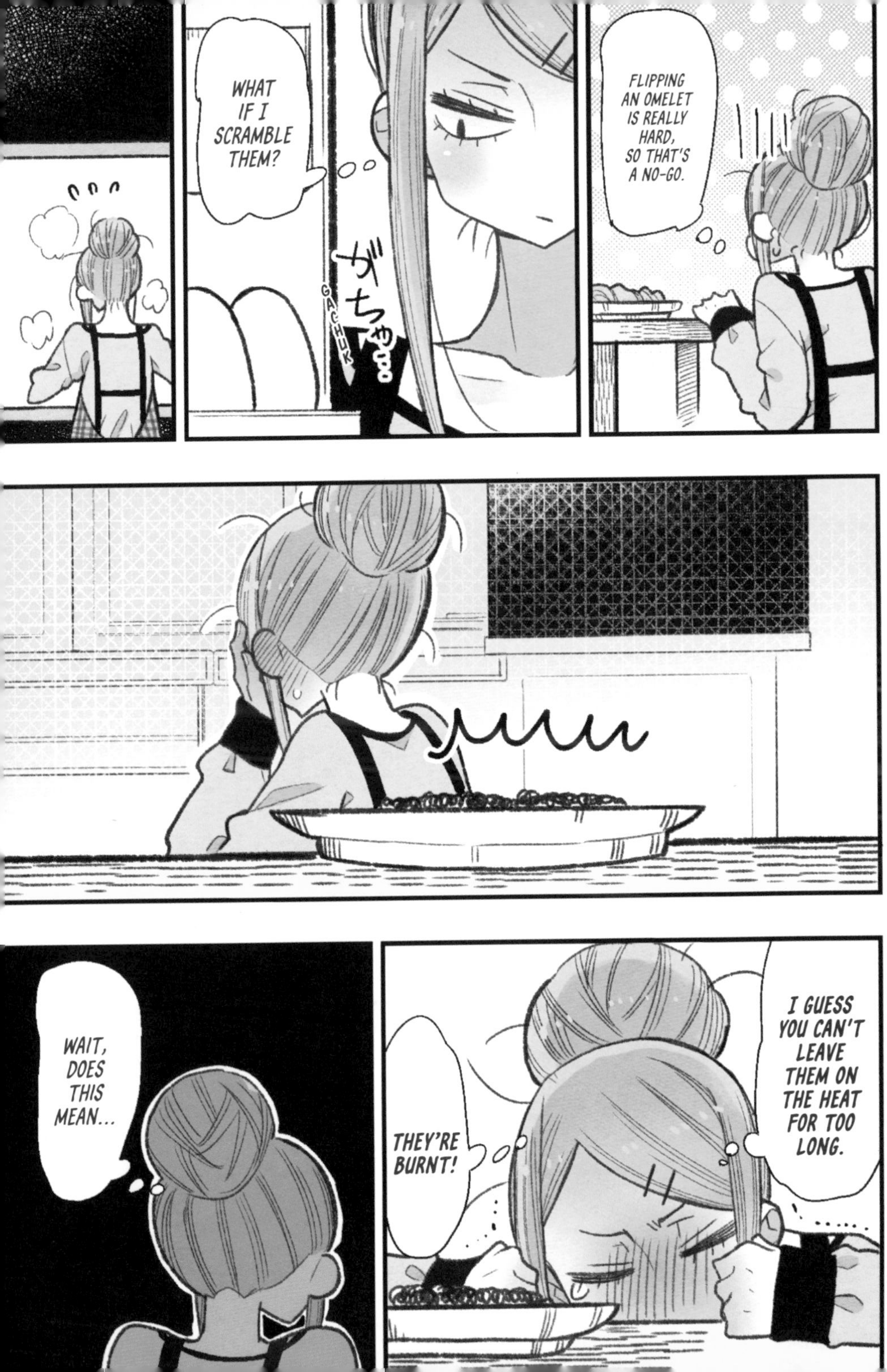
FLIPPING AN OMELET IS REALLY HARD, SO THAT'S A NO-GO.
WHAT IF I SCRAMBLE THEM?
がちゃ
GACHUK
I GUESS YOU CAN'T LEAVE THEM ON THE HEAT FOR TOO LONG.
THEY'RE BURNT!
WAIT, DOES THIS MEAN...

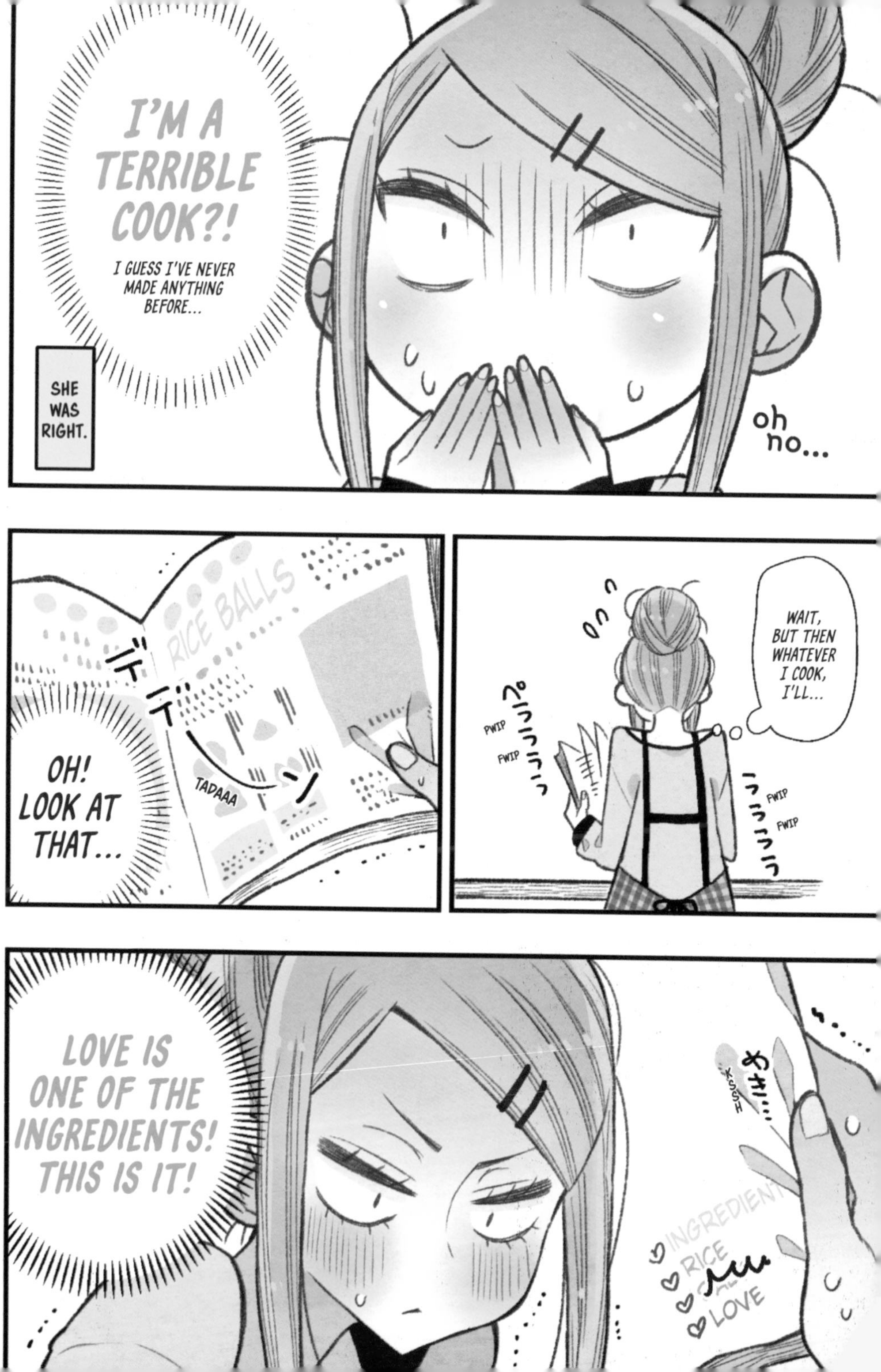
I'M A TERRIBLE COOK?!
I GUESS I'VE NEVER MADE ANYTHING BEFORE...
SHE WAS RIGHT.
oh no...
WAIT, BUT THEN WHATEVER I COOK, I'LL...
PWIP
FWIP
FWIP
FWIP
RICE BALLS
TADAAA
OH! LOOK AT THAT...
KSSH
LOVE IS ONE OF THE INGREDIENTS! THIS IS IT!
INGREDIENT
RICE
LOVE

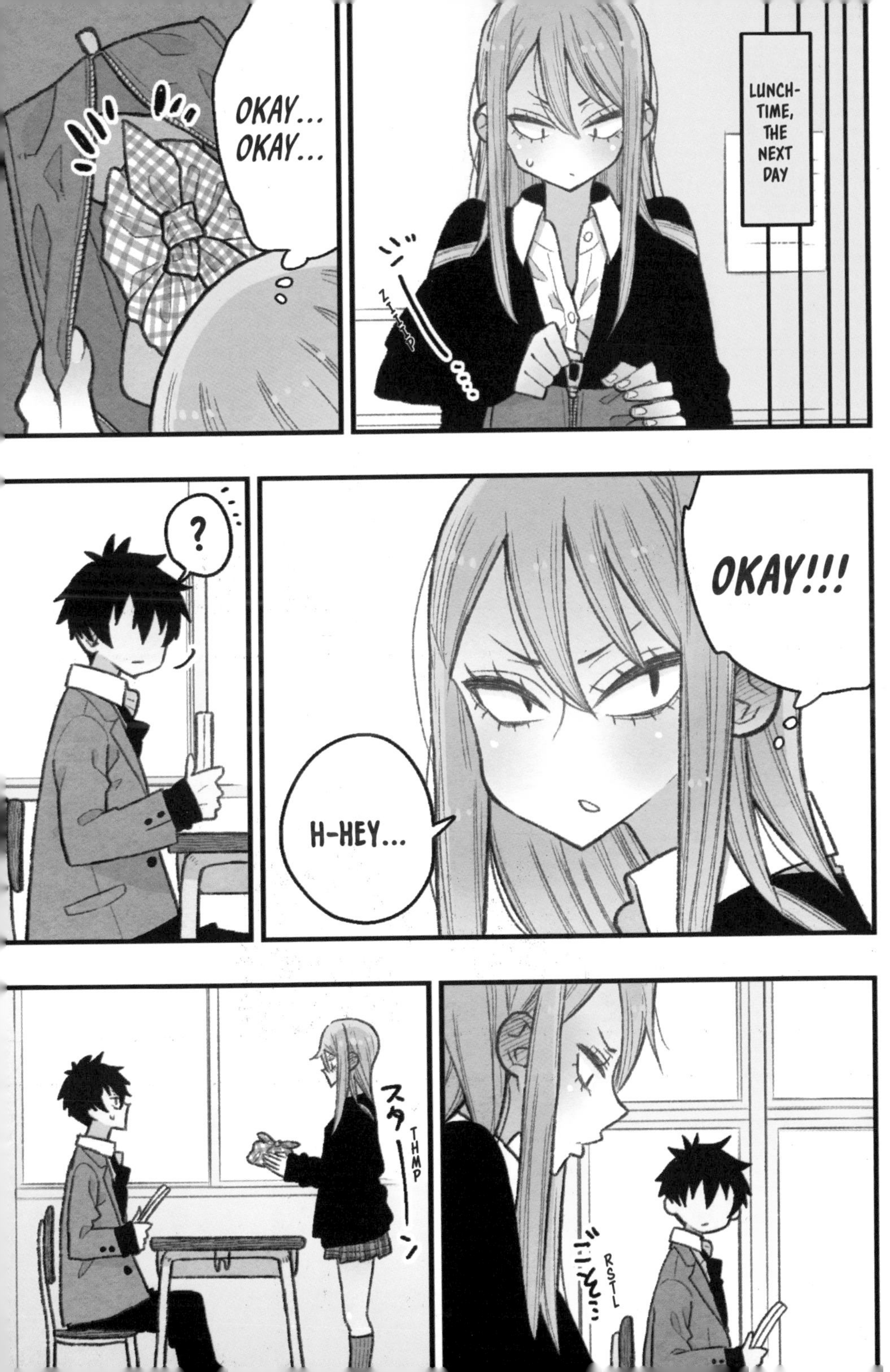
LUNCH-TIME, THE NEXT DAY
ZIIIP
OKAY... OKAY...
OKAY!!!
H-HEY...
?
RSTL
THMP

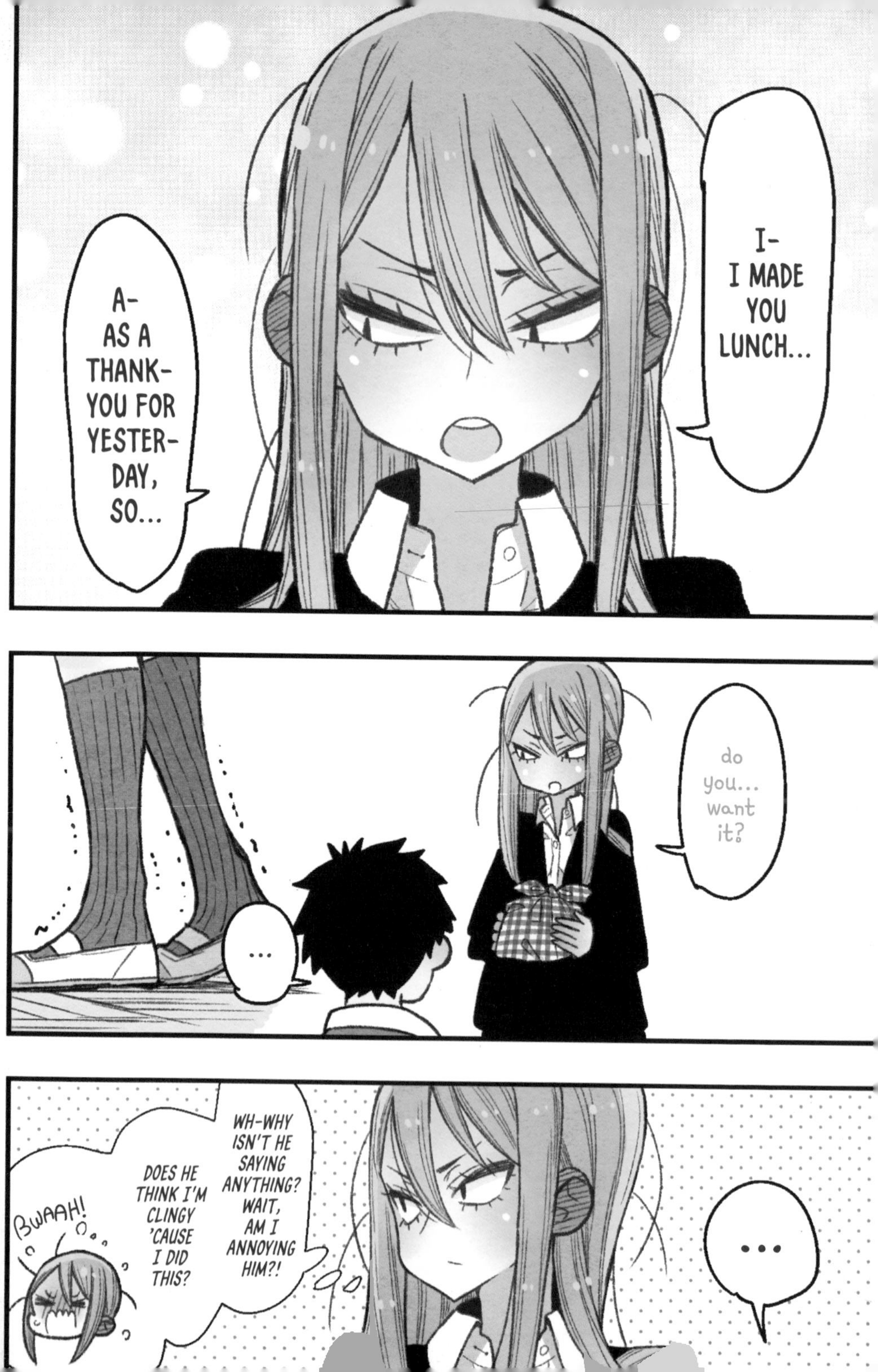
I- I MADE YOU LUNCH...
A- AS A THANK-YOU FOR YESTER-DAY, SO...
do you... want it?
...
...
WH-WHY ISN'T HE SAYING ANYTHING? WAIT, AM I ANNOYING HIM?!
DOES HE THINK I'M CLINGY 'CAUSE I DID THIS?
BWAAH!

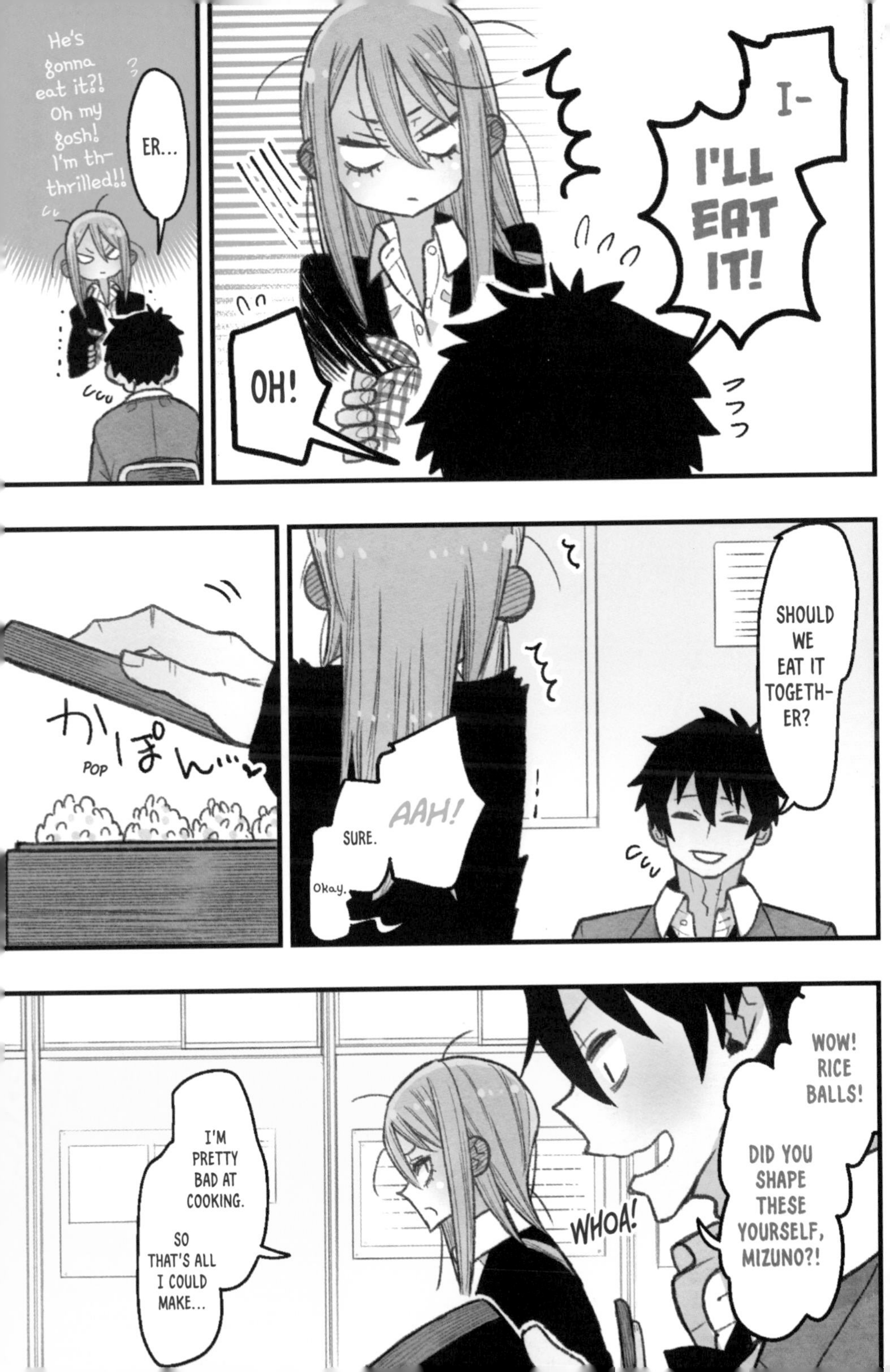
I-
I'LL EAT IT!
OH!
ER...
He's gonna eat it?! Oh my gosh! I'm th-thrilled!!
SHOULD WE EAT IT TOGETH-ER?
AAH!
SURE.
Okay.
かぽん
POP
WOW! RICE BALLS!
DID YOU SHAPE THESE YOURSELF, MIZUNO?!
WHOA!
I'M PRETTY BAD AT COOKING.
SO THAT'S ALL I COULD MAKE...

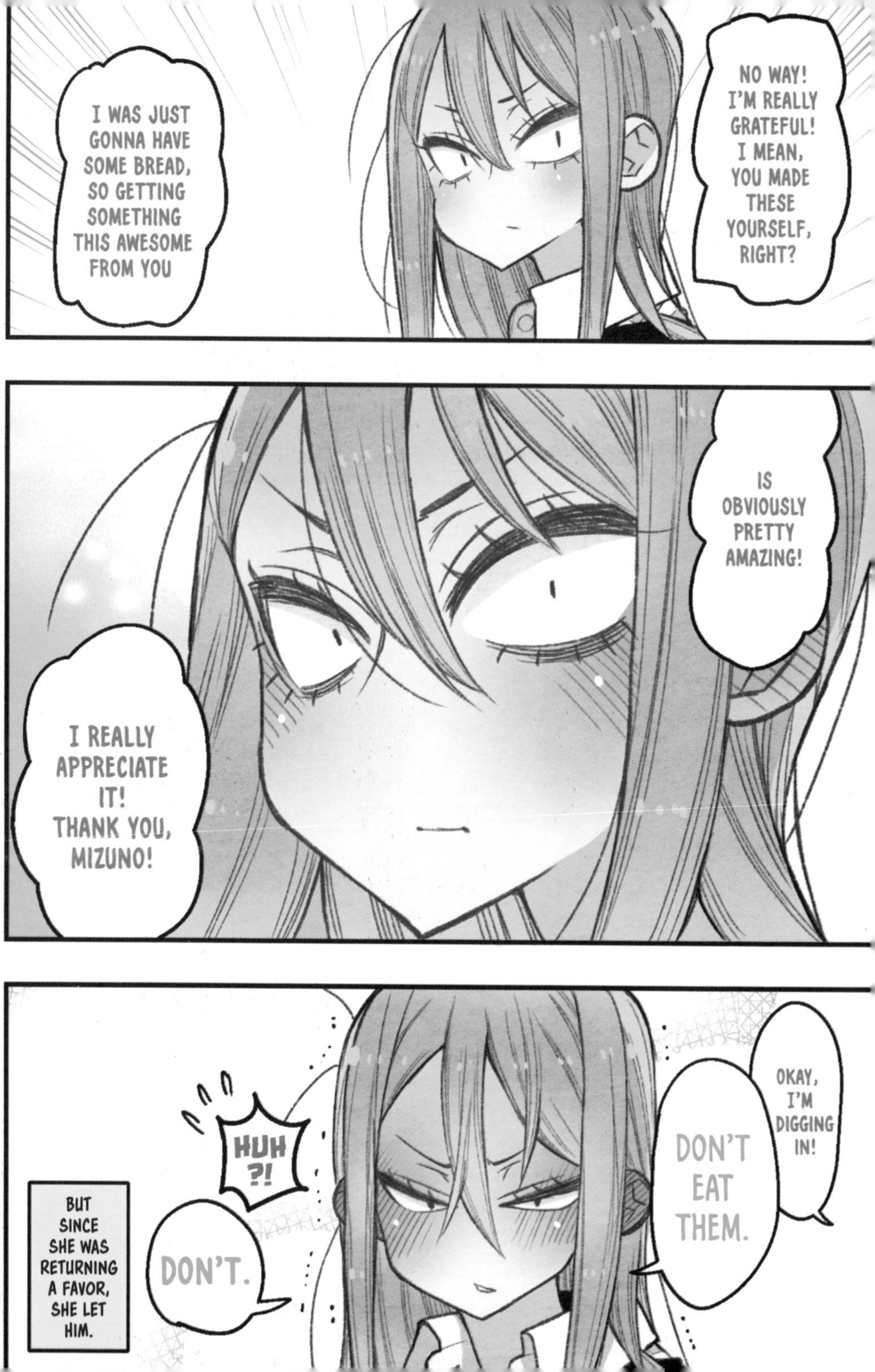
NO WAY! I'M REALLY GRATEFUL! I MEAN, YOU MADE THESE YOURSELF, RIGHT?
I WAS JUST GONNA HAVE SOME BREAD, SO GETTING SOMETHING THIS AWESOME FROM YOU
IS OBVIOUSLY PRETTY AMAZING!
I REALLY APPRECIATE IT! THANK YOU, MIZUNO!
OKAY, I'M DIGGING IN!
DON'T EAT THEM.
HUH ?!
DON'T.
BUT SINCE SHE WAS RETURNING A FAVOR, SHE LET HIM.

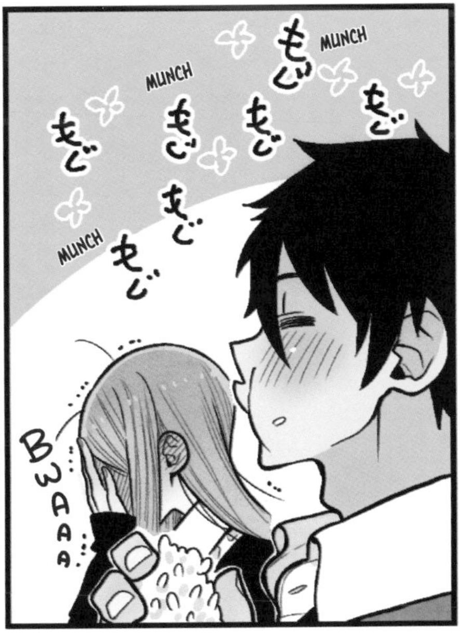
もぐ
MUNCH
もぐ
もぐ
もぐ
MUNCH
もぐ
もぐ
もぐ
MUNCH
BWAAAA

THE GiRL
WiTH THE
SANPAKu
EyES

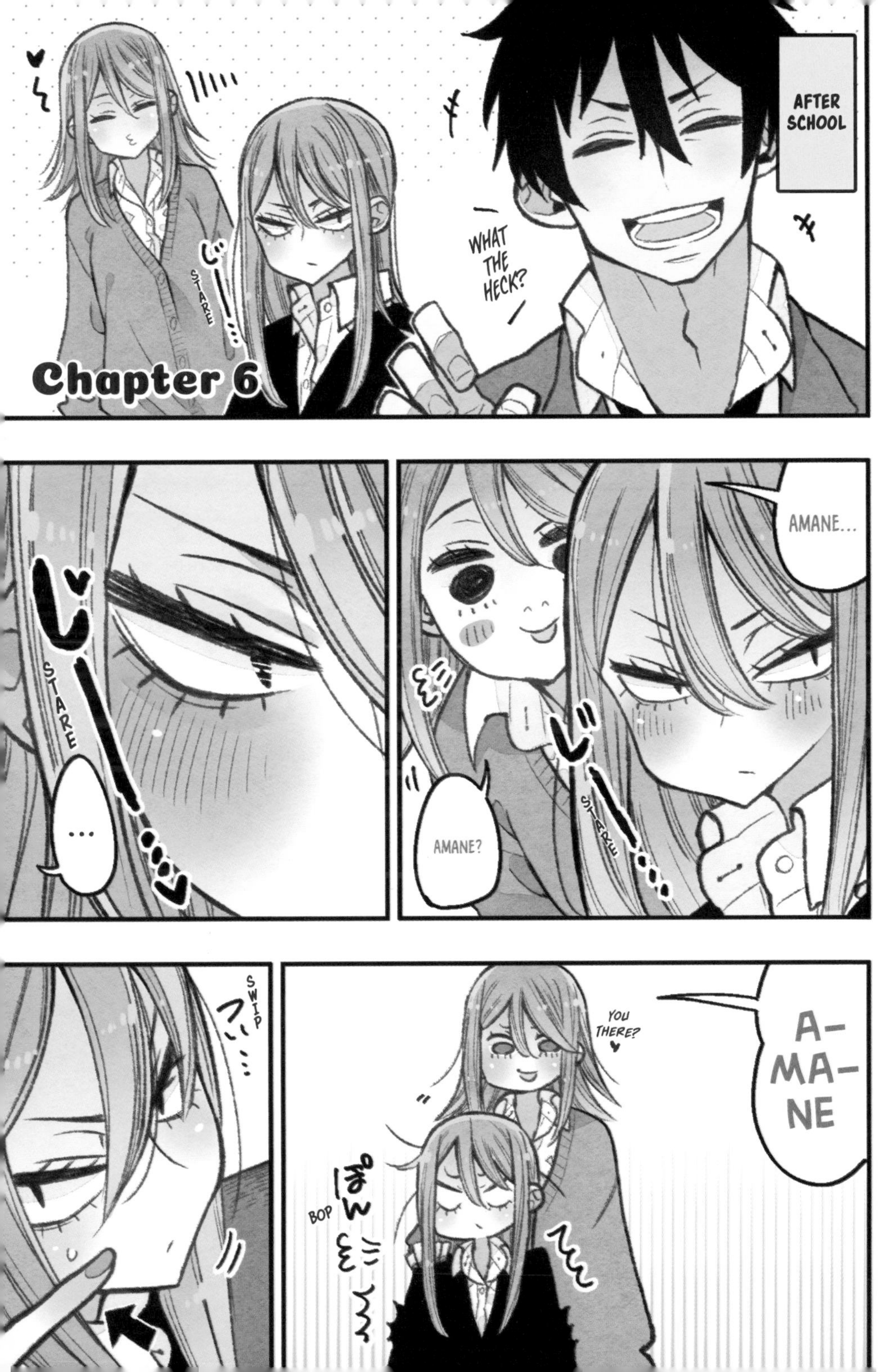
AFTER SCHOOL
WHAT THE HECK?
STARE
Chapter 6
AMANE...
STARE
AMANE?
STARE
...
A-MA-NE
YOU THERE?
BOP
SWIP

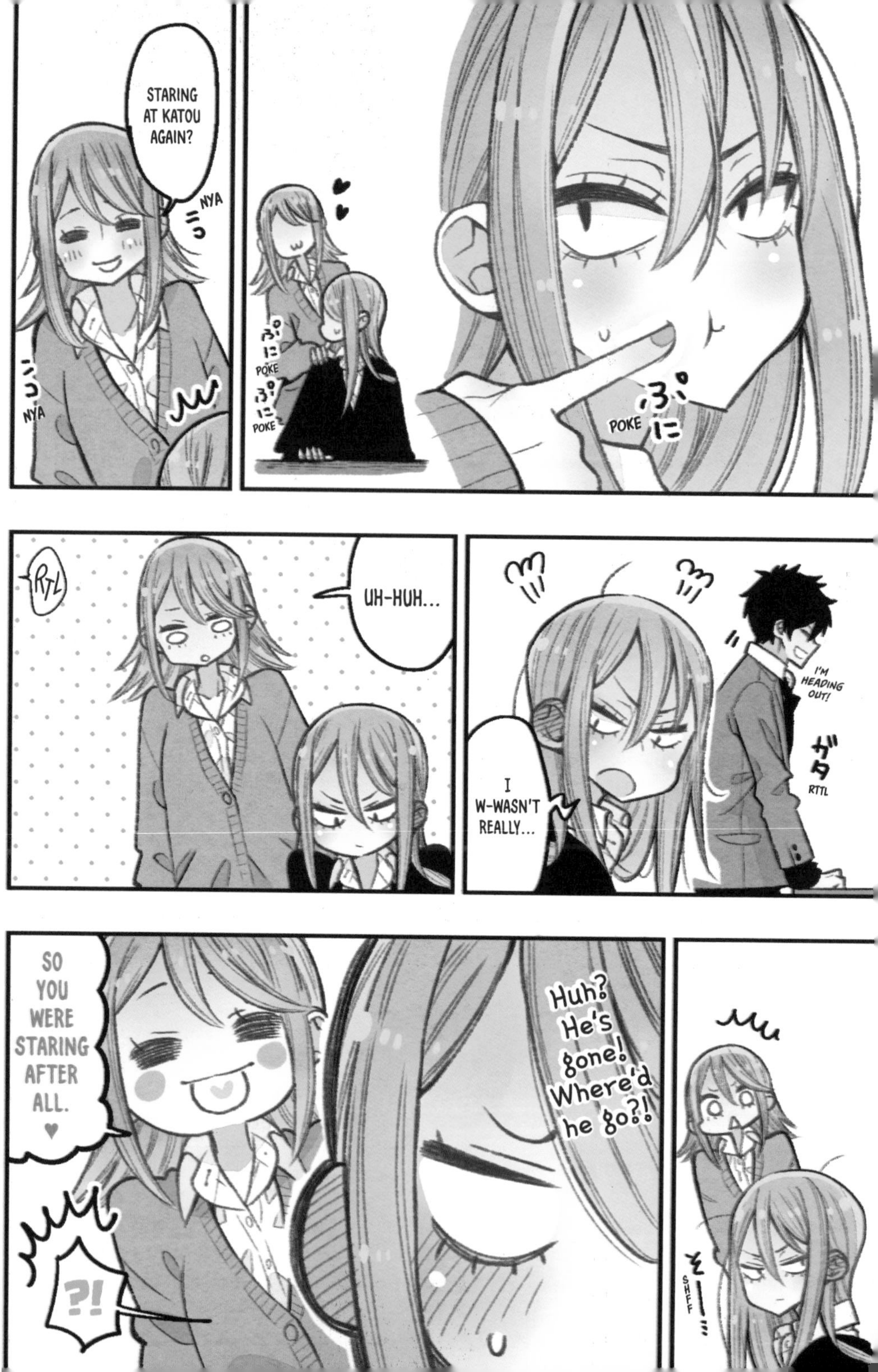
ぷに
POKE
ぷに
POKE
ぷに
POKE
STARING AT KATOU AGAIN?
NYA
NYA
I'M HEADING OUT!
ガタ
RTTL
I W-WASN'T REALLY...
UH-HUH...
RTL
SHFF
Huh? He's gone! Where'd he go?!
SO YOU WERE STARING AFTER ALL. ♥
?!

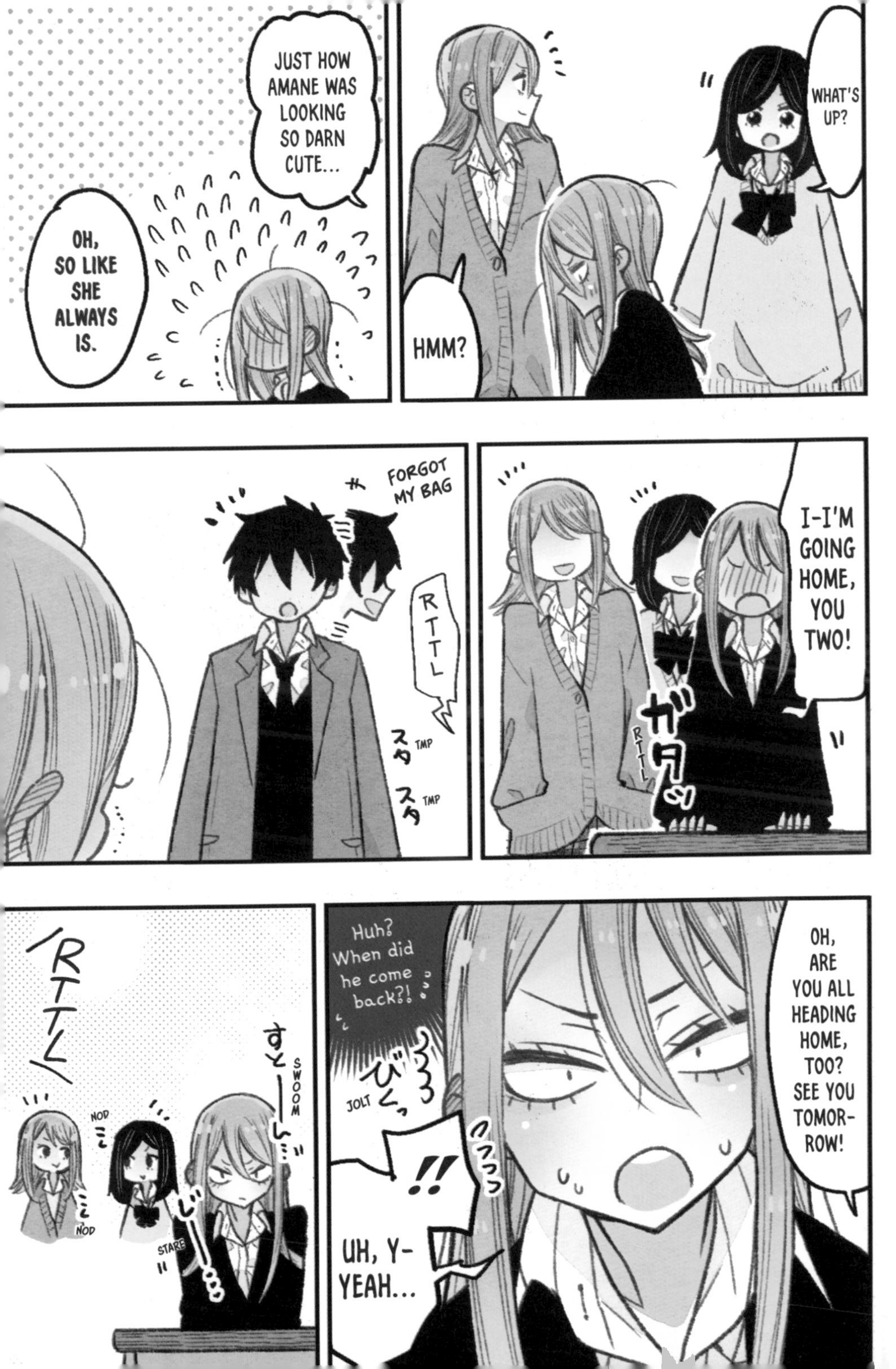
WHAT'S UP?
HMM?
JUST HOW AMANE WAS LOOKING SO DARN CUTE...
OH, SO LIKE SHE ALWAYS IS.
I-I'M GOING HOME, YOU TWO!
ガタッ
RTTL
FORGOT MY BAG
RTTL
スタ
TMP
スタ
TMP
OH, ARE YOU ALL HEADING HOME, TOO? SEE YOU TOMOR-ROW!
Huh? When did he come back?!
びくっ
JOLT
!!
UH, Y-YEAH...
RTTL
すとーん
SWOOM
NOD
NOD
STARE

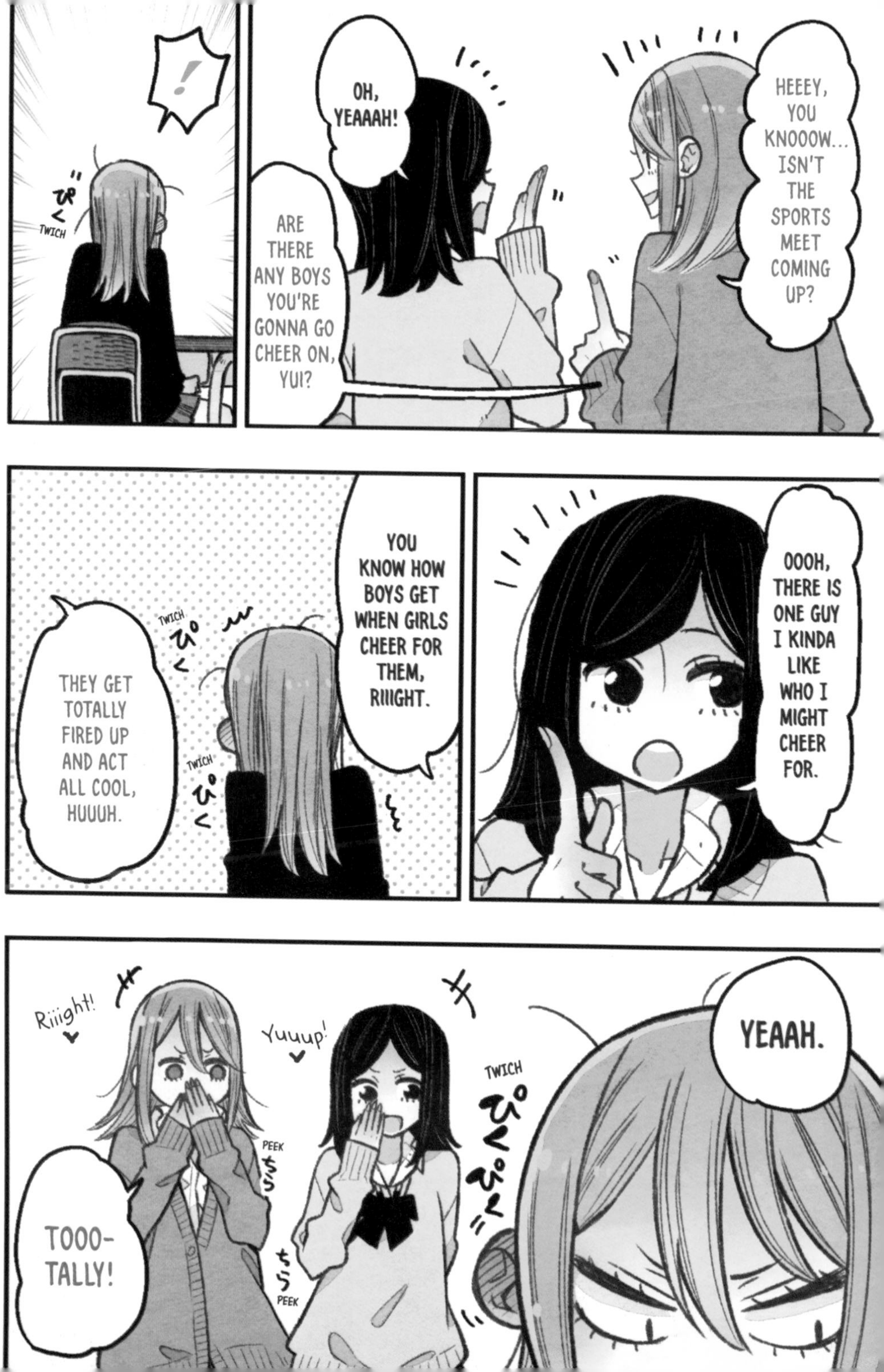
HEEEY, YOU KNOOOW... ISN'T THE SPORTS MEET COMING UP?
OH, YEAAAH!
ARE THERE ANY BOYS YOU'RE GONNA GO CHEER ON, YUI?
!
ぴく
TWICH
OOOH, THERE IS ONE GUY I KINDA LIKE WHO I MIGHT CHEER FOR.
YOU KNOW HOW BOYS GET WHEN GIRLS CHEER FOR THEM, RIIIGHT.
TWICH
ぴく
THEY GET TOTALLY FIRED UP AND ACT ALL COOL, HUUUH.
TWICH
ぴく
YEAAH.
TWICH
ぴくぴくぴく
Yuuup!
PEEK
ちら
Riiight!
TOOO-TALLY!
ちら
PEEK

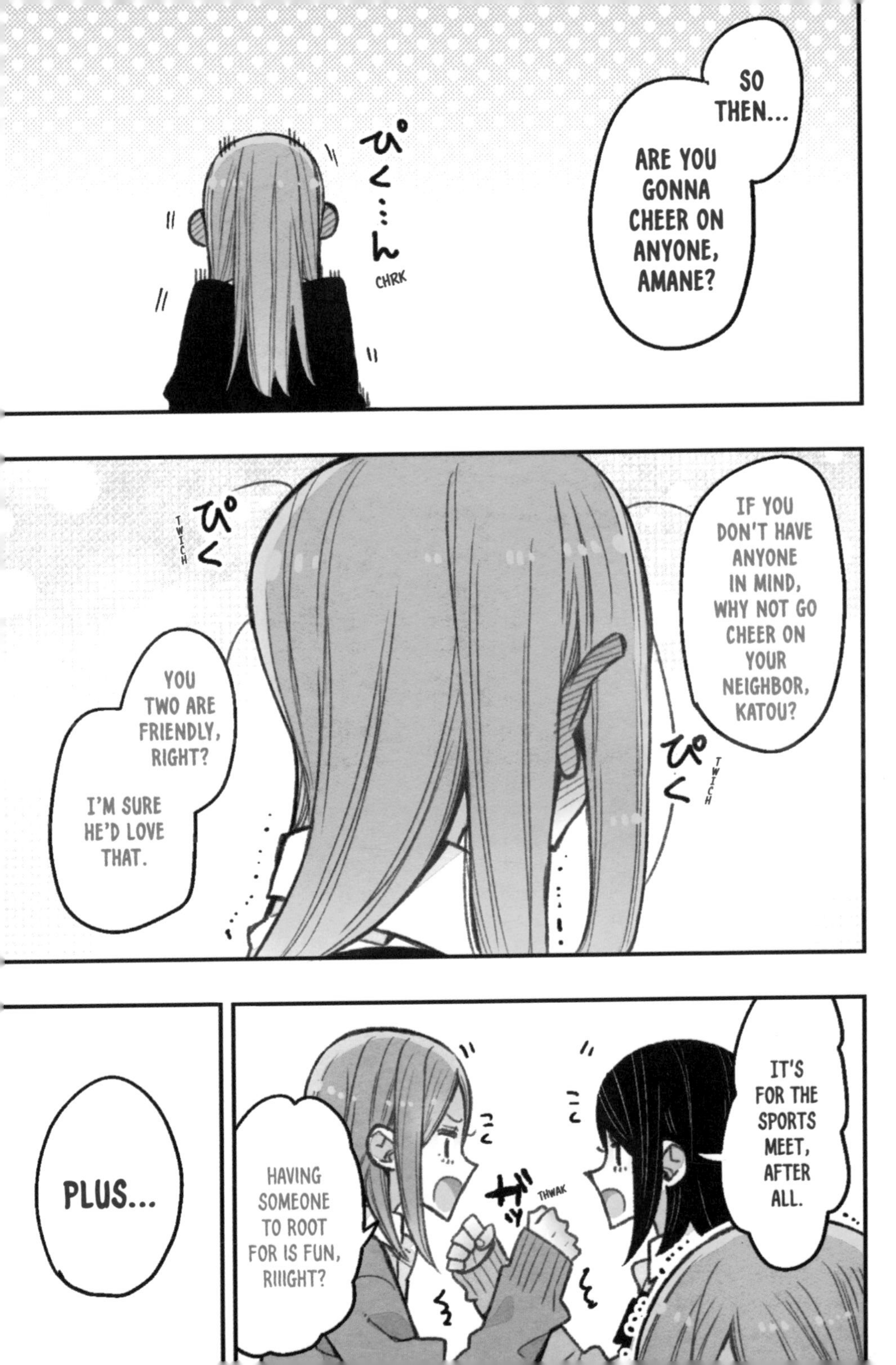
SO THEN...
ARE YOU GONNA CHEER ON ANYONE, AMANE?
ぴく…ん
CHRK
IF YOU DON'T HAVE ANYONE IN MIND, WHY NOT GO CHEER ON YOUR NEIGHBOR, KATOU?
ぴく
TWICH
ぴく
TWICH
YOU TWO ARE FRIENDLY, RIGHT?
I'M SURE HE'D LOVE THAT.
IT'S FOR THE SPORTS MEET, AFTER ALL.
ガッ
THWAK
HAVING SOMEONE TO ROOT FOR IS FUN, RIIIGHT?
PLUS...

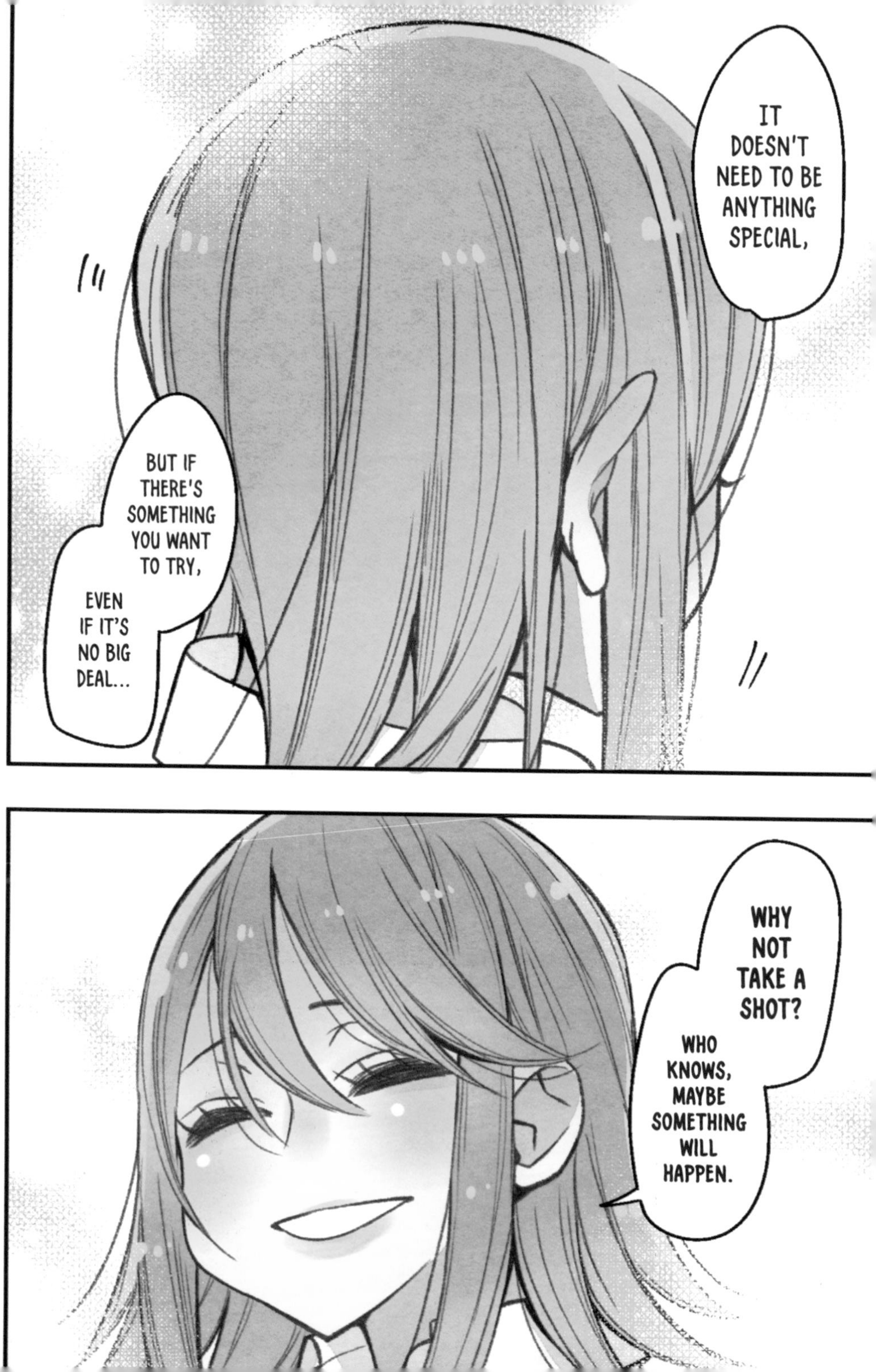
IT DOESN'T NEED TO BE ANYTHING SPECIAL,
BUT IF THERE'S SOMETHING YOU WANT TO TRY,
EVEN IF IT'S NO BIG DEAL...
WHY NOT TAKE A SHOT?
WHO KNOWS, MAYBE SOMETHING WILL HAPPEN.

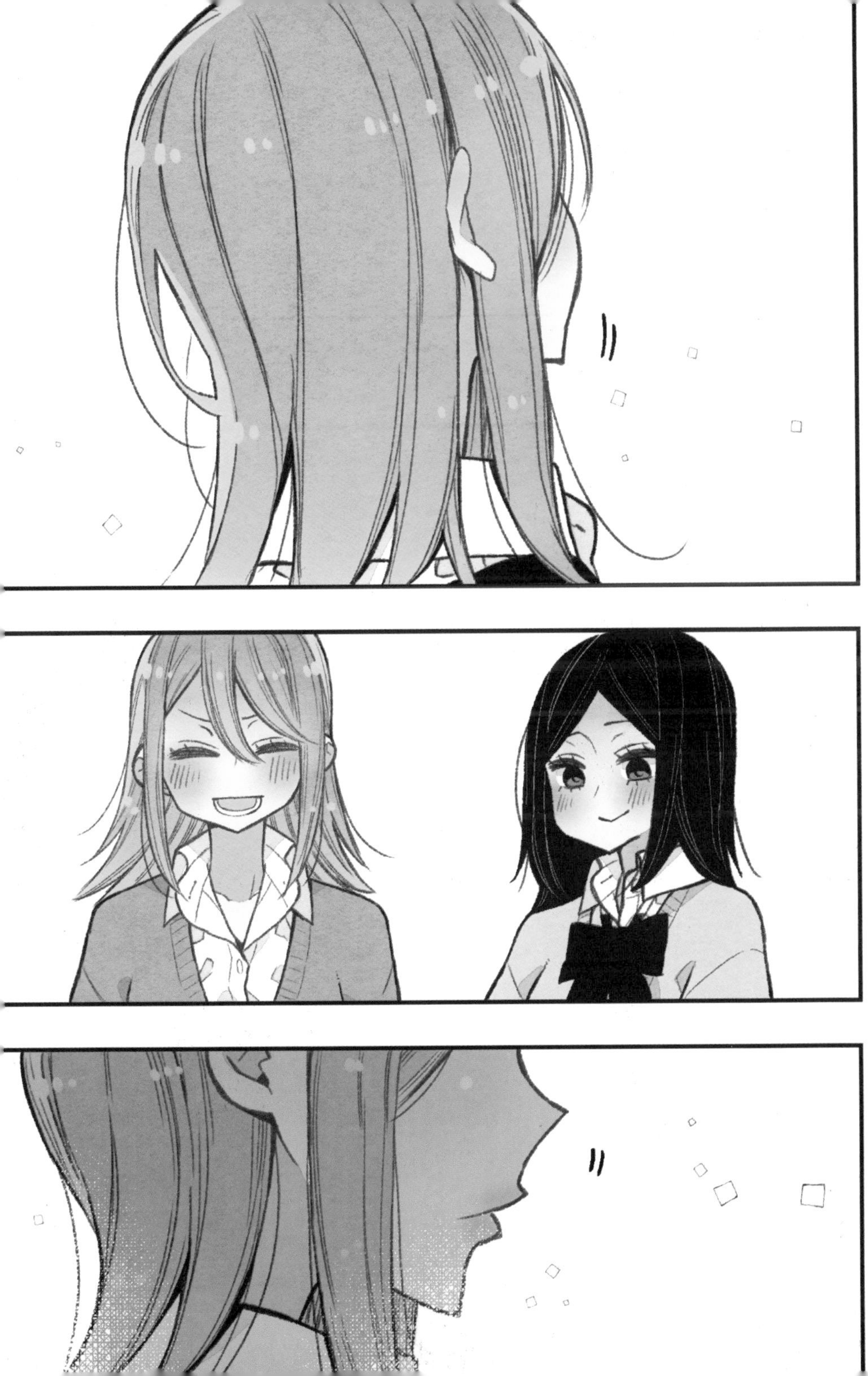

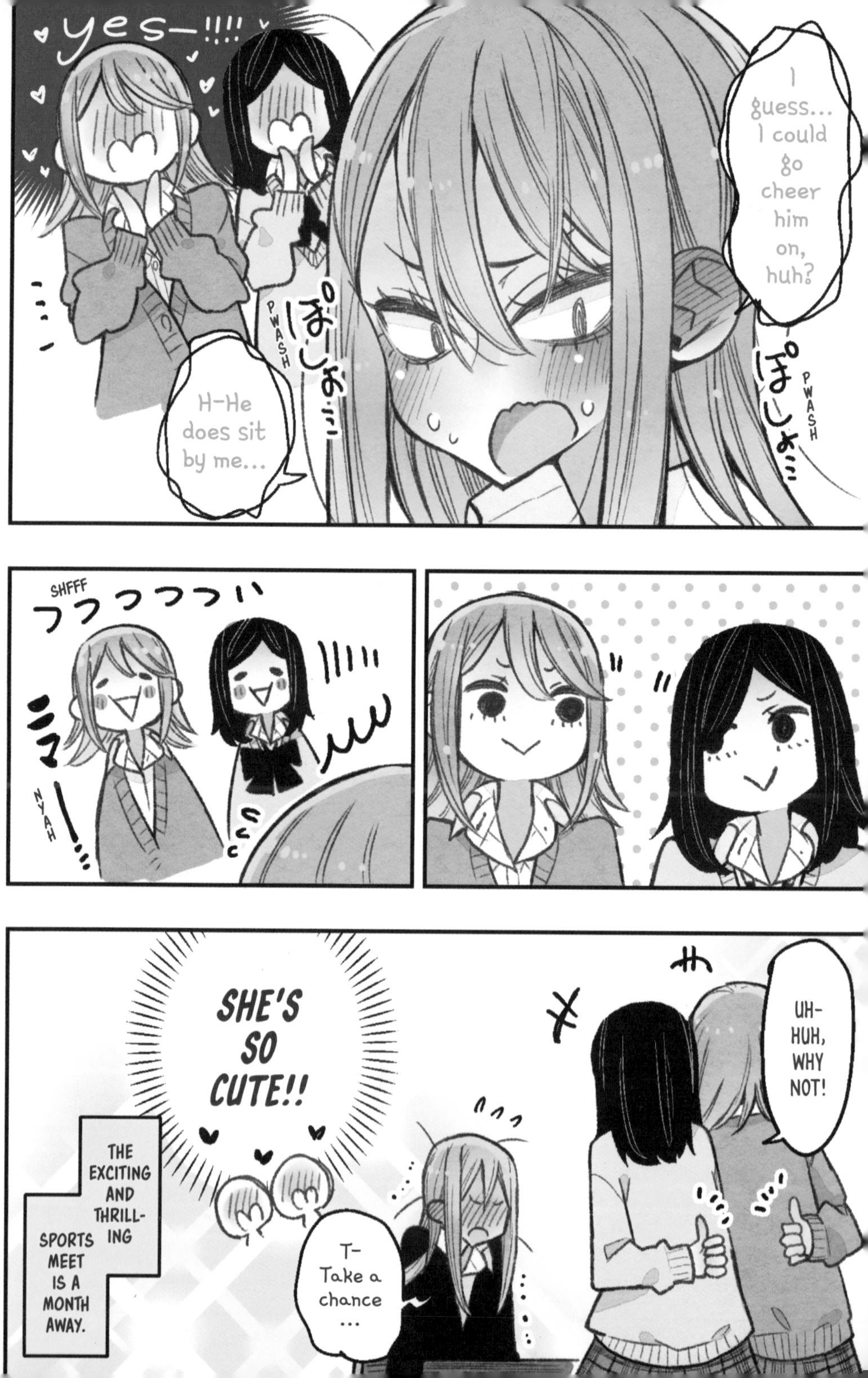
I guess... I could go cheer him on, huh?
PWASH
H-He does sit by me...
PWASH
yes—!!!!
SHFFF
NYAH
UH-HUH, WHY NOT!
SHE'S SO CUTE!!
T-Take a chance...
THE EXCITING AND THRILL-ING SPORTS MEET IS A MONTH AWAY.

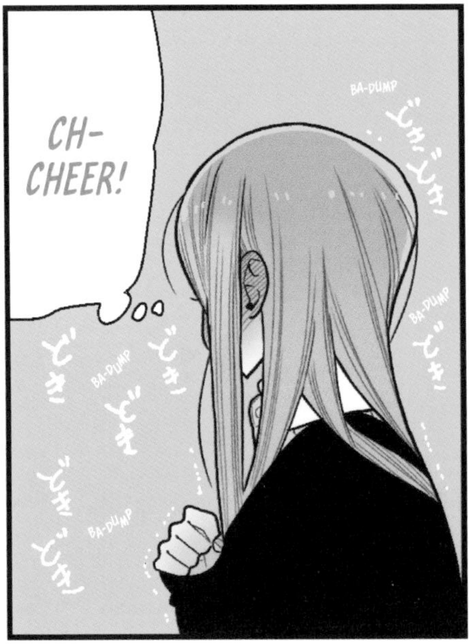
CH- CHEER!
BA-DUMP
BA-DUMP
BA-DUMP
BA-DUMP

THE GiRL
WiTH THE
SANPAKu
EyES

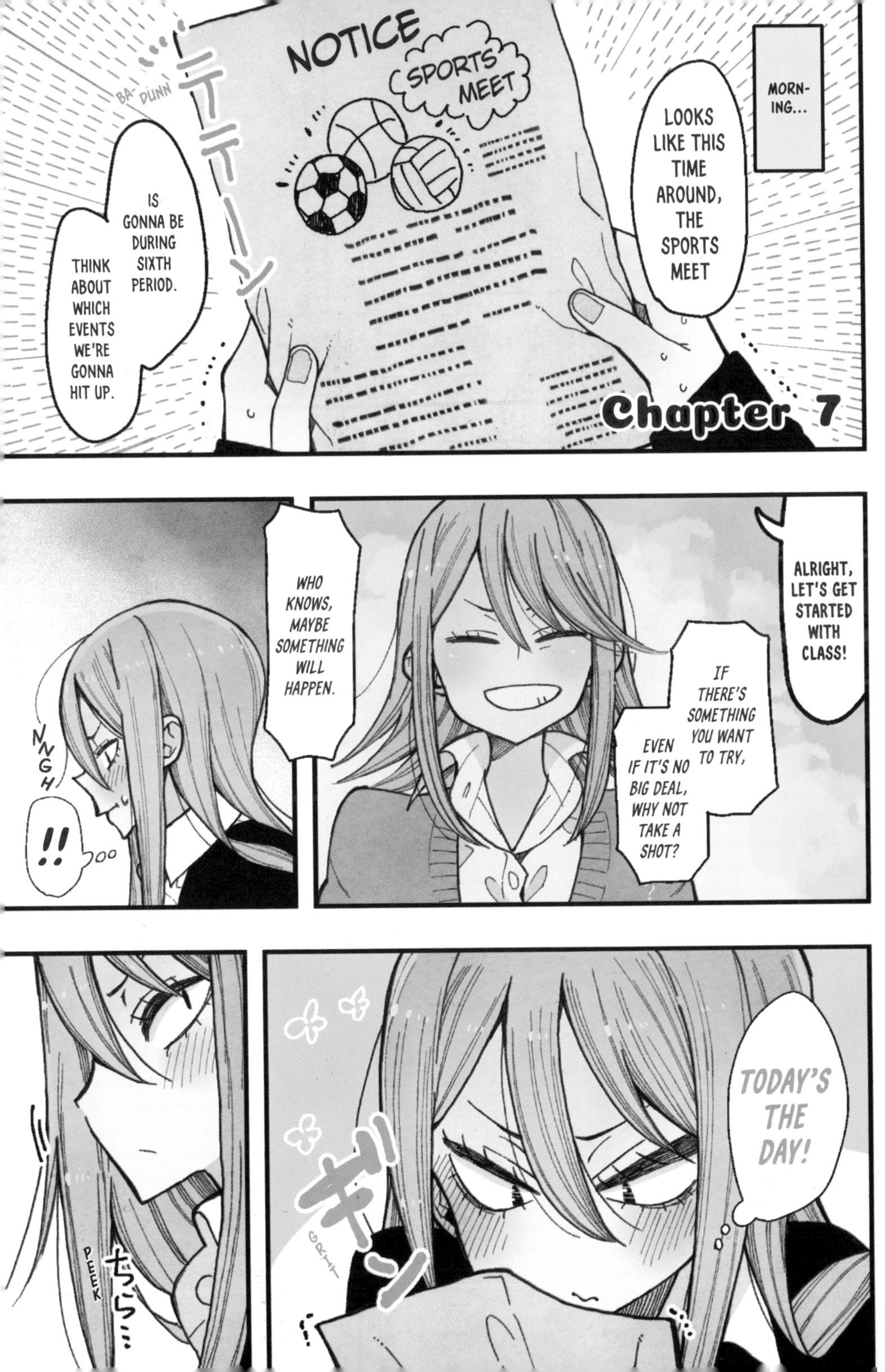
MORN-ING...
LOOKS LIKE THIS TIME AROUND, THE SPORTS MEET
NOTICE
SPORTS MEET
BA-DUNN
IS GONNA BE DURING SIXTH PERIOD.
THINK ABOUT WHICH EVENTS WE'RE GONNA HIT UP.
Chapter 7
ALRIGHT, LET'S GET STARTED WITH CLASS!
IF THERE'S SOMETHING YOU WANT TO TRY,
EVEN IF IT'S NO BIG DEAL, WHY NOT TAKE A SHOT?
WHO KNOWS, MAYBE SOMETHING WILL HAPPEN.
NNGH
!!
TODAY'S THE DAY!
GRIT
PEEK
ちら…

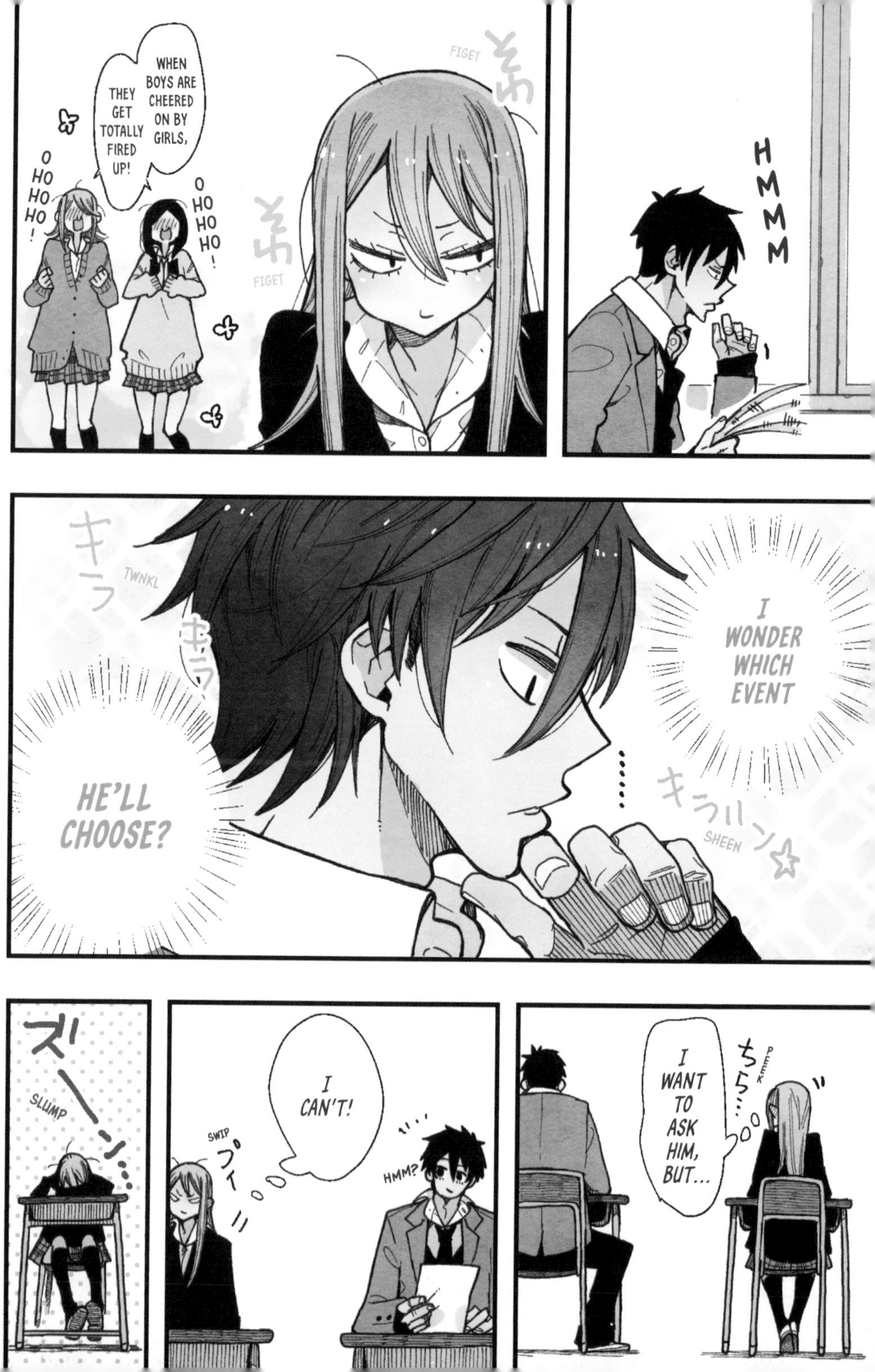
HMMM
そわ
FIGET
そわ
FIGET
WHEN BOYS ARE CHEERED ON BY GIRLS,
THEY GET TOTALLY FIRED UP!
O HO HO HO!
O HO HO HO!
I WONDER WHICH EVENT
キラ
TWNKL
キラ
......
キラリーン
SHEEN
HE'LL CHOOSE?
I WANT TO ASK HIM, BUT...
ちら
PEEK
HMM?
I CAN'T!
プイ
SWIP
ズーン
SLUMP

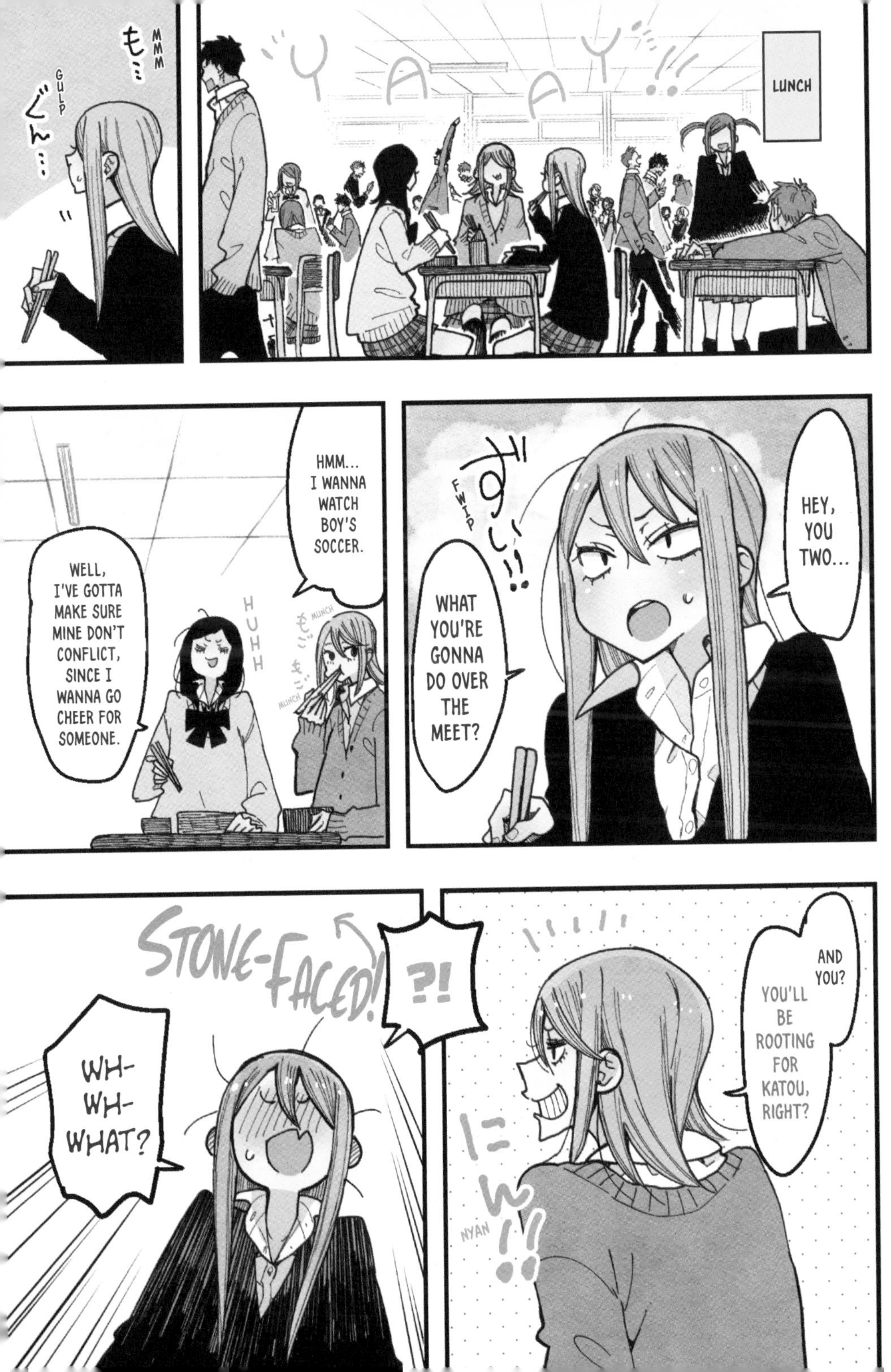
LUNCH
YAAY!!
もぐ…
MMM
ぐん…
GULP
ずい!!
FWIP
HEY, YOU TWO...
WHAT YOU'RE GONNA DO OVER THE MEET?
HMM... I WANNA WATCH BOY'S SOCCER.
もごもご
MUNCH MUNCH
HUHH
WELL, I'VE GOTTA MAKE SURE MINE DON'T CONFLICT, SINCE I WANNA GO CHEER FOR SOMEONE.
AND YOU?
YOU'LL BE ROOTING FOR KATOU, RIGHT?
にん!!
NYAN
?!
STONE-FACED!!
WH-WH-WHAT?

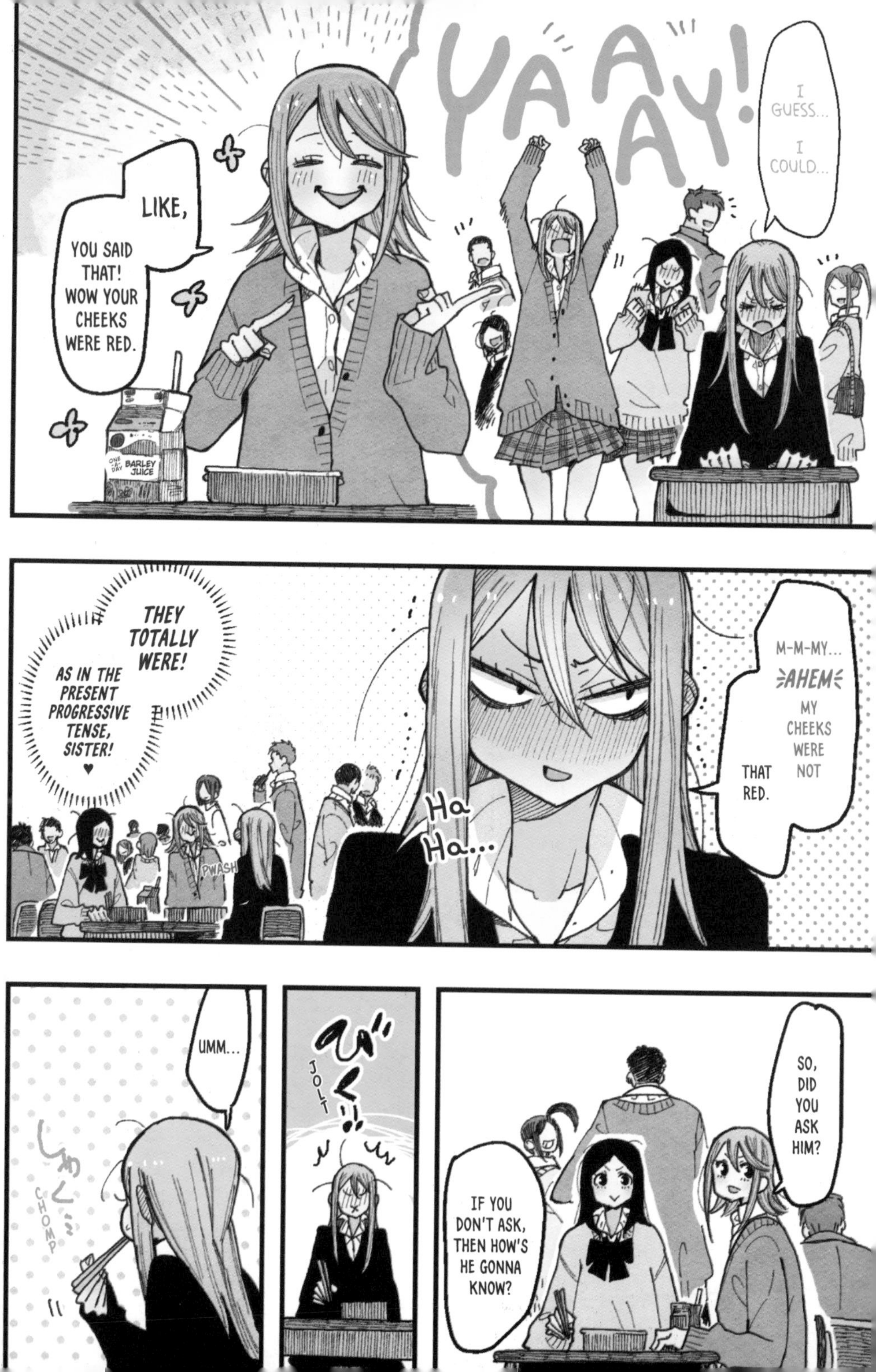
I GUESS... I COULD...
YAAAAY!
LIKE,
YOU SAID THAT! WOW YOUR CHEEKS WERE RED.
ONE-A-DAY BARLEY JUICE
M-M-MY... AHEM MY CHEEKS WERE NOT THAT RED.
Ha Ha...
THEY TOTALLY WERE!
AS IN THE PRESENT PROGRESSIVE TENSE, SISTER! ♥
PWASH
SO, DID YOU ASK HIM?
IF YOU DON'T ASK, THEN HOW'S HE GONNA KNOW?
JOLT
UMM...
CHOMP

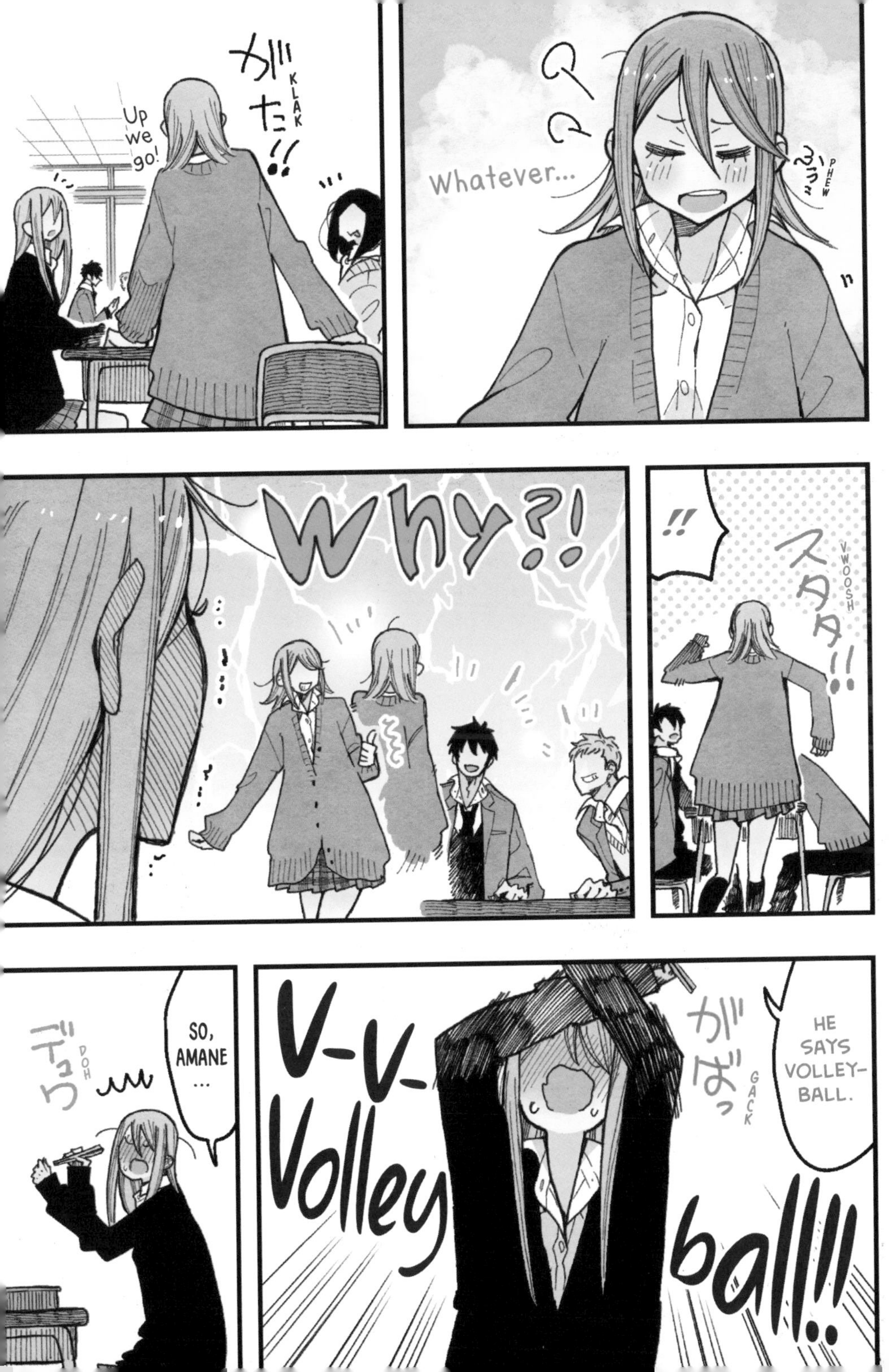
Whatever...
PHEW
Up we go!
がた!!
KLAK
!!
スタタ!!
VWOOSH
Why?!
HE SAYS VOLLEY-BALL.
がばっ
GACK
V-V-Volleyball!!
SO, AMANE ...
DOH

WHICH EVENT ARE YOU GONNA DO?

IF YOU'RE GONNA GO CHEER ON KATOU

Wait.

Should we go?

TRY NOT TO PICK SOMETHING THAT OVERLAPS, OKAY...

STARE

I- I GUESS SO...

I...

CHOMP

AMANE?

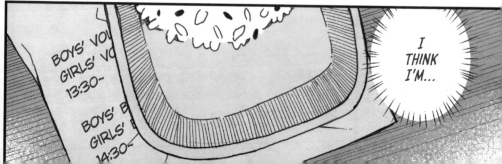

BOYS' VO
GIRLS' VO
13:30~

BOYS' B
GIRLS' B
14:30~

I THINK I'M...

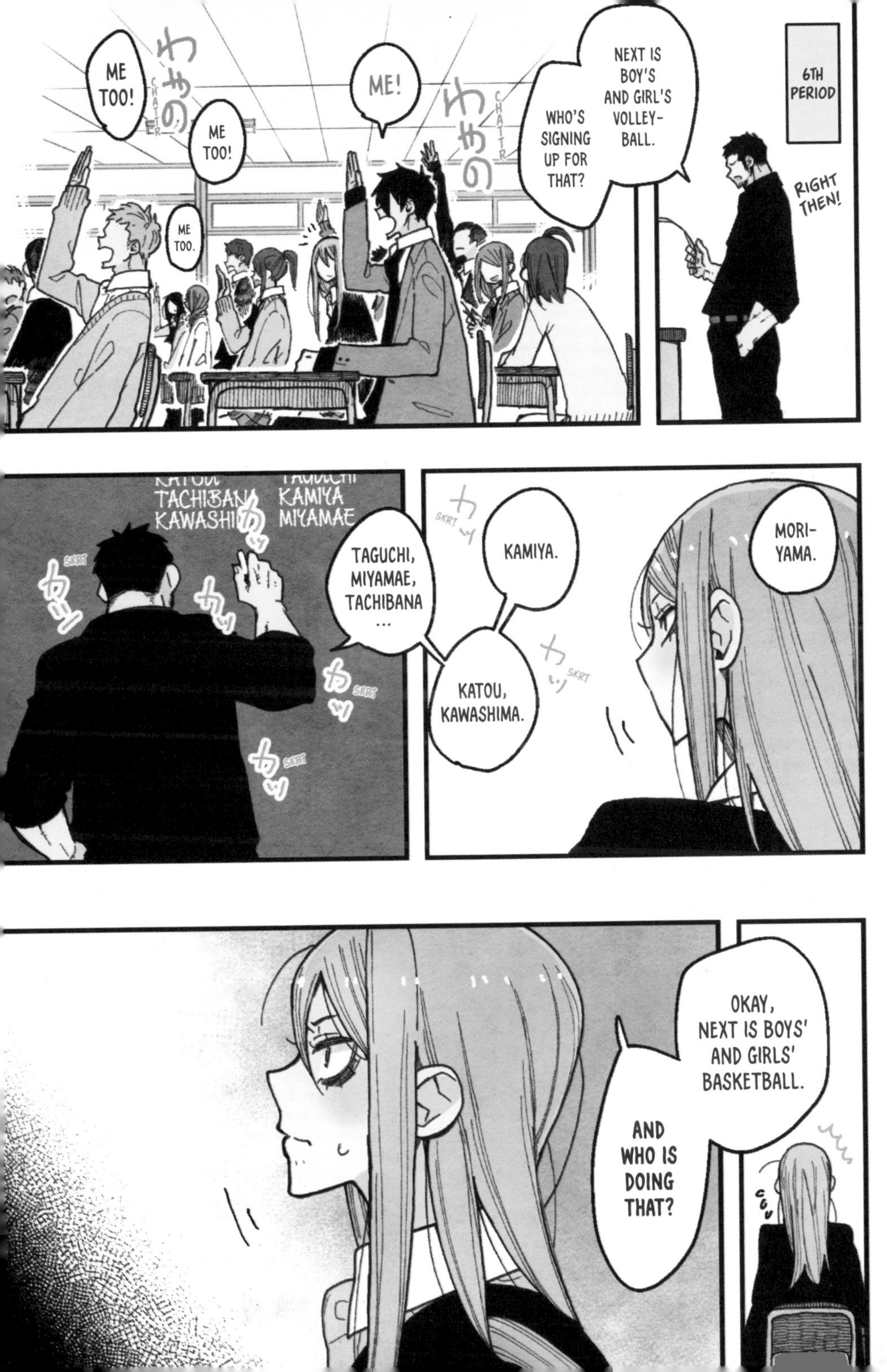
6TH PERIOD
RIGHT THEN!
NEXT IS BOY'S AND GIRL'S VOLLEY-BALL.
WHO'S SIGNING UP FOR THAT?
CHATTR
ME!
CHATTR
ME TOO!
ME TOO!
ME TOO.
MORI-YAMA.
SKRT
KAMIYA.
SKRT
KATOU, KAWASHIMA.
TAGUCHI, MIYAMAE, TACHIBANA ...
KAMIYA
MIYAMAE
TACHIBANA
SKRT
SKRT
SKRT
OKAY, NEXT IS BOYS' AND GIRLS' BASKETBALL.
AND WHO IS DOING THAT?

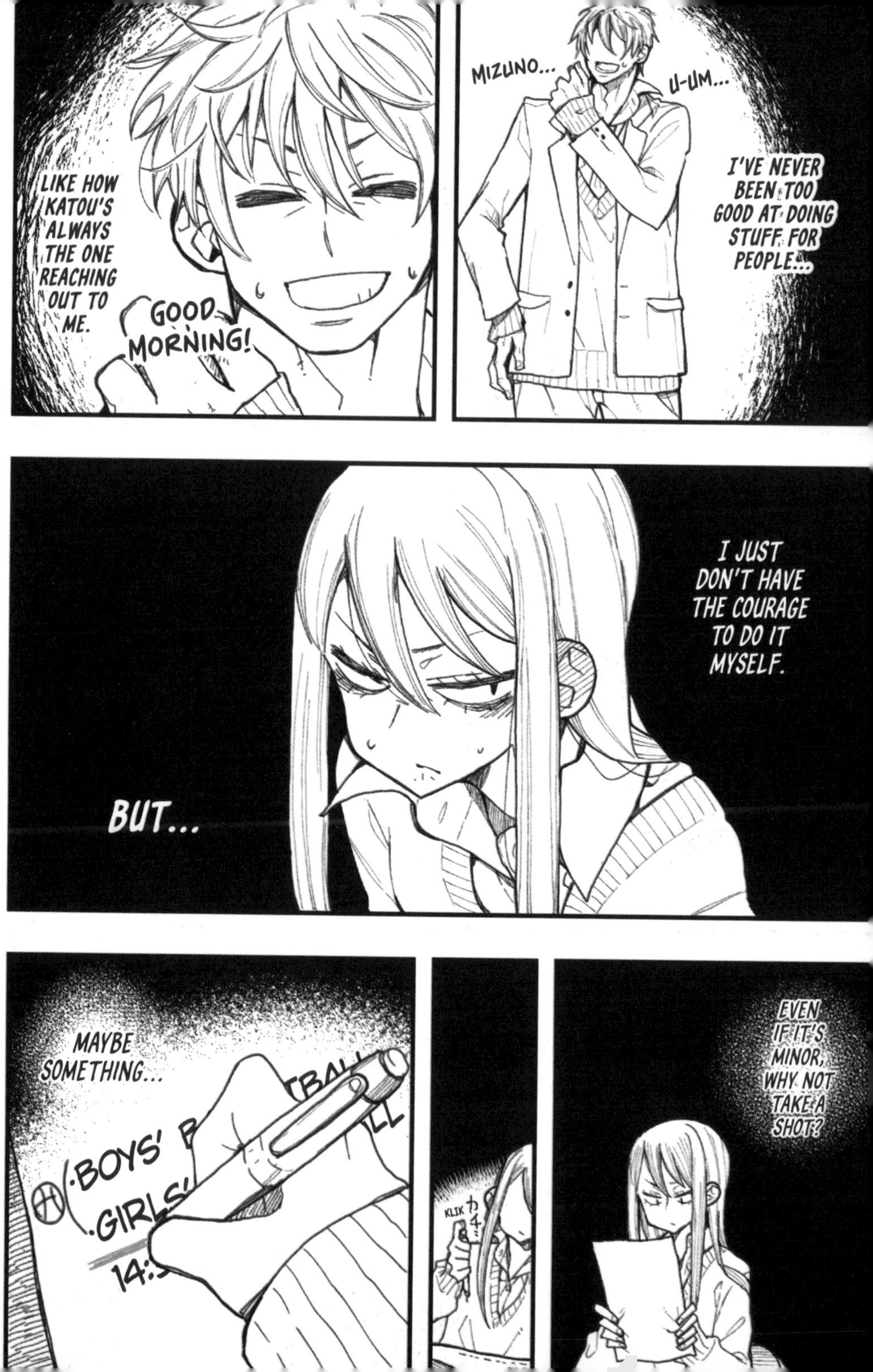
MIZUNO...
U-UM...
I'VE NEVER BEEN TOO GOOD AT DOING STUFF FOR PEOPLE...
LIKE HOW KATOU'S ALWAYS THE ONE REACHING OUT TO ME.
GOOD MORNING!
I JUST DON'T HAVE THE COURAGE TO DO IT MYSELF.
BUT...
EVEN IF IT'S MINOR, WHY NOT TAKE A SHOT?
KLIK
カチ
MAYBE SOMETHING...
·BOYS'
·GIRLS'

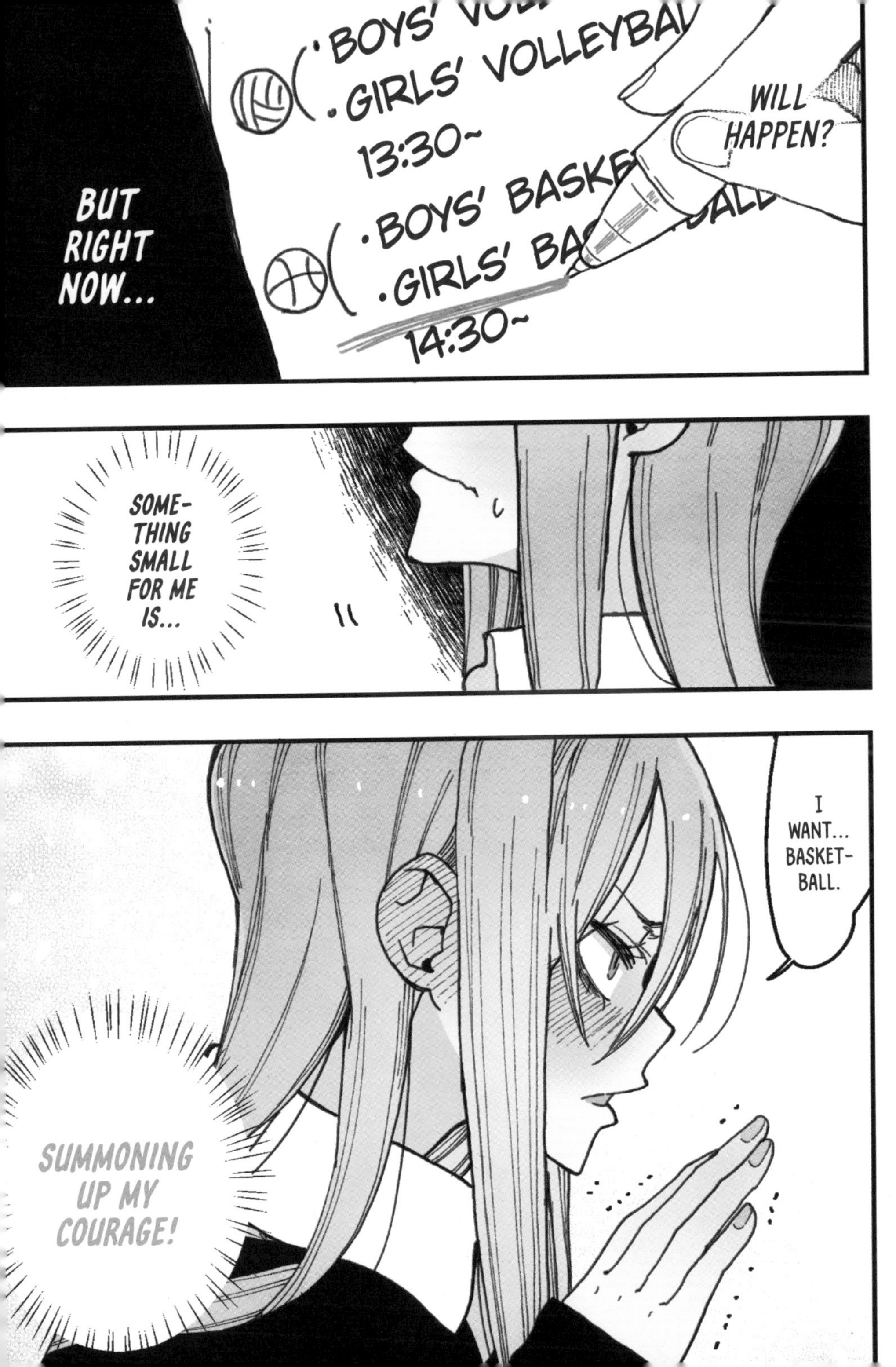
WILL HAPPEN?
·BOYS' VOL
·GIRLS' VOLLEYBA
13:30~
·BOYS' BASKE
·GIRLS' BAS
14:30~
BUT RIGHT NOW...
SOME-THING SMALL FOR ME IS...
I WANT... BASKET-BALL.
SUMMONING UP MY COURAGE!

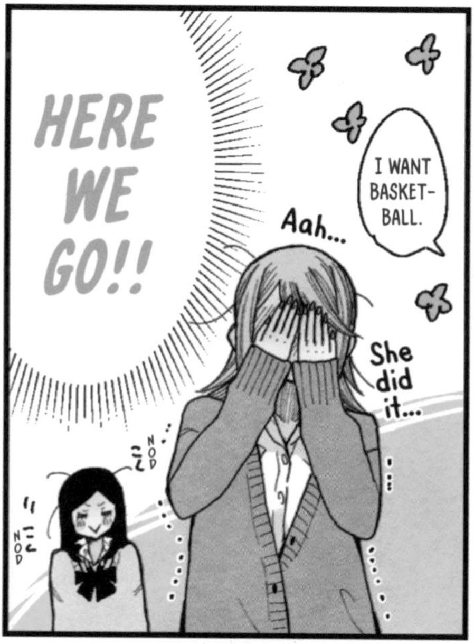
I WANT BASKET-BALL.
Aah...
She did it...
HERE WE GO!!
NOD
NOD

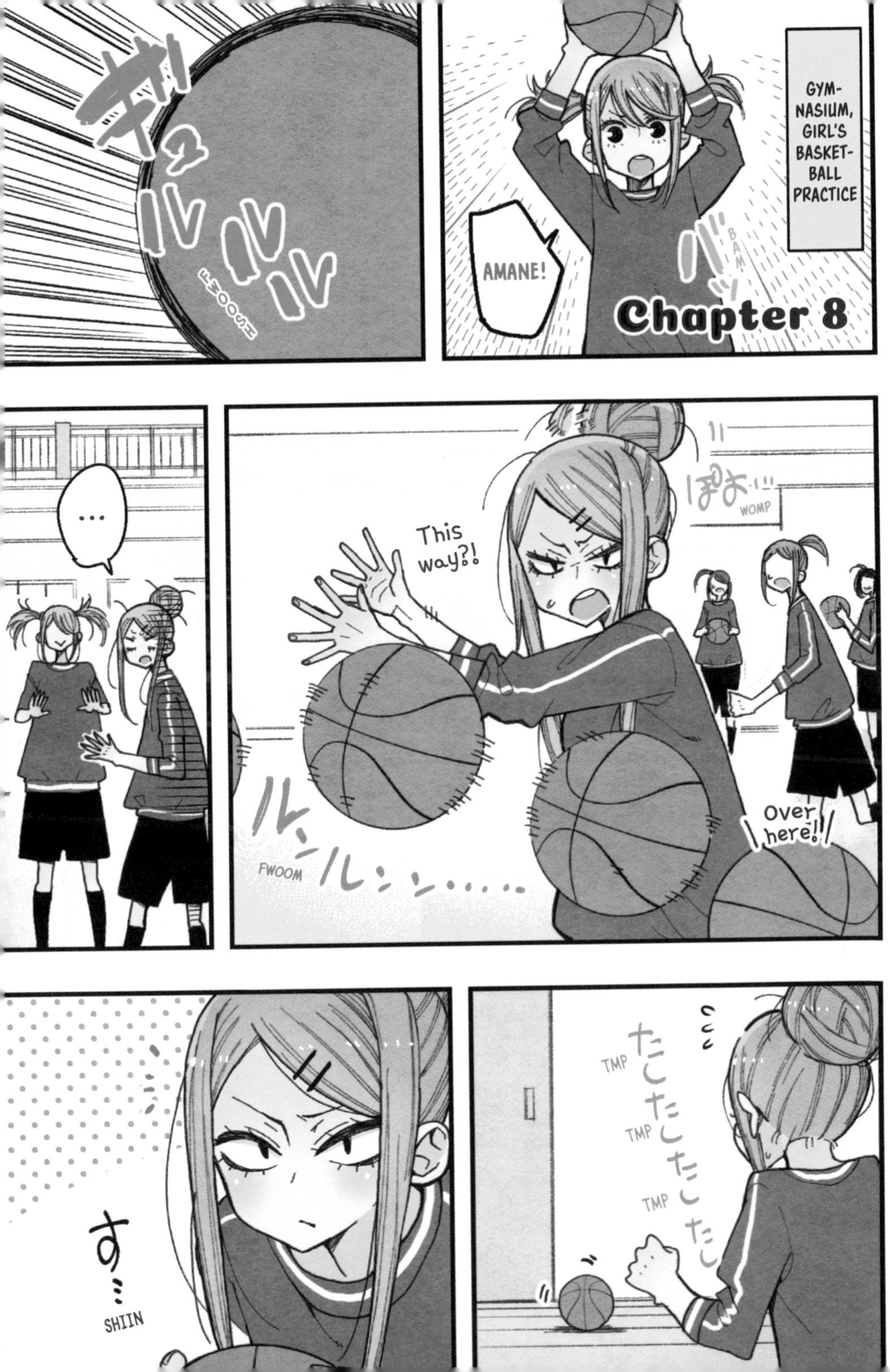
GYM-
NASIUM,
GIRL'S
BASKET-
BALL
PRACTICE
AMANE!
BAM
Chapter 8
FWOOSH
This way?!
WOMP
Over here!
FWOOM
...
TMP
TMP
TMP
SHIIN

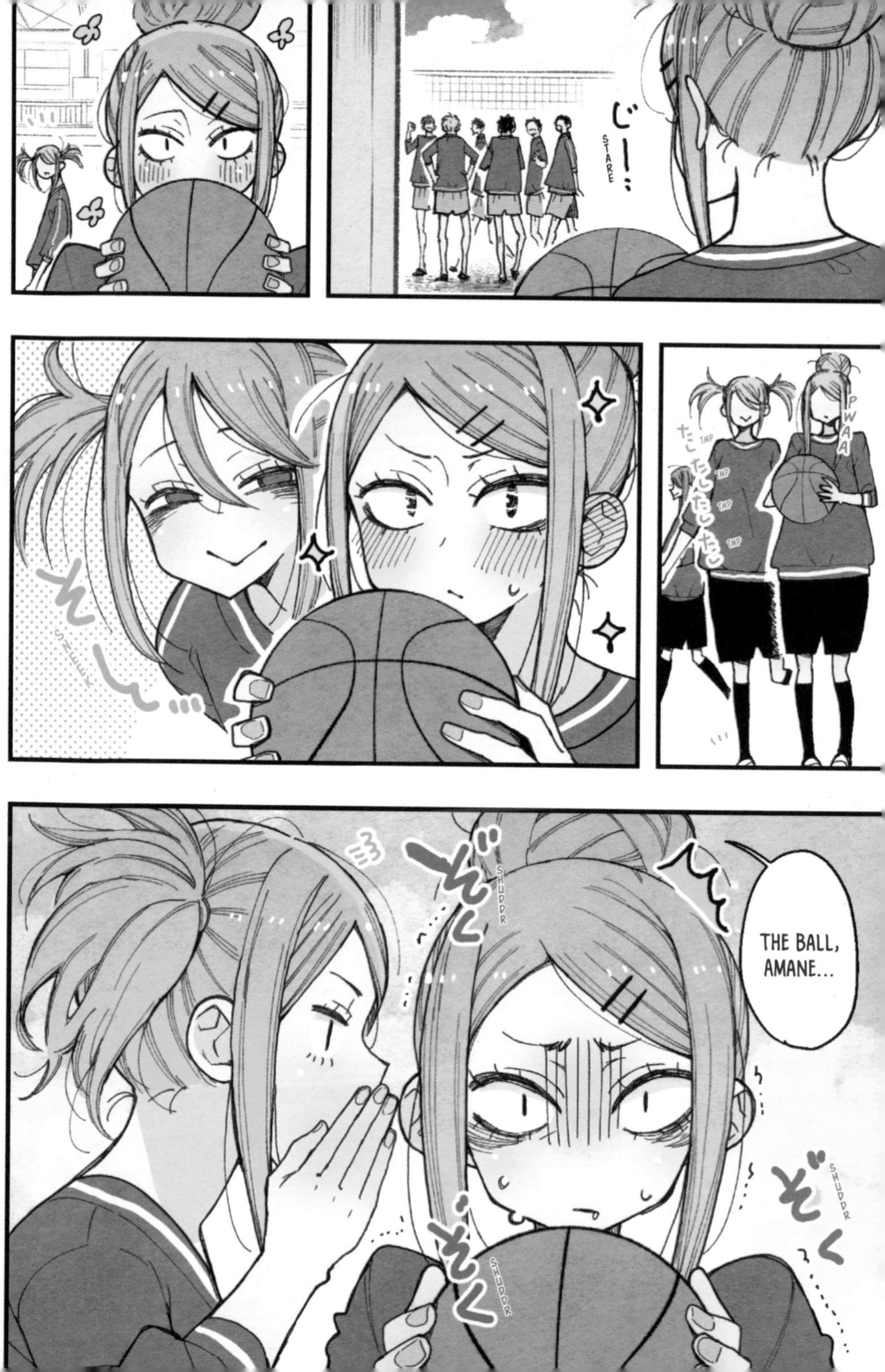
じー…
STARE
PWAA
たしたしたし
TMP
TMP
TMP
TMP
そー…
SNEEK
THE BALL, AMANE...
ぞく
SHUDDR
ぞく
SHUDDR
ぞく
SHUDDR

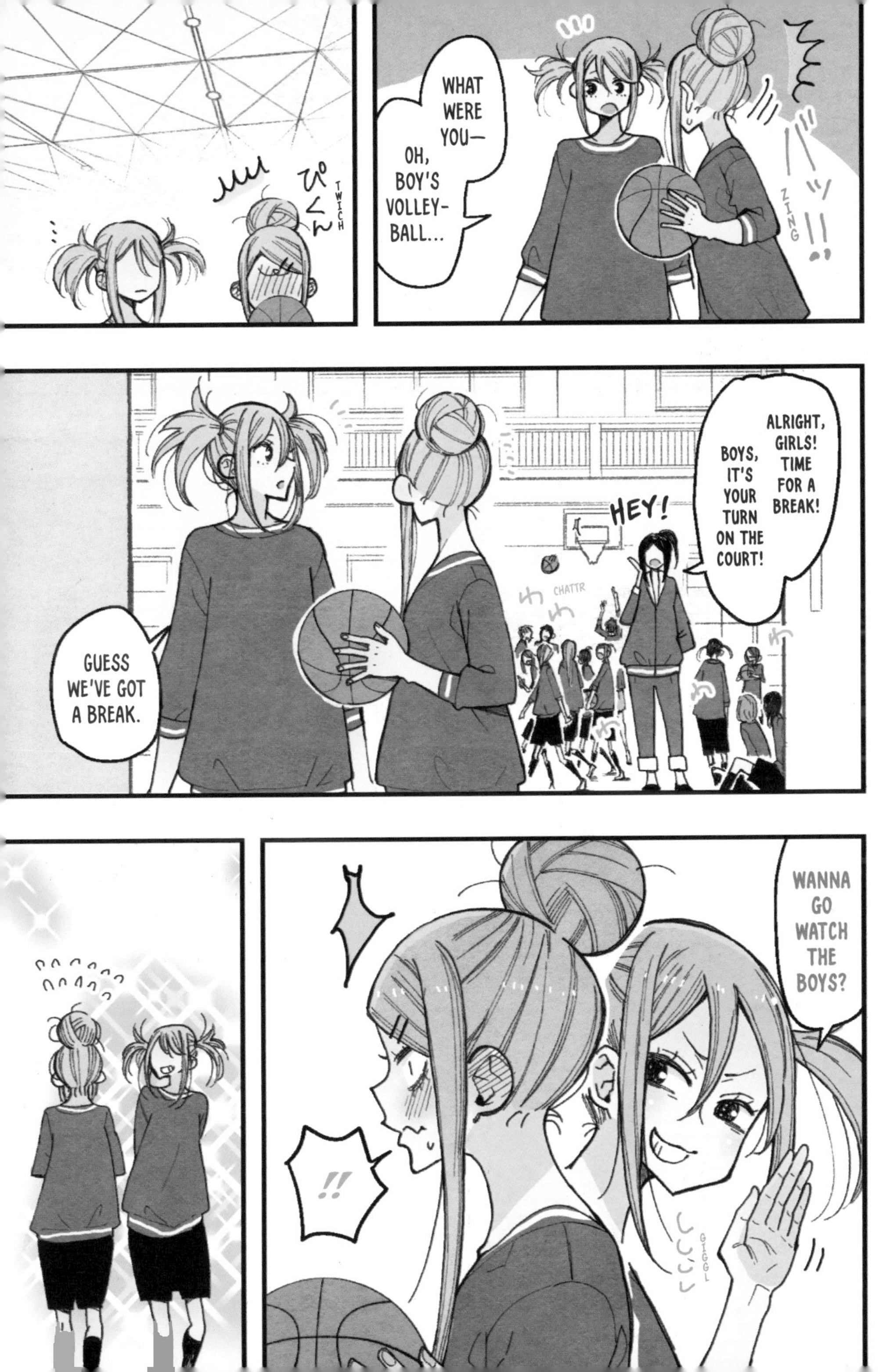
WHAT WERE YOU—
OH, BOY'S VOLLEY-BALL...
バッ!!
ZING
ぴくん
TWICH
ALRIGHT, GIRLS! TIME FOR A BREAK!
BOYS, IT'S YOUR TURN ON THE COURT!
HEY!
CHATTR
GUESS WE'VE GOT A BREAK.
WANNA GO WATCH THE BOYS?
GIGGL
!!

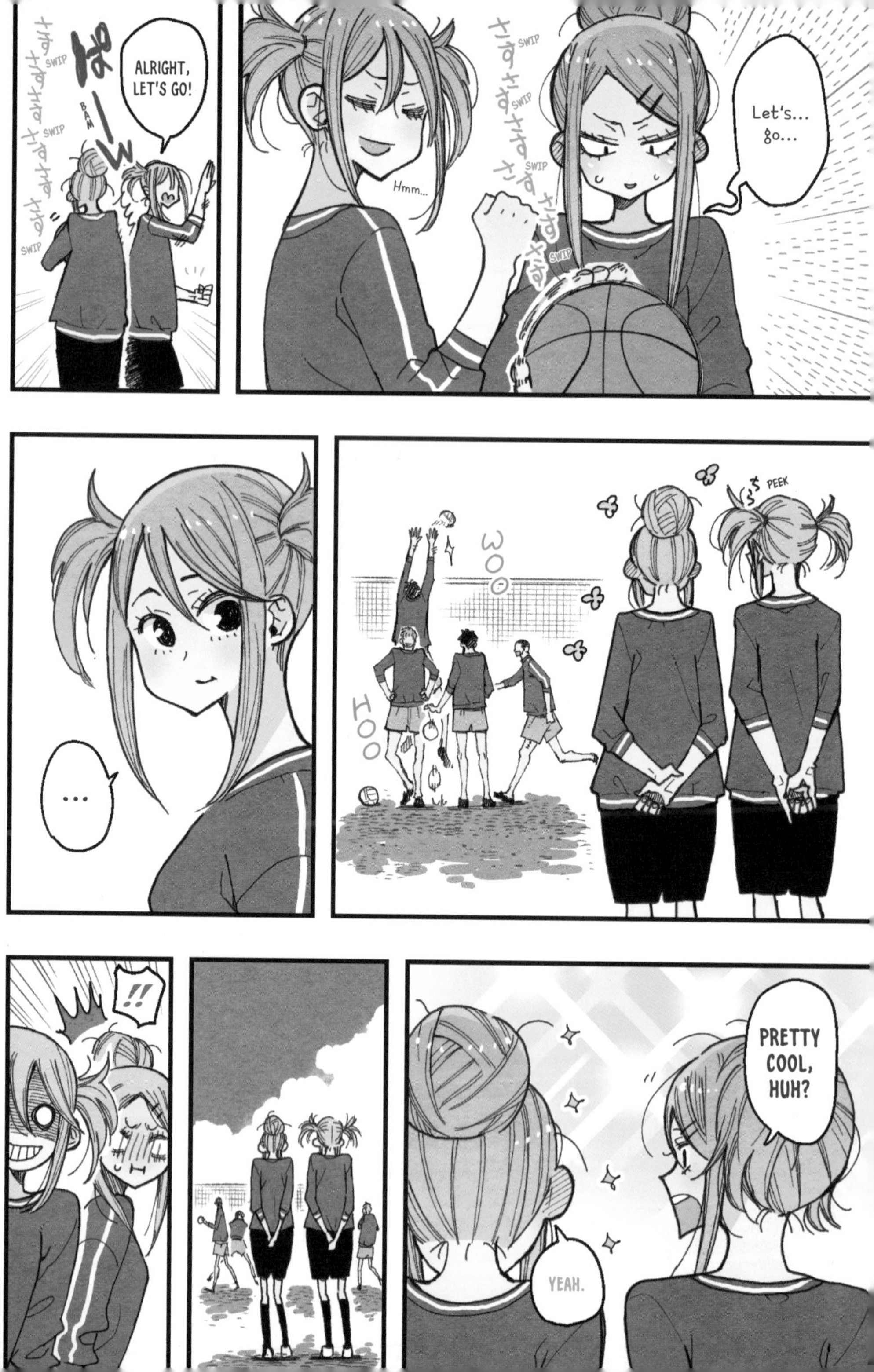
Let's... go...
SWIP
SWIP
SWIP
Hmm...
SWIP
ALRIGHT, LET'S GO!
BAM
SWIP
SWIP
PEEK
WOO
HOO
...
PRETTY COOL, HUH?
YEAH.
!!

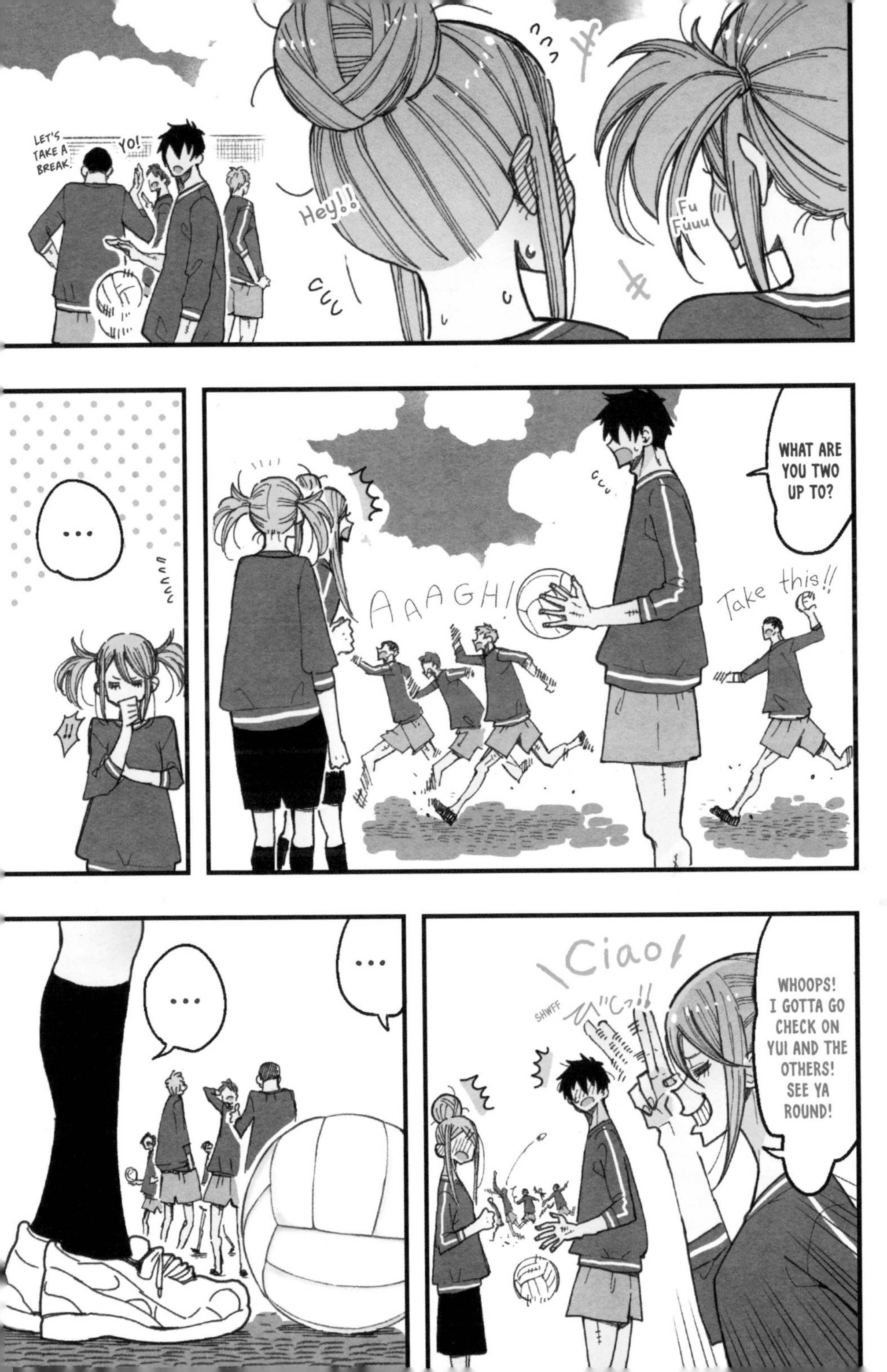
Fu Fuuu
Hey!!
YO!
LET'S TAKE A BREAK
WHAT ARE YOU TWO UP TO?
Take this!!
AAAGH!
...
WHOOPS! I GOTTA GO CHECK ON YUI AND THE OTHERS! SEE YA ROUND!
Ciao
SHWFF
...
...

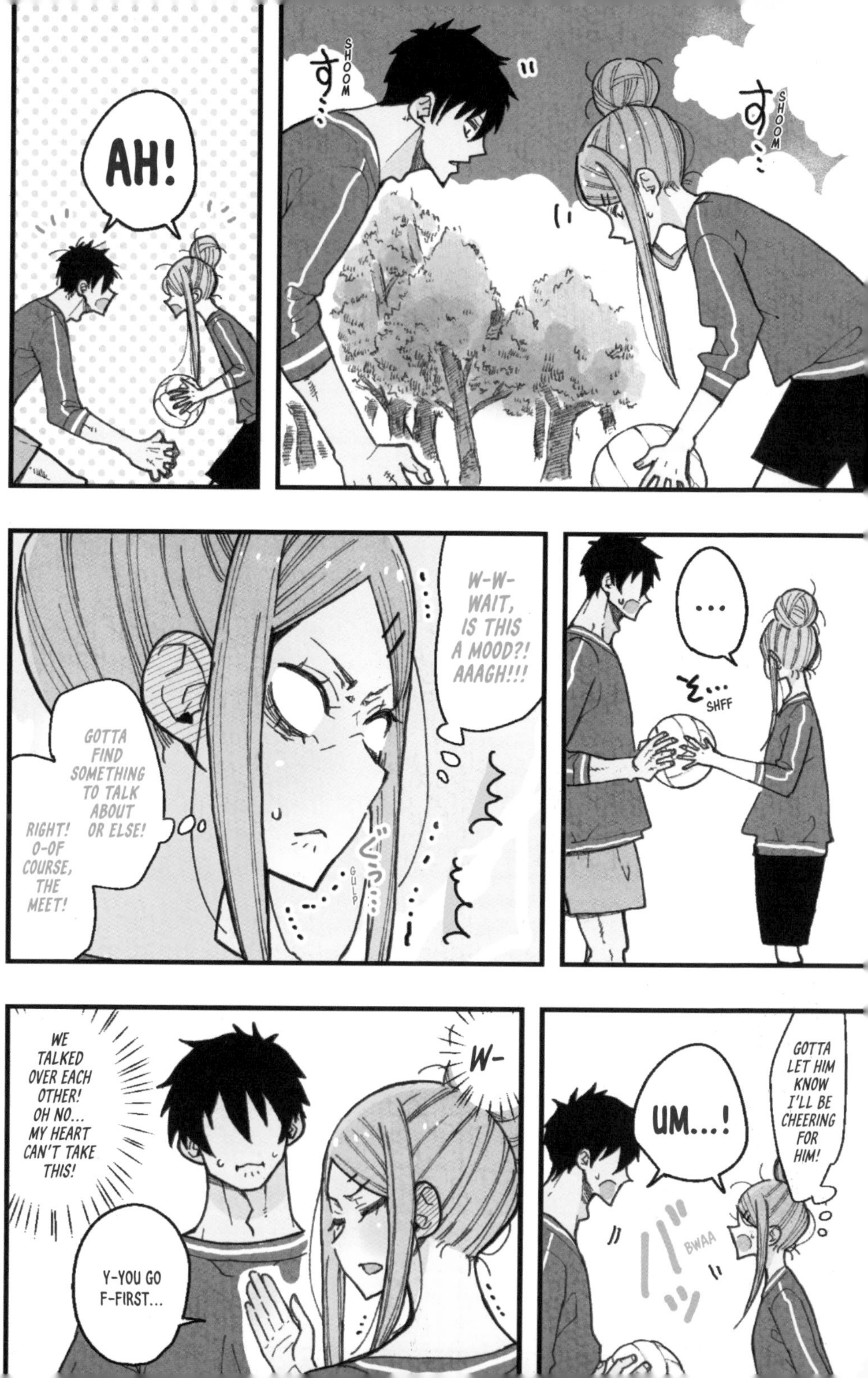

SHOOM
SHOOM
AH!
...
SHFF
W-W-WAIT, IS THIS A MOOD?! AAAGH!!!
GOTTA FIND SOMETHING TO TALK ABOUT OR ELSE!
RIGHT! O-OF COURSE, THE MEET!
GULP
GOTTA LET HIM KNOW I'LL BE CHEERING FOR HIM!
UM...!
BWAA
W-
WE TALKED OVER EACH OTHER! OH NO... MY HEART CAN'T TAKE THIS!
Y-YOU GO F-FIRST...

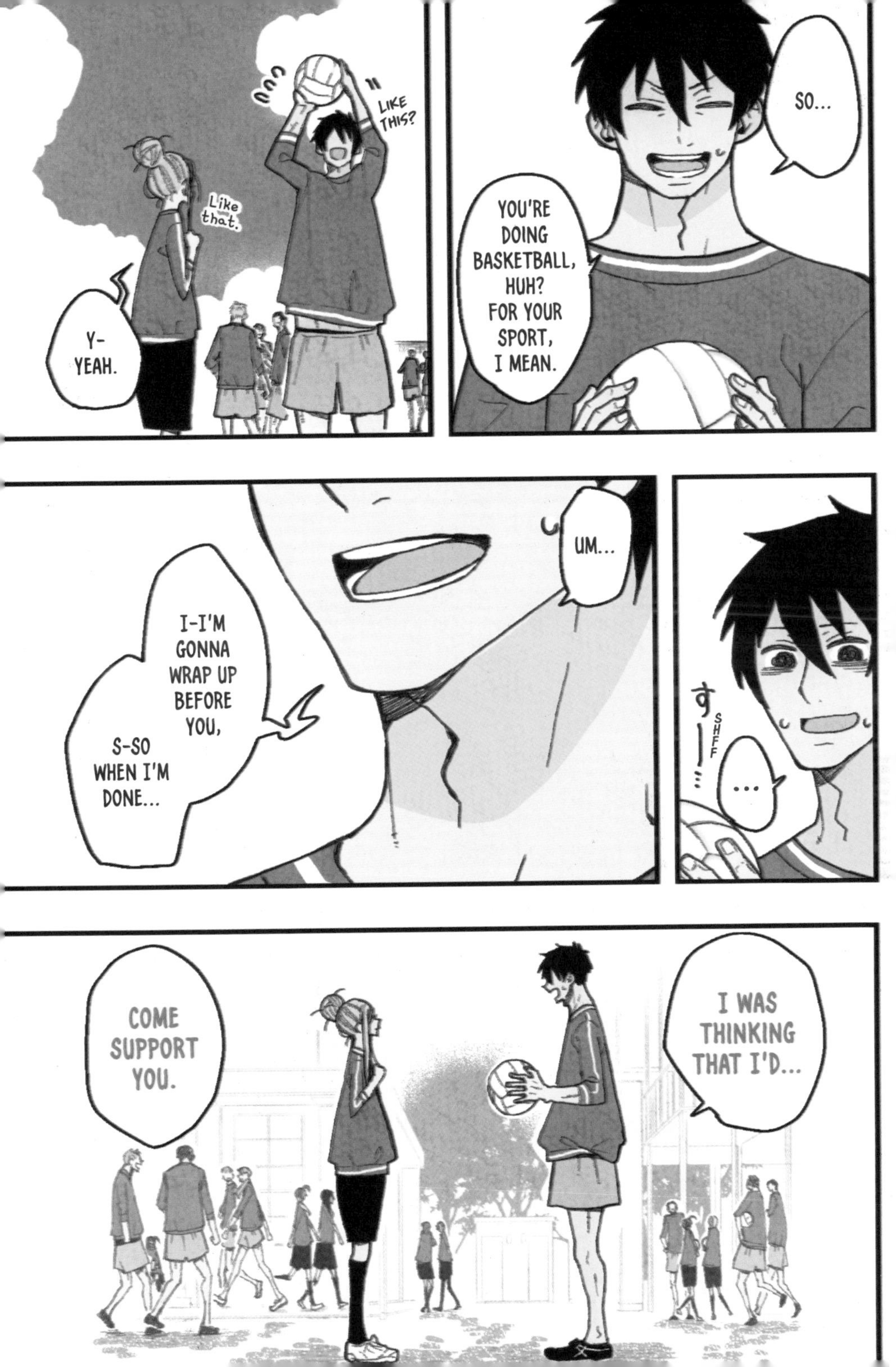
SO...
YOU'RE DOING BASKETBALL, HUH? FOR YOUR SPORT, I MEAN.
LIKE THIS?
Like that.
Y- YEAH.
すー SHFF
...
UM...
I-I'M GONNA WRAP UP BEFORE YOU,
S-SO WHEN I'M DONE...
I WAS THINKING THAT I'D...
COME SUPPORT YOU.

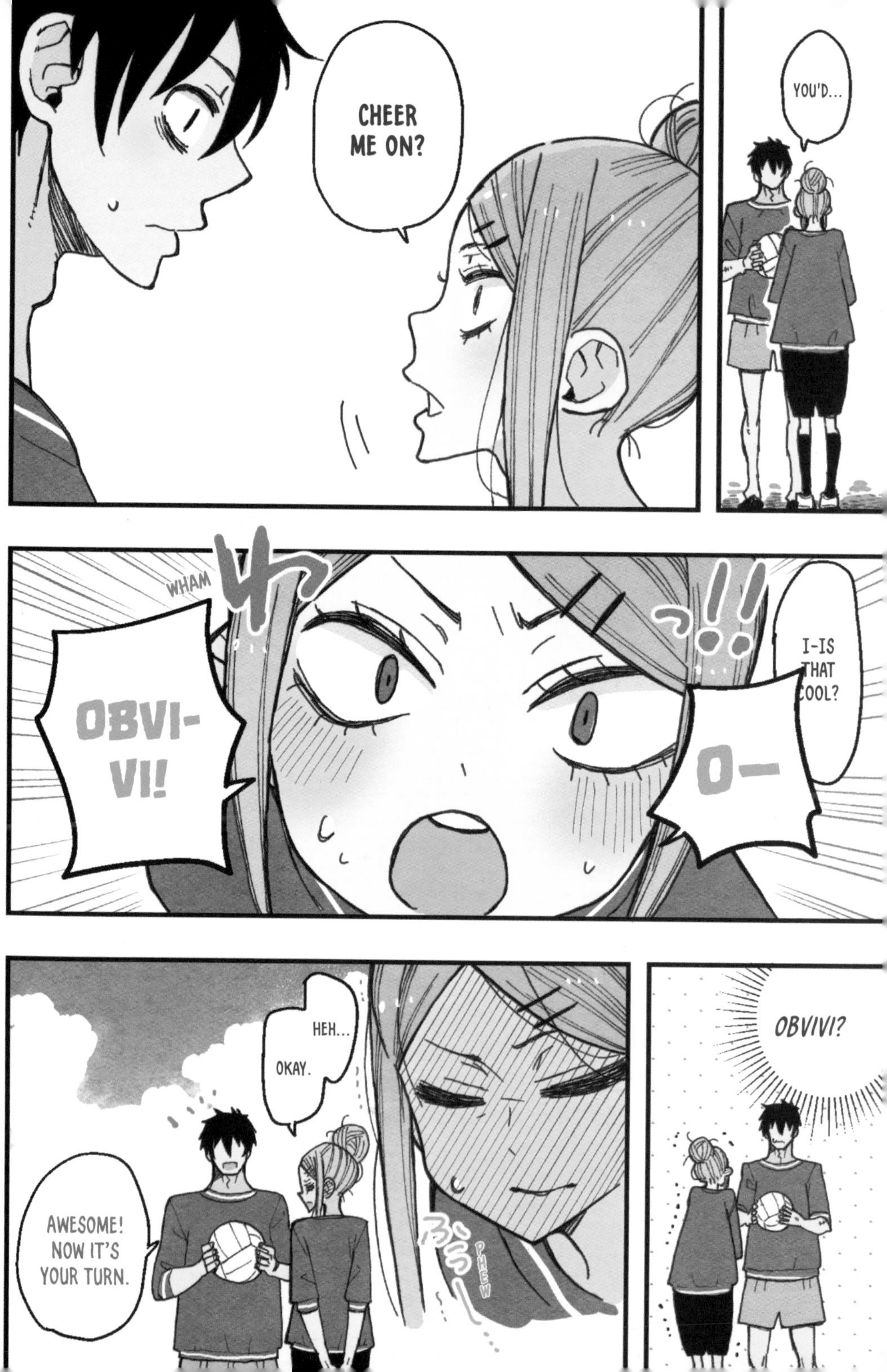
YOU'D...
CHEER ME ON?
I-IS THAT COOL?
O—
WHAM
OBVI-VI!
OBVIVI?
HEH... OKAY.
PHEW
AWESOME! NOW IT'S YOUR TURN.

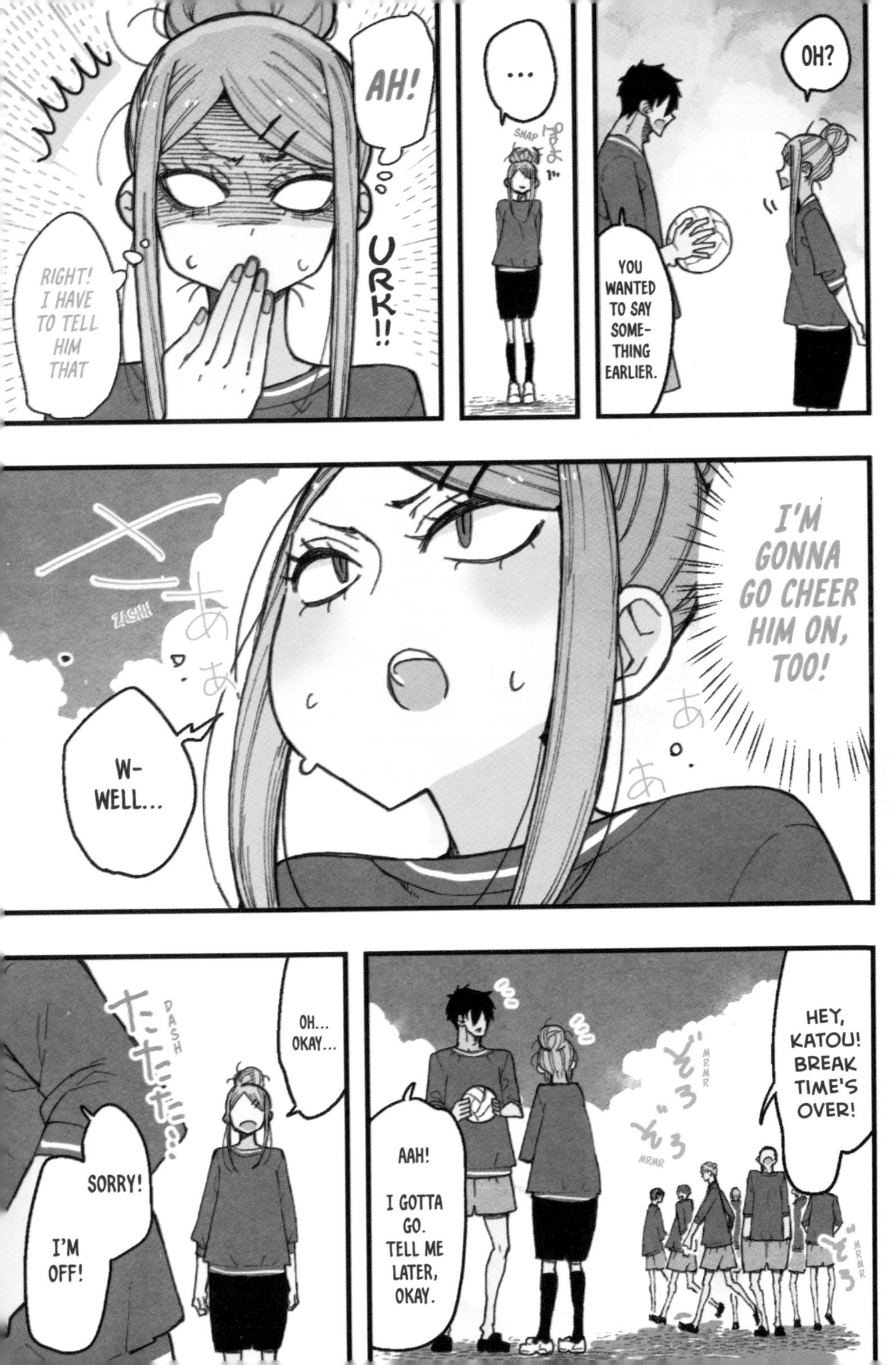
OH?
YOU WANTED TO SAY SOME-THING EARLIER.
...
SNAP
AH!
URK!!
RIGHT! I HAVE TO TELL HIM THAT
I'M GONNA GO CHEER HIM ON, TOO!
あ あ
ZASHH
あ あ
W-WELL...
HEY, KATOU! BREAK TIME'S OVER!
ぞろ MRMR
ぞろ MRMR
ぞろ MRMR
AAH! I GOTTA GO. TELL ME LATER, OKAY.
OH... OKAY...
DASH
SORRY! I'M OFF!

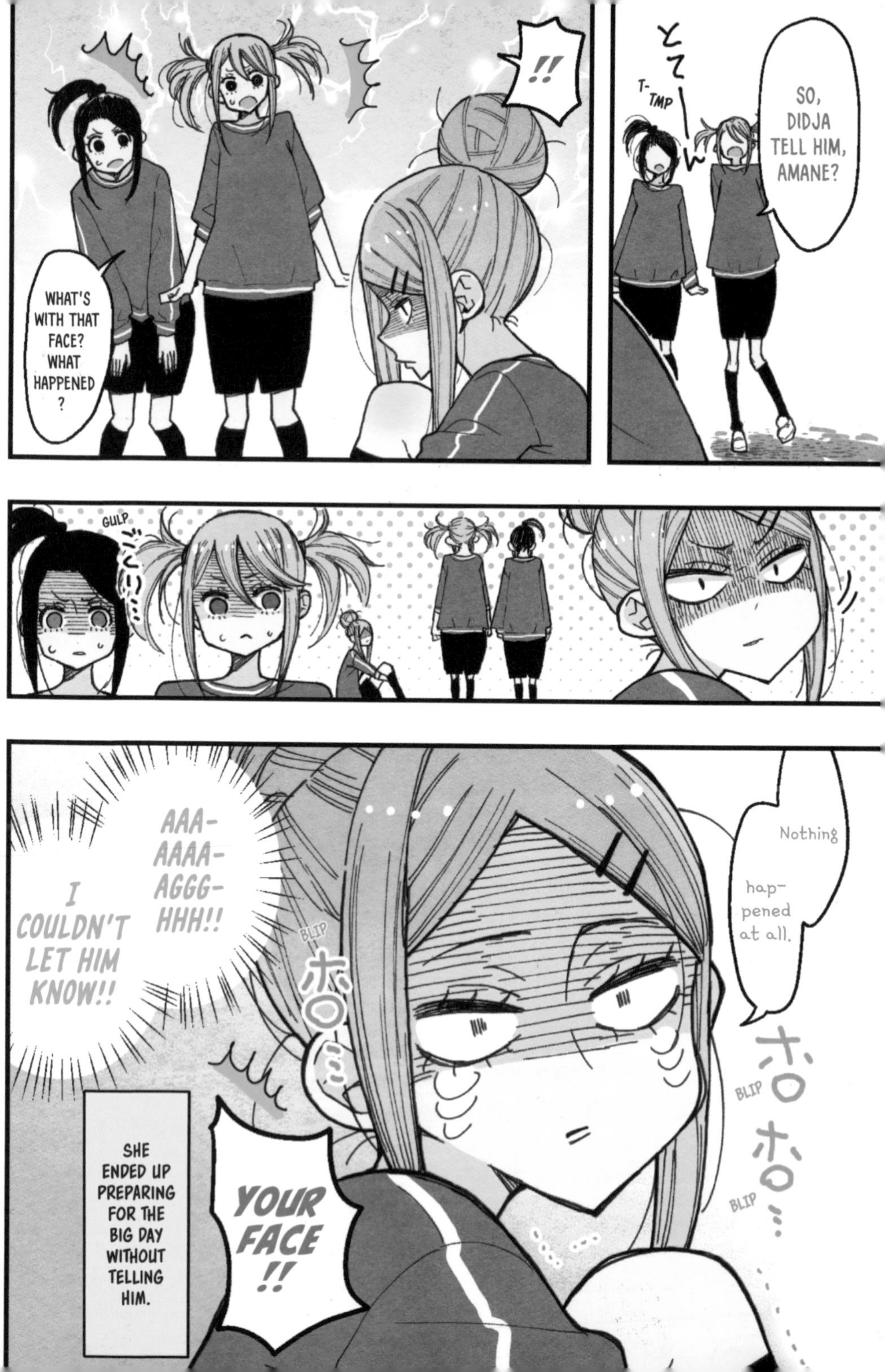
T-TMP
SO, DIDJA TELL HIM, AMANE?
!!
WHAT'S WITH THAT FACE? WHAT HAPPENED?
GULP
Nothing hap-pened at all.
BLIP
BLIP
AAA-AAAA-AGGG-HHH!!
BLIP
I COULDN'T LET HIM KNOW!!
YOUR FACE!!
SHE ENDED UP PREPARING FOR THE BIG DAY WITHOUT TELLING HIM.

Encouragement

AMANE...
...
SHUMP
ARE THEY TRYING TO CHEER ME UP?
YOUR FACE IS SCARY.
NOD
NOD
THEY'RE NOT!

JUST KIDDING! YOU'LL GET IT NEXT TIME, AMANE.
HELL YEAH!
...UH-HUH.

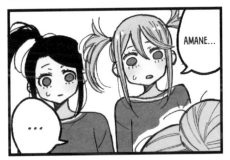

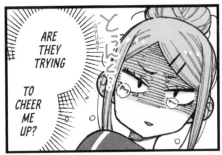

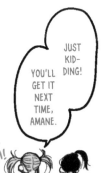

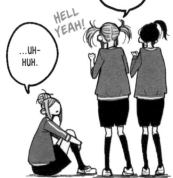

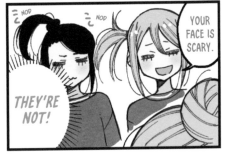

THE GIRL
WITH THE
SANPAKU
EYES

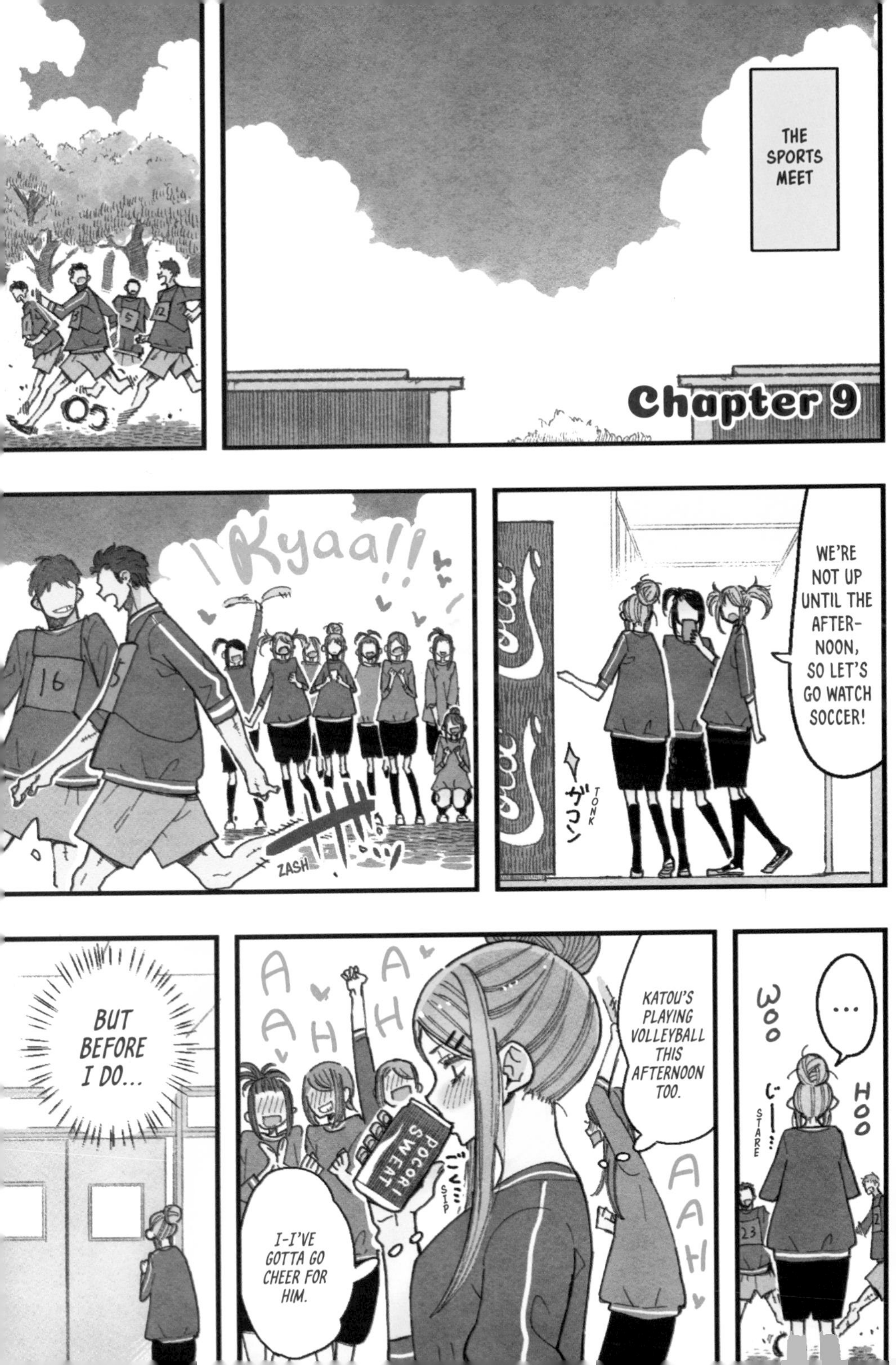
THE SPORTS MEET
Chapter 9
WE'RE NOT UP UNTIL THE AFTER-NOON, SO LET'S GO WATCH SOCCER!
ザコン
TONK
Kyaa!!
ZASH
...
WOO HOO
STARE
KATOU'S PLAYING VOLLEYBALL THIS AFTERNOON TOO.
AAH
AAH
POCORI SWEAT
SIP
I-I'VE GOTTA GO CHEER FOR HIM.
AAH
BUT BEFORE I DO...

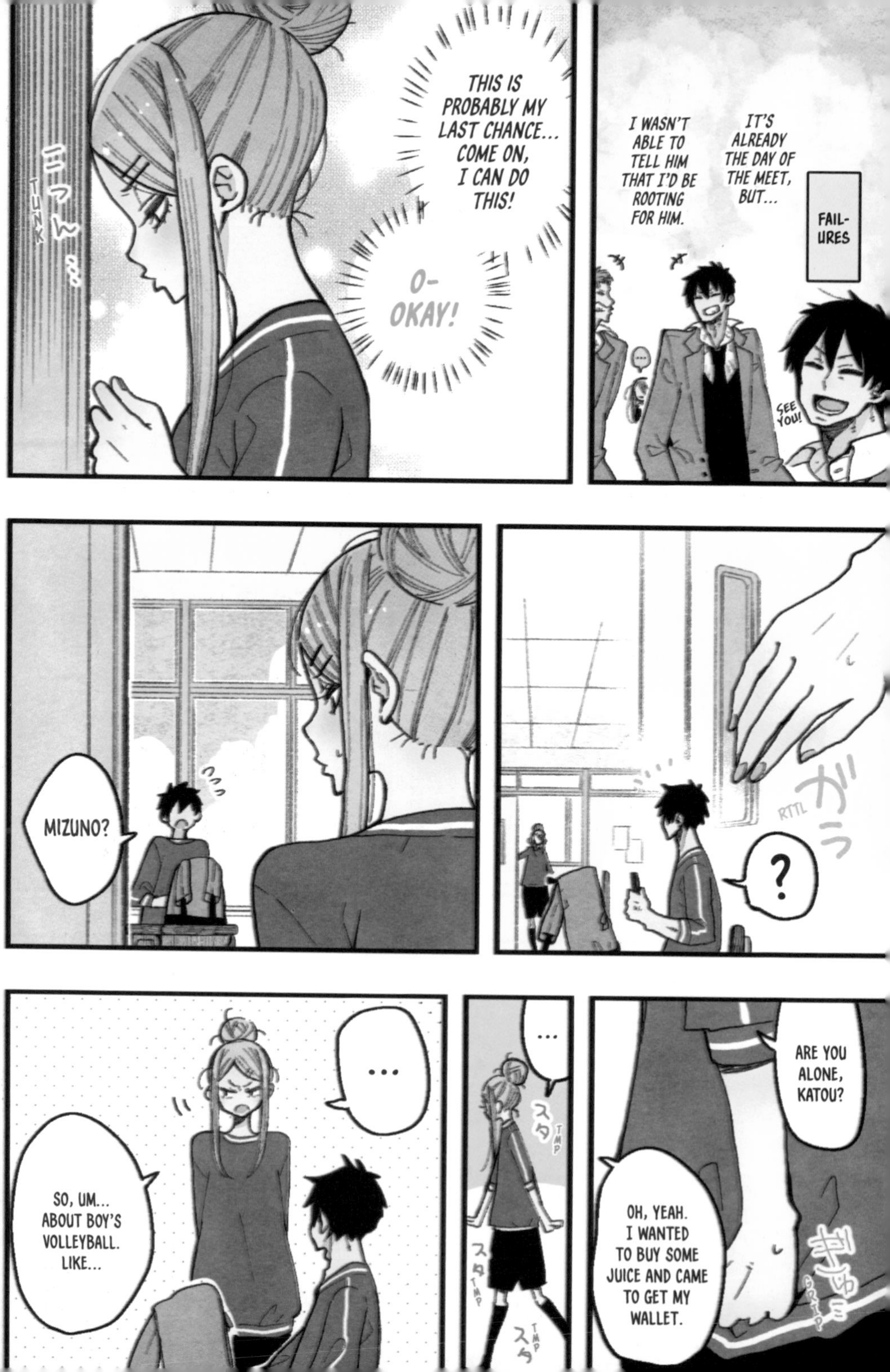
FAIL-URES
IT'S ALREADY THE DAY OF THE MEET, BUT...
I WASN'T ABLE TO TELL HIM THAT I'D BE ROOTING FOR HIM.
SEE YOU!
...
THIS IS PROBABLY MY LAST CHANCE... COME ON, I CAN DO THIS!
O-OKAY!
TUNK
RTTL
?
MIZUNO?
ARE YOU ALONE, KATOU?
OH, YEAH. I WANTED TO BUY SOME JUICE AND CAME TO GET MY WALLET.
...
TMP
TMP
TMP
...
SO, UM... ABOUT BOY'S VOLLEYBALL. LIKE...

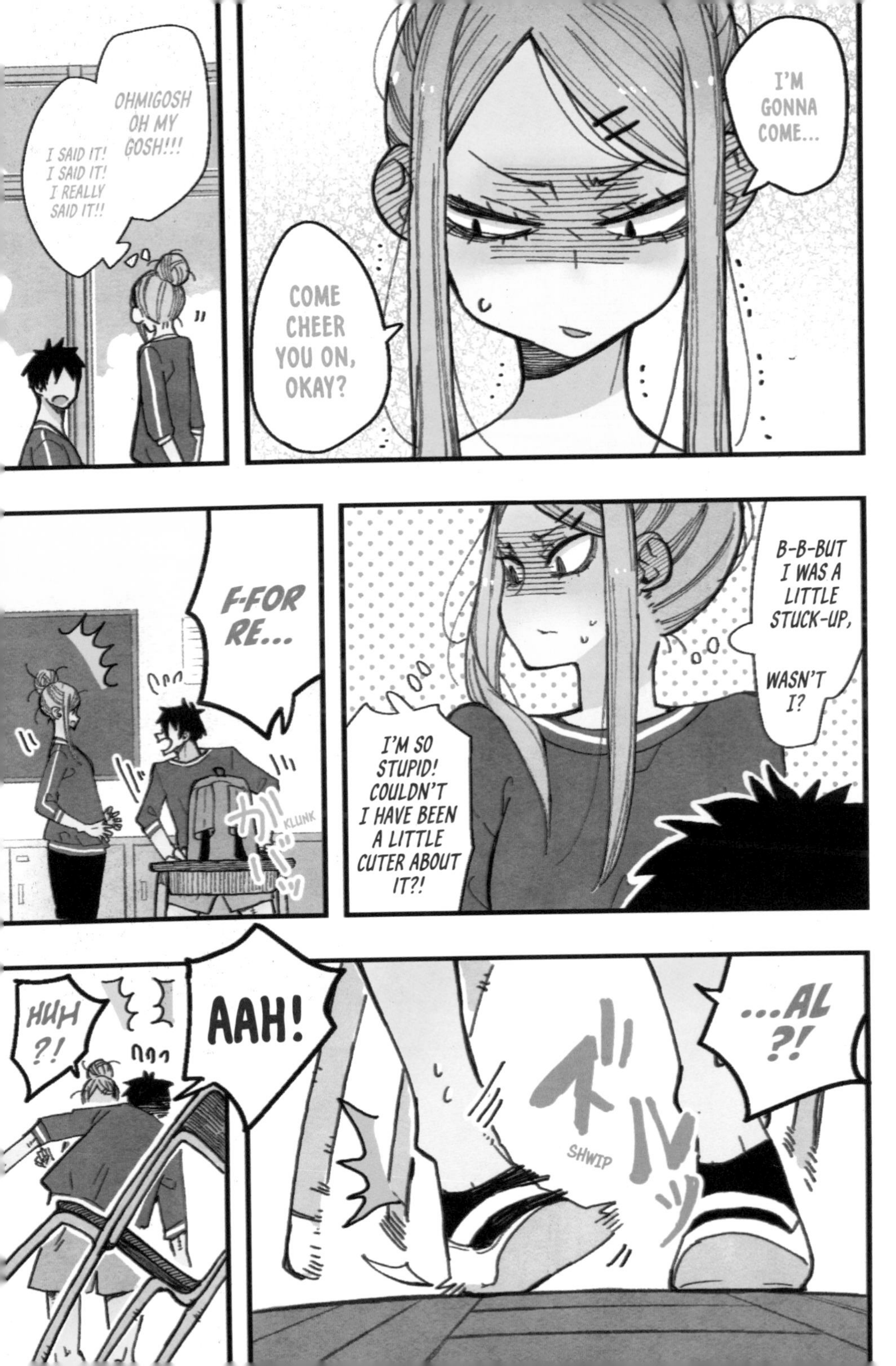
I'M GONNA COME...
COME CHEER YOU ON, OKAY?
OHMIGOSH OH MY GOSH!!!
I SAID IT! I SAID IT! I REALLY SAID IT!!
B-B-BUT I WAS A LITTLE STUCK-UP,
WASN'T I?
I'M SO STUPID! COULDN'T I HAVE BEEN A LITTLE CUTER ABOUT IT?!
F-FOR RE...
KLUNK
...AL ?!
SHWIP
AAH!
HUH ?!

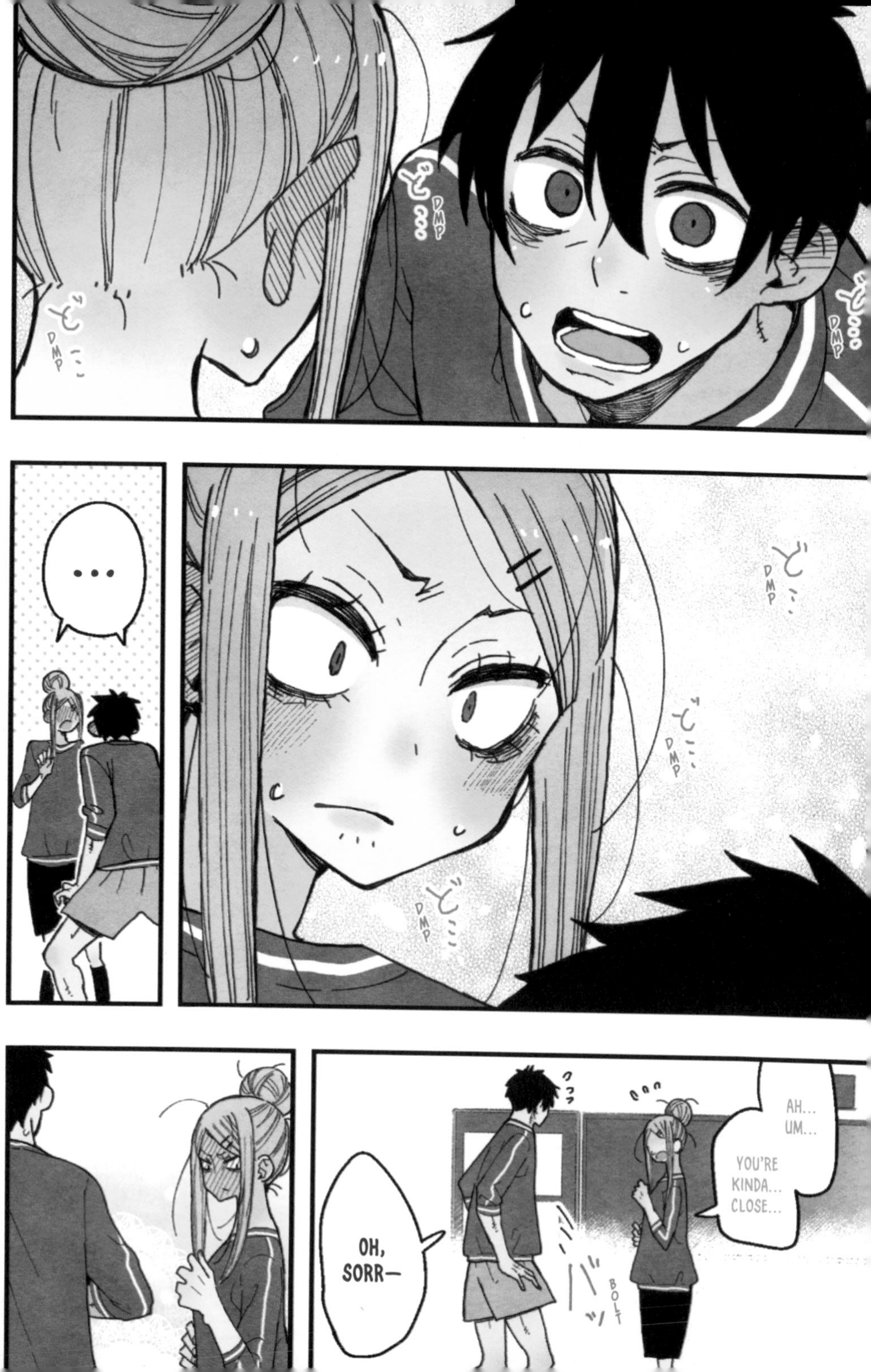

DMP
DMP
DMP
DMP
DMP
DMP
...
AH... UM...
YOU'RE KINDA... CLOSE...
BOLT
OH, SORR—

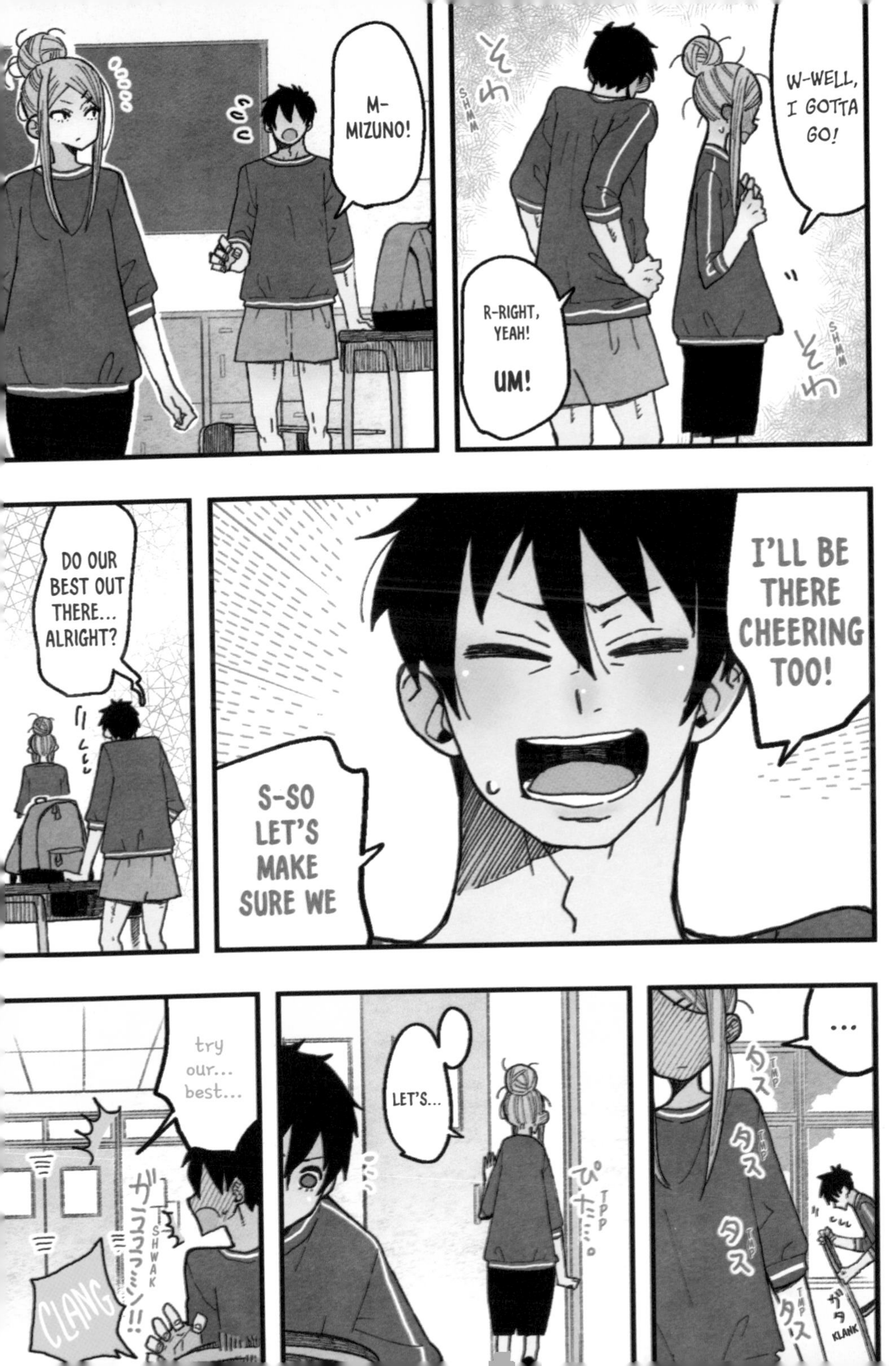
W-WELL, I GOTTA GO!
SHMM
SHMM
R-RIGHT, YEAH!
UM!
M-MIZUNO!
I'LL BE THERE CHEERING TOO!
S-SO LET'S MAKE SURE WE
DO OUR BEST OUT THERE... ALRIGHT?
...
TMP
TMP
TMP
TMP
KLANK
LET'S...
TPP
try our... best...
SHWAK
CLANG

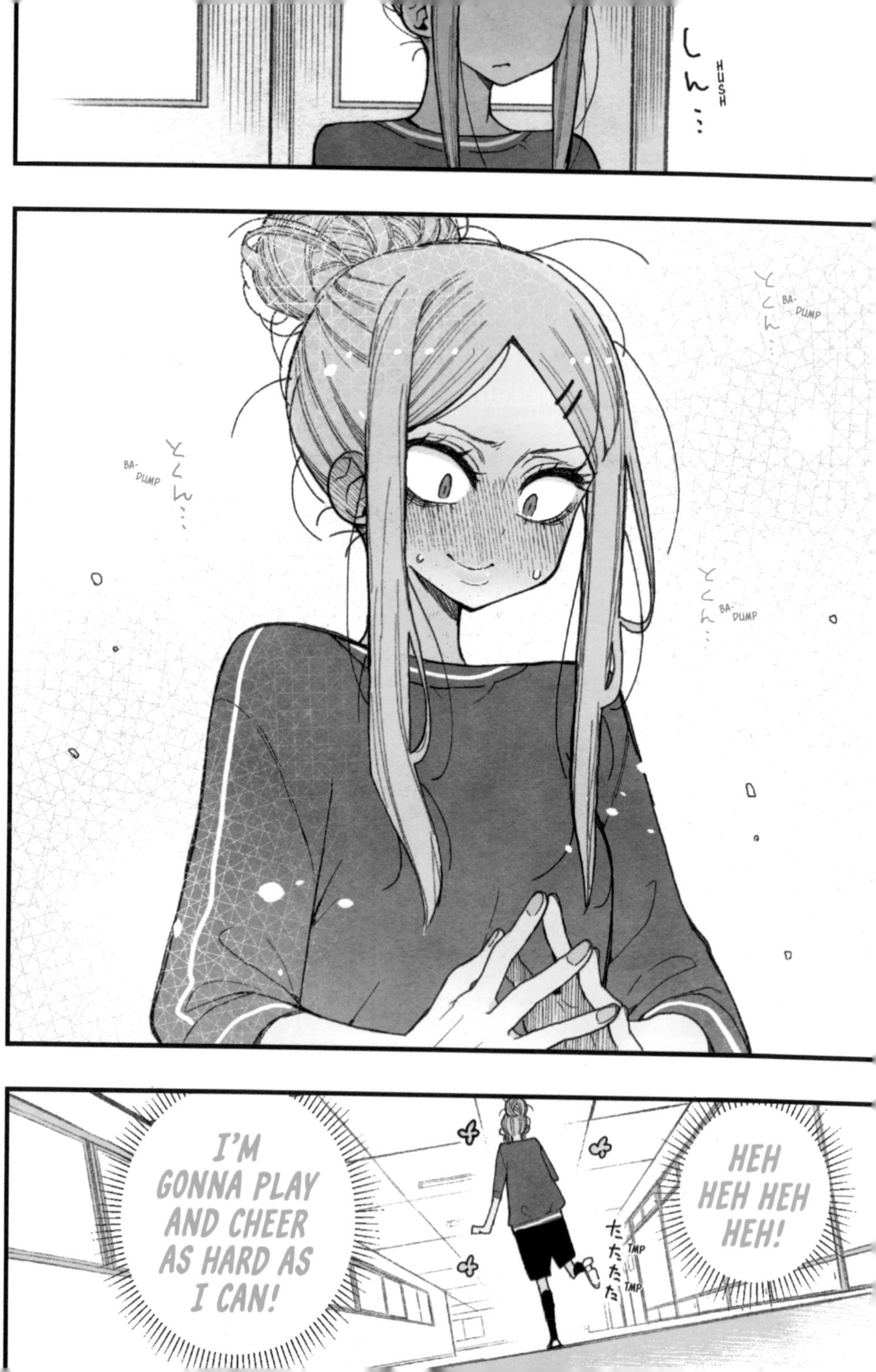

しん…
HUSH
とくん…
BA-DUMP
とくん…
BA-DUMP
とくん…
BA-DUMP
HEH HEH HEH HEH!
たたたた
TMP TMP
I'M GONNA PLAY AND CHEER AS HARD AS I CAN!

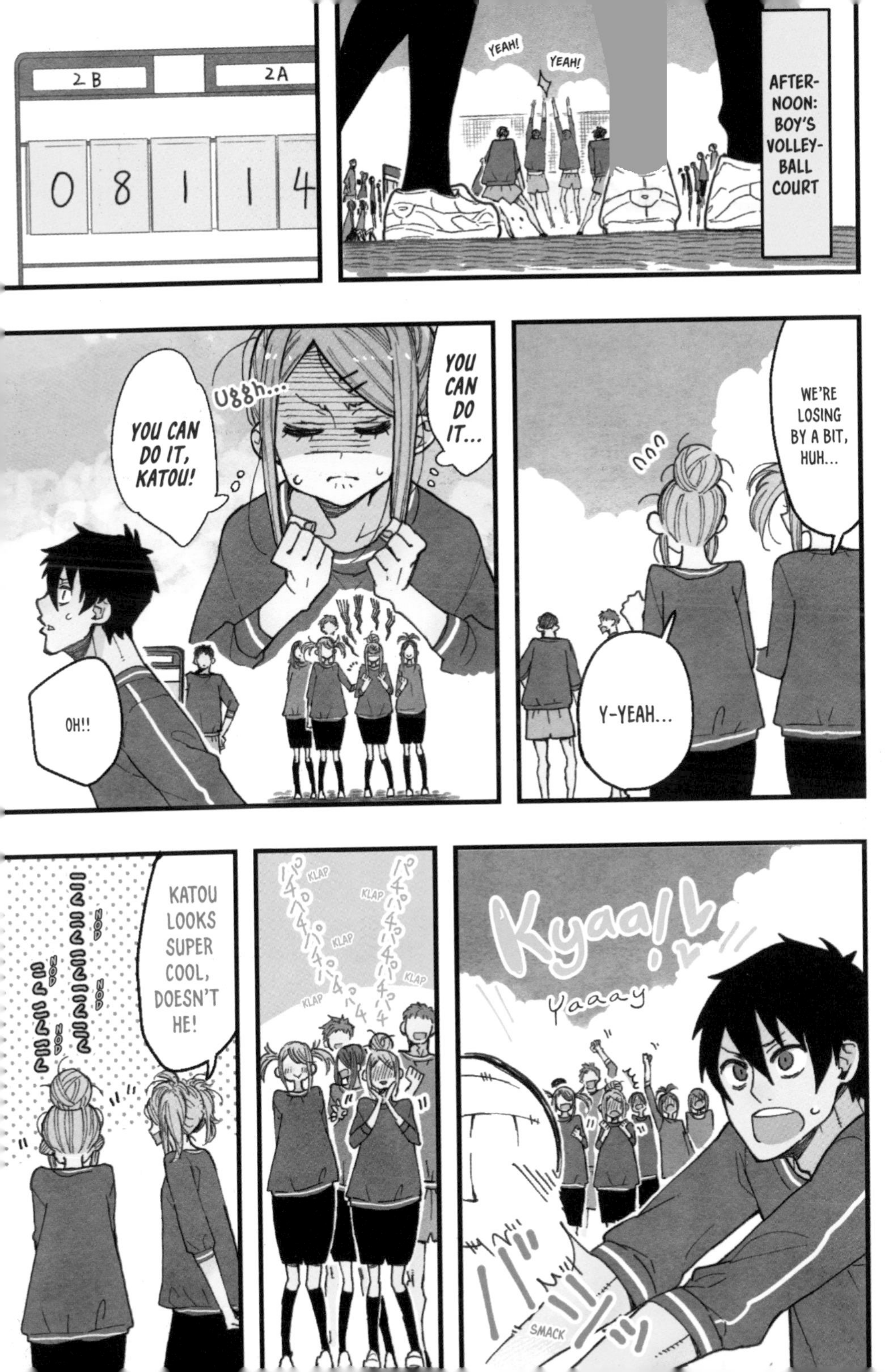

AFTER-NOON: BOY'S VOLLEY-BALL COURT
YEAH!
YEAH!
2B
2A
0 8 1 1 4
WE'RE LOSING BY A BIT, HUH...
Y-YEAH...
YOU CAN DO IT...
Uggh...
YOU CAN DO IT, KATOU!
OH!!
Kyaa!
Yaaay
SMACK
KLAP
KLAP
KLAP
KLAP
KLAP
KATOU LOOKS SUPER COOL, DOESN'T HE!
NOD
NOD
NOD
NOD

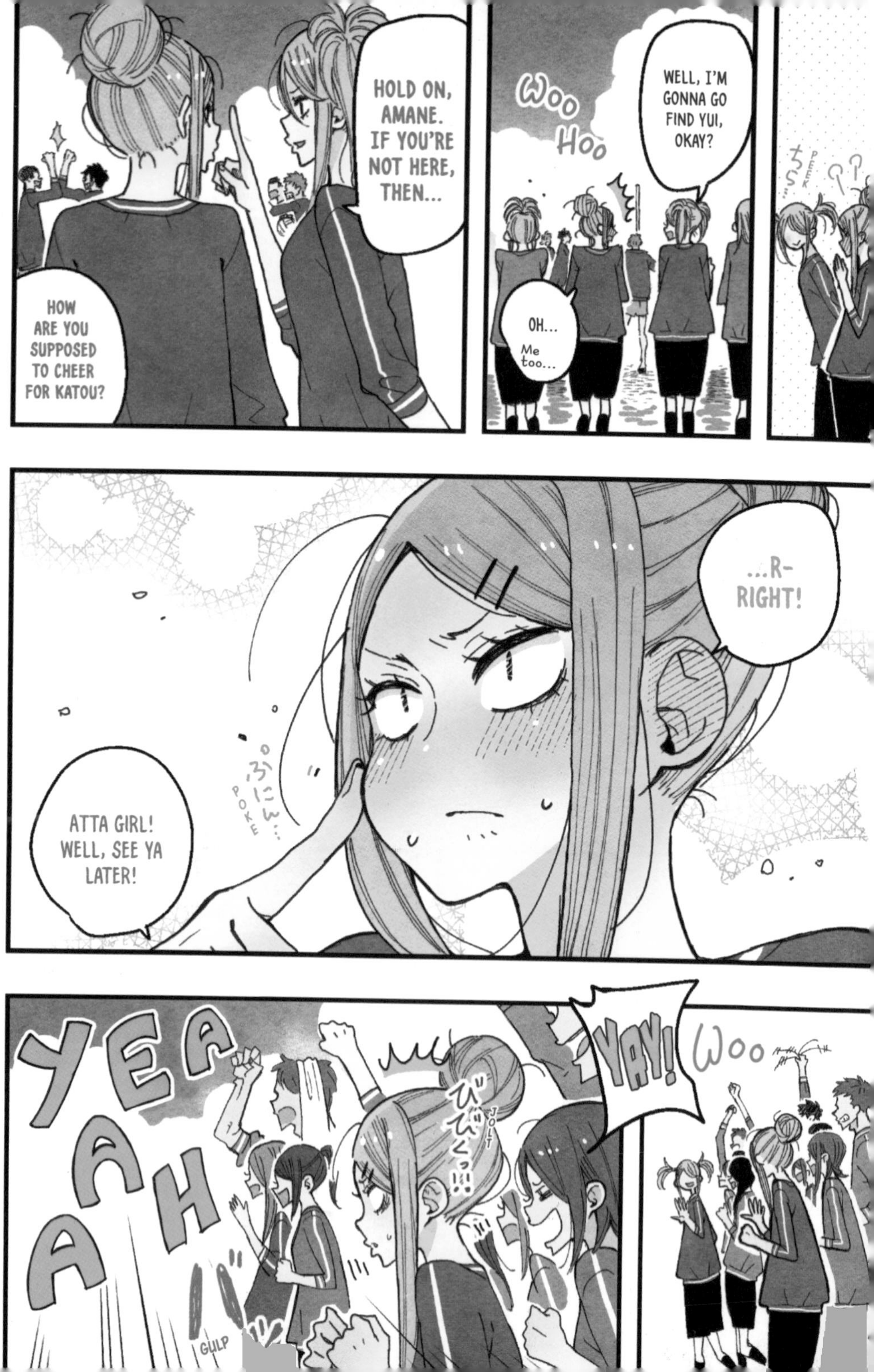
PEEK
WELL, I'M GONNA GO FIND YUI, OKAY?
Woo Hoo
OH... Me too...
HOLD ON, AMANE. IF YOU'RE NOT HERE, THEN...
HOW ARE YOU SUPPOSED TO CHEER FOR KATOU?
...R-RIGHT!
POKE
ATTA GIRL! WELL, SEE YA LATER!
Woo
YAY!
JOLT
YEAAAAH
GULP

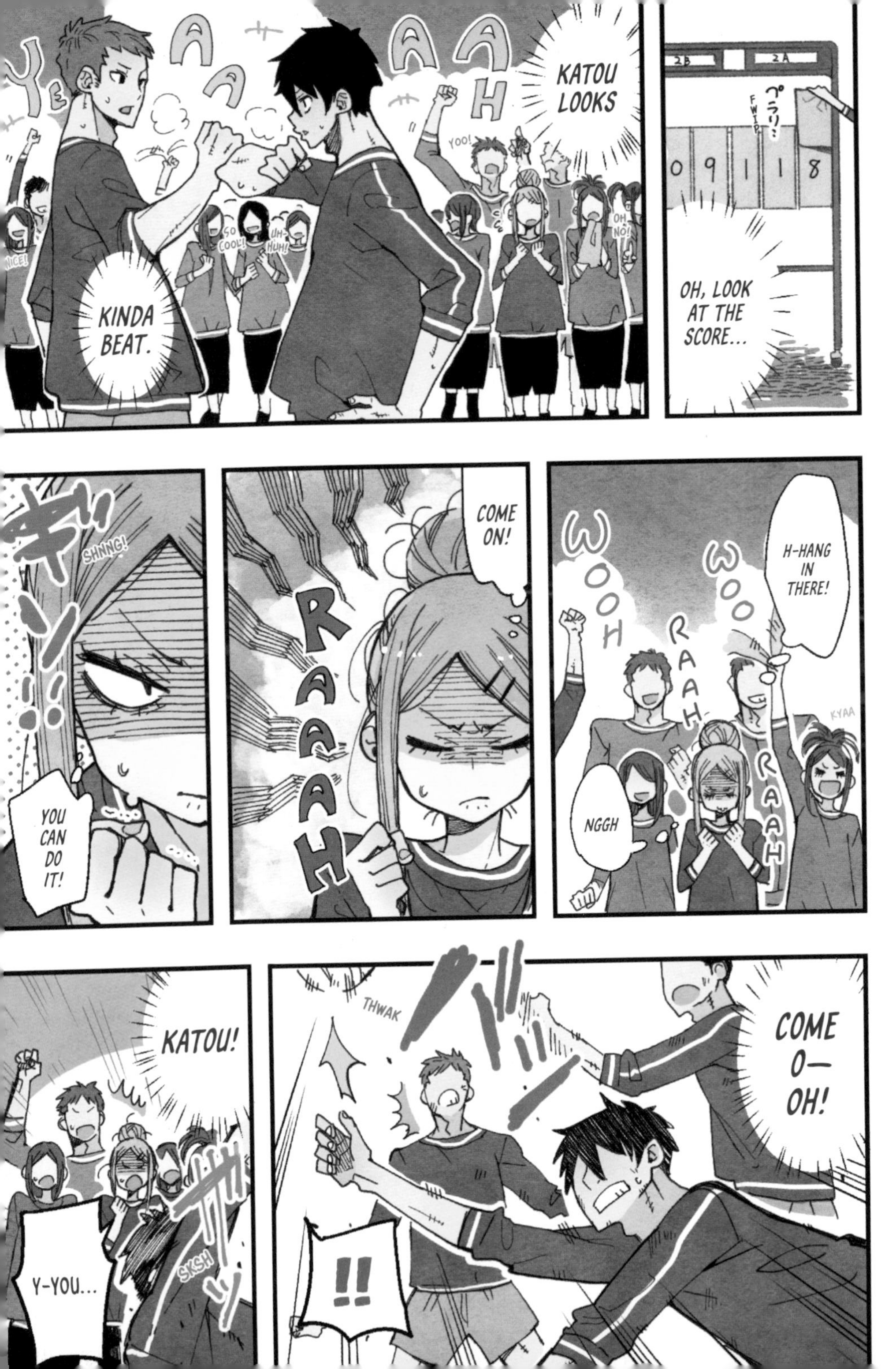
プラリ
FWIP
OH, LOOK AT THE SCORE...
YEAAAAAH
KATOU LOOKS
KINDA BEAT.
YOO!
OH NO!
SO COOL!
UH-HUH!
NICE!
H-HANG IN THERE!
WOOO
WOOOH
RAAAH
RAAAH
KYAA
NGGH
COME ON!
RAAAAH
SHNNG!
YOU CAN DO IT!
COME O—OH!
THWAK
!!
KATOU!
SKSH
Y-YOU...

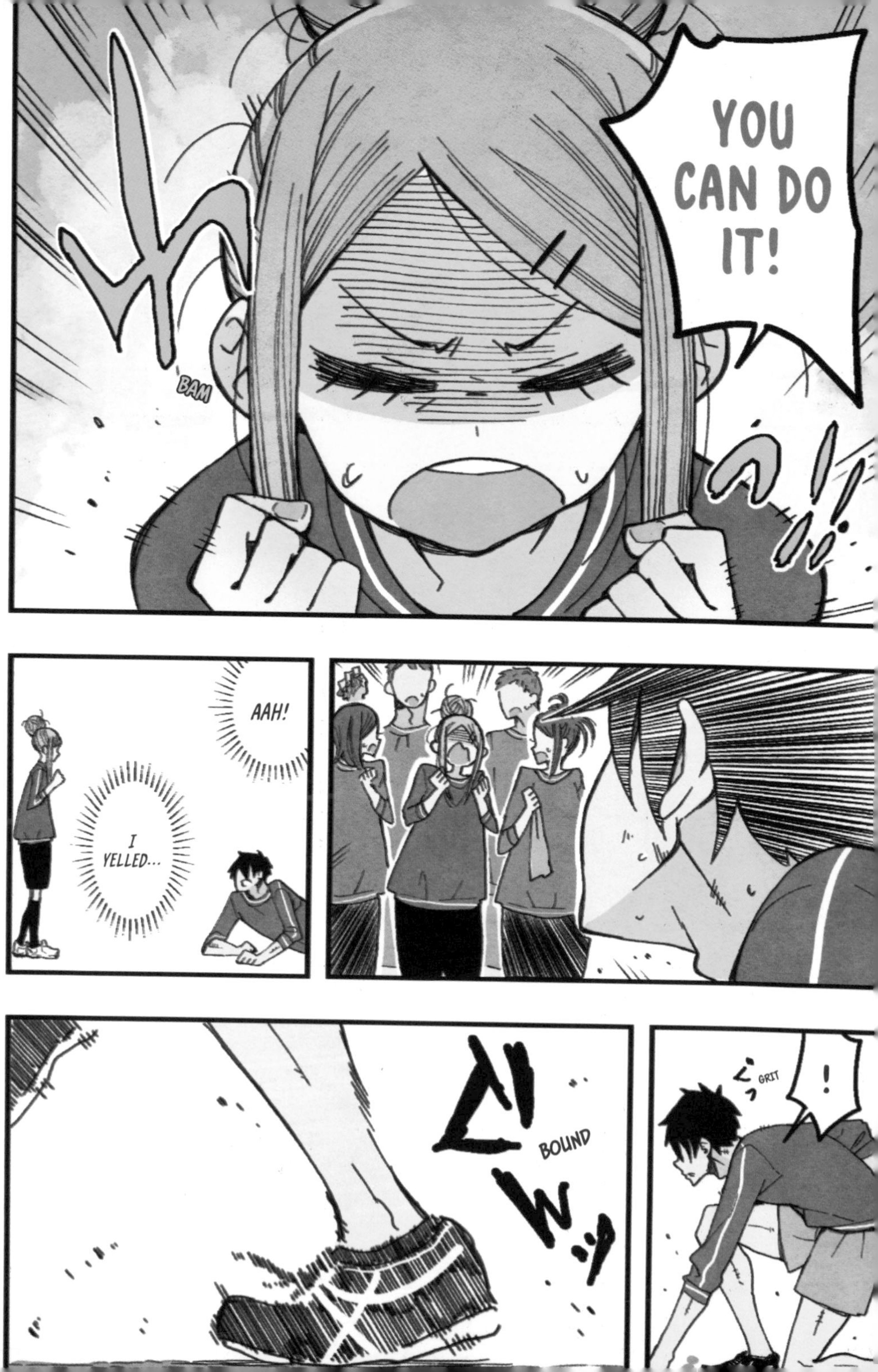
YOU CAN DO IT!
BAM
AAH!
I YELLED...
GRIT
!
BOUND

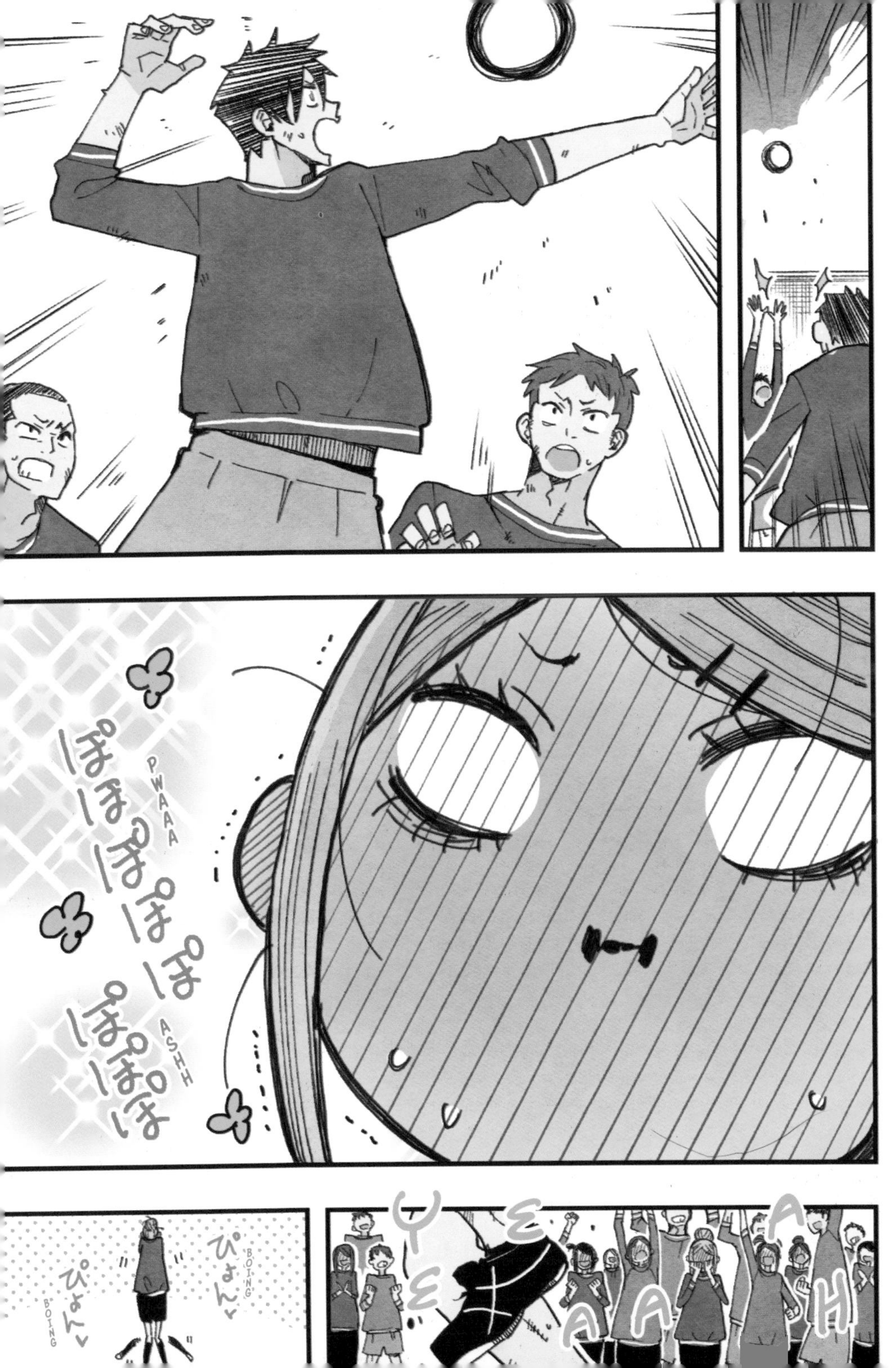
ぽーぽーぽぽーぽー
PWAAA
ぽーぽーぽ
ASHH
YEEAAAH
ぴょん
BOING
ぴょん
BOING

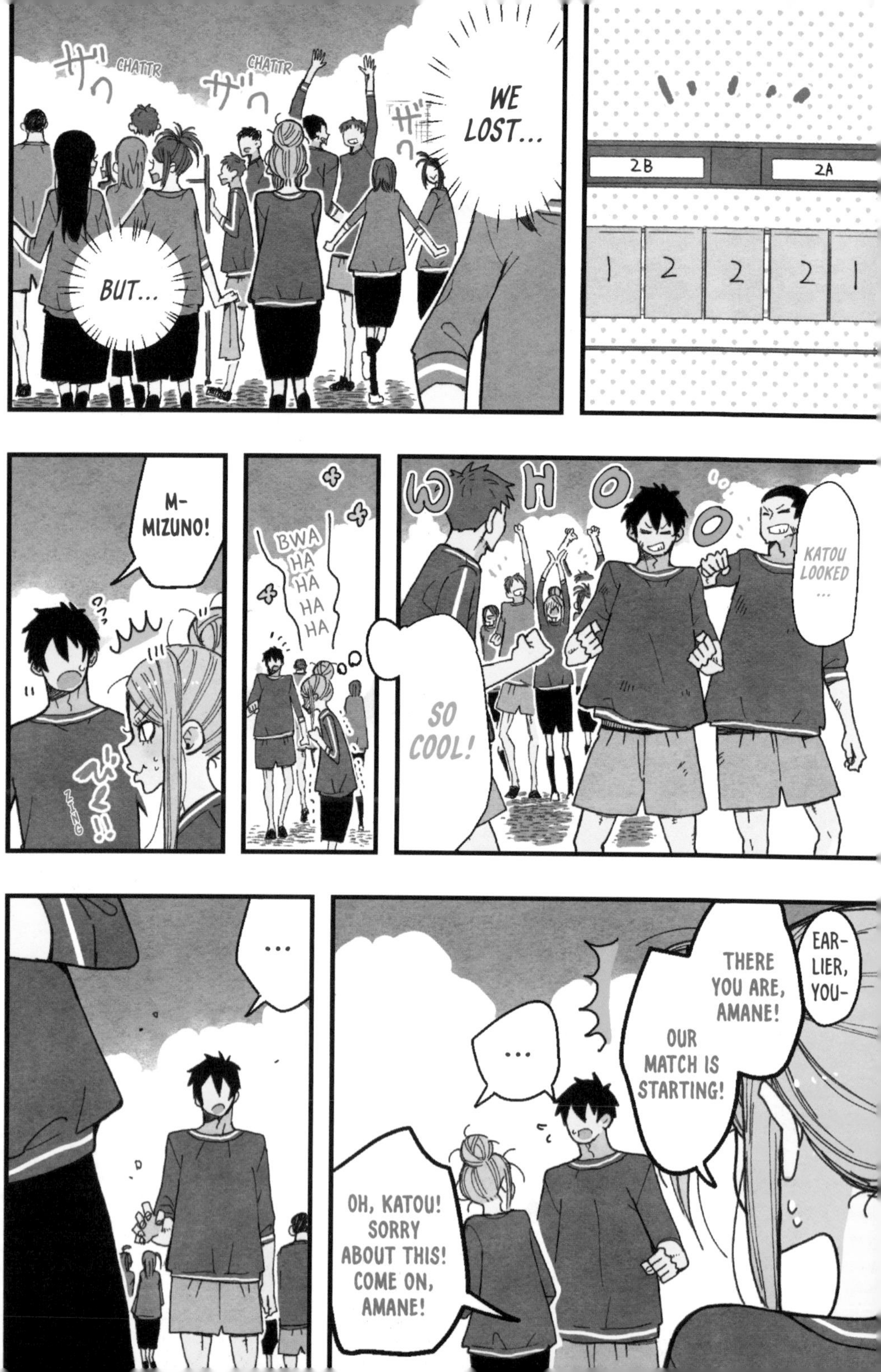
2B
2A
1
2
2
2
1
WE LOST...
CHATTR
CHATTR
BUT...
KATOU LOOKED...
WHOO
SO COOL!
BWA HA HA HA HA HA
M-MIZUNO!
ZING
EAR-LIER, YOU-
THERE YOU ARE, AMANE!
OUR MATCH IS STARTING!
...
OH, KATOU! SORRY ABOUT THIS! COME ON, AMANE!
...

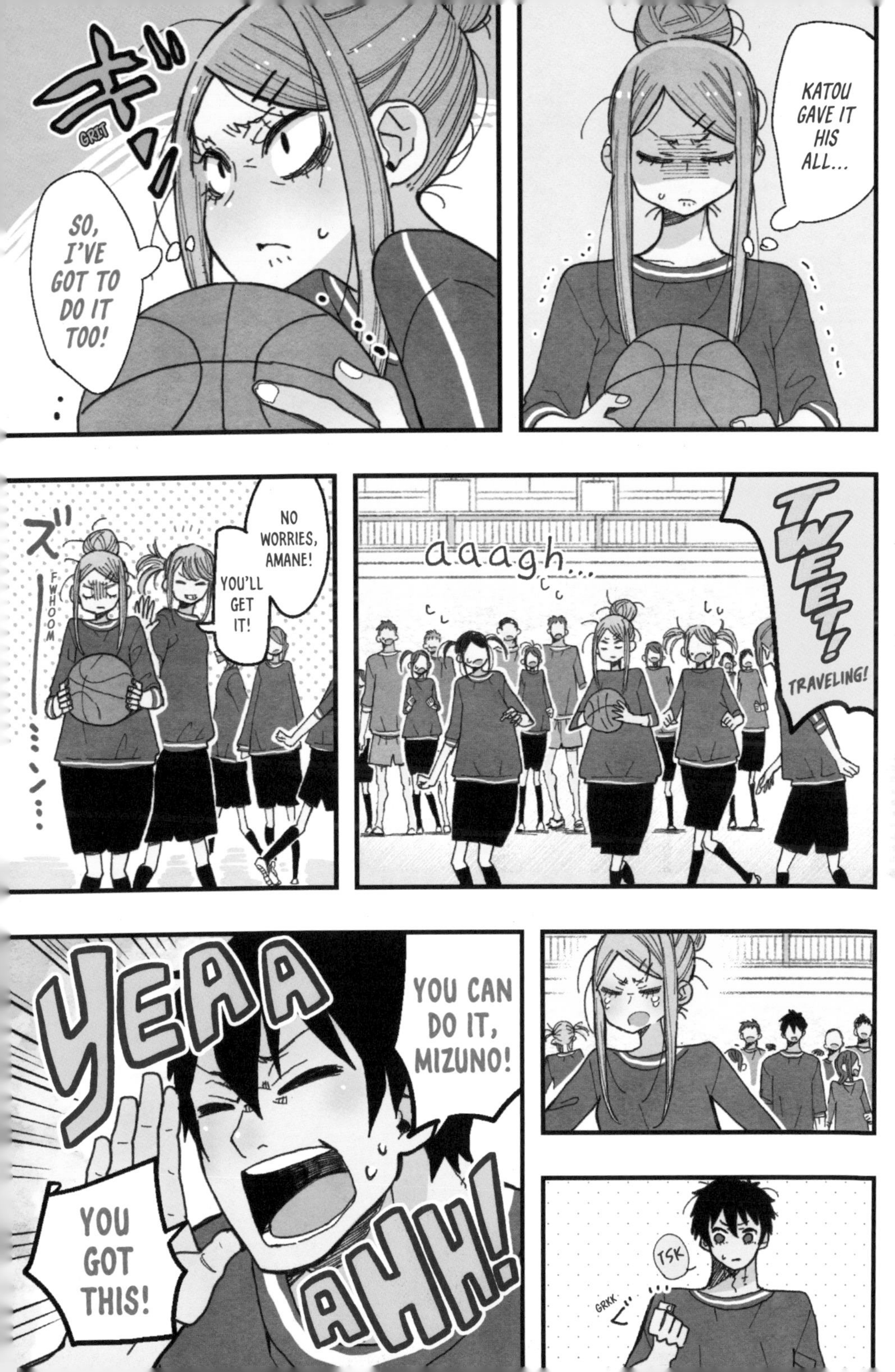
KATOU GAVE IT HIS ALL...
ギッ
GRIT
SO, I'VE GOT TO DO IT TOO!
TWEET!
TRAVELING!
aaagh...
NO WORRIES, AMANE!
YOU'LL GET IT!
ズ
FWHOOM
TSK
GRKK
YOU CAN DO IT, MIZUNO!
YEAA
AHH!
YOU GOT THIS!

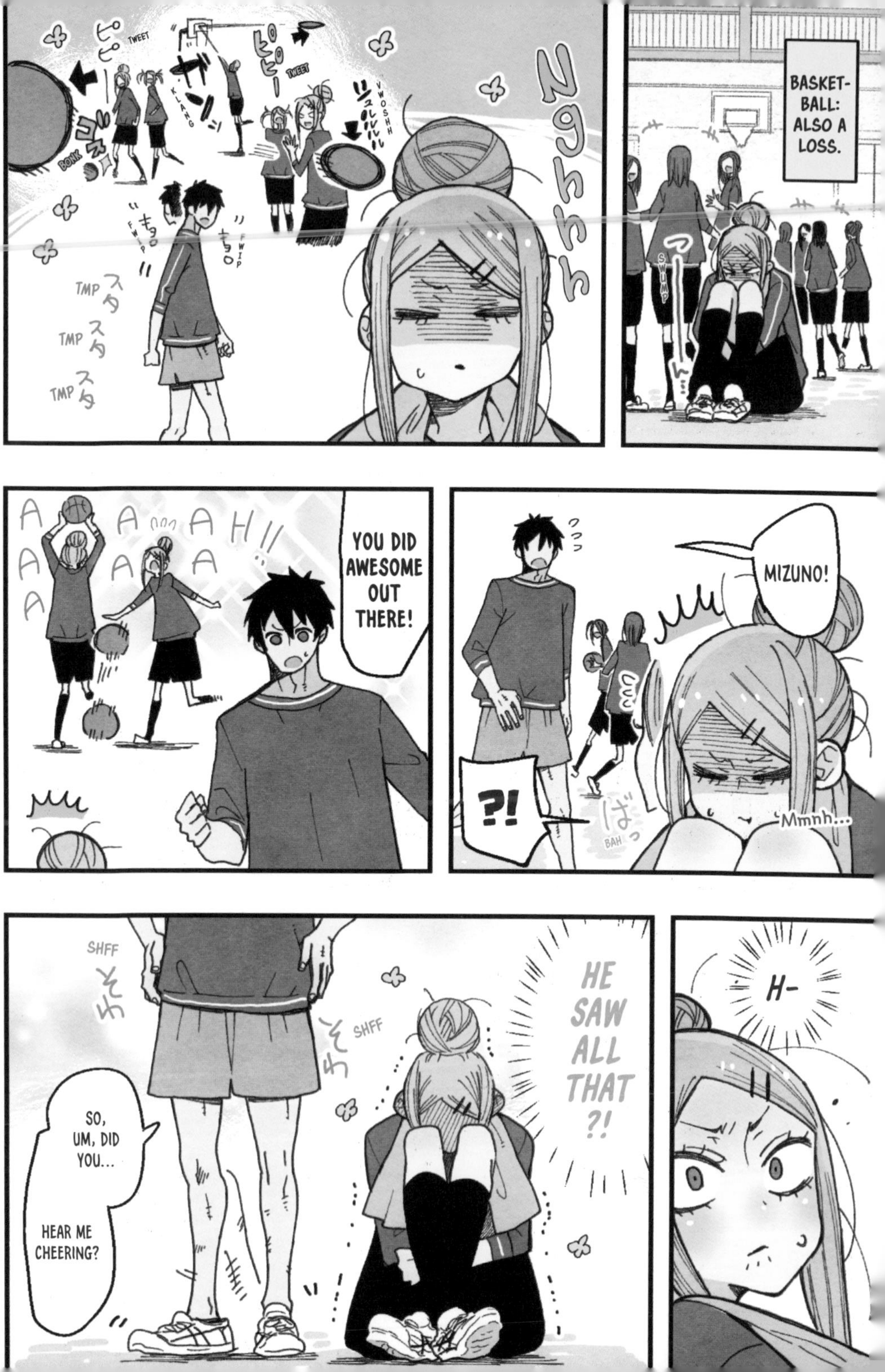

BASKET-BALL: ALSO A LOSS.
SWUMP
Nghhhh
TWEET
TWEET
KLANG
VWOSHH
BONK
FWIP
FWIP
TMP
TMP
TMP
MIZUNO!
?!
BAH
Mmnh...
YOU DID AWESOME OUT THERE!
AAAAAAH!!
H-
HE SAW ALL THAT?!
SHFF
SHFF
SO, UM, DID YOU...
HEAR ME CHEERING?

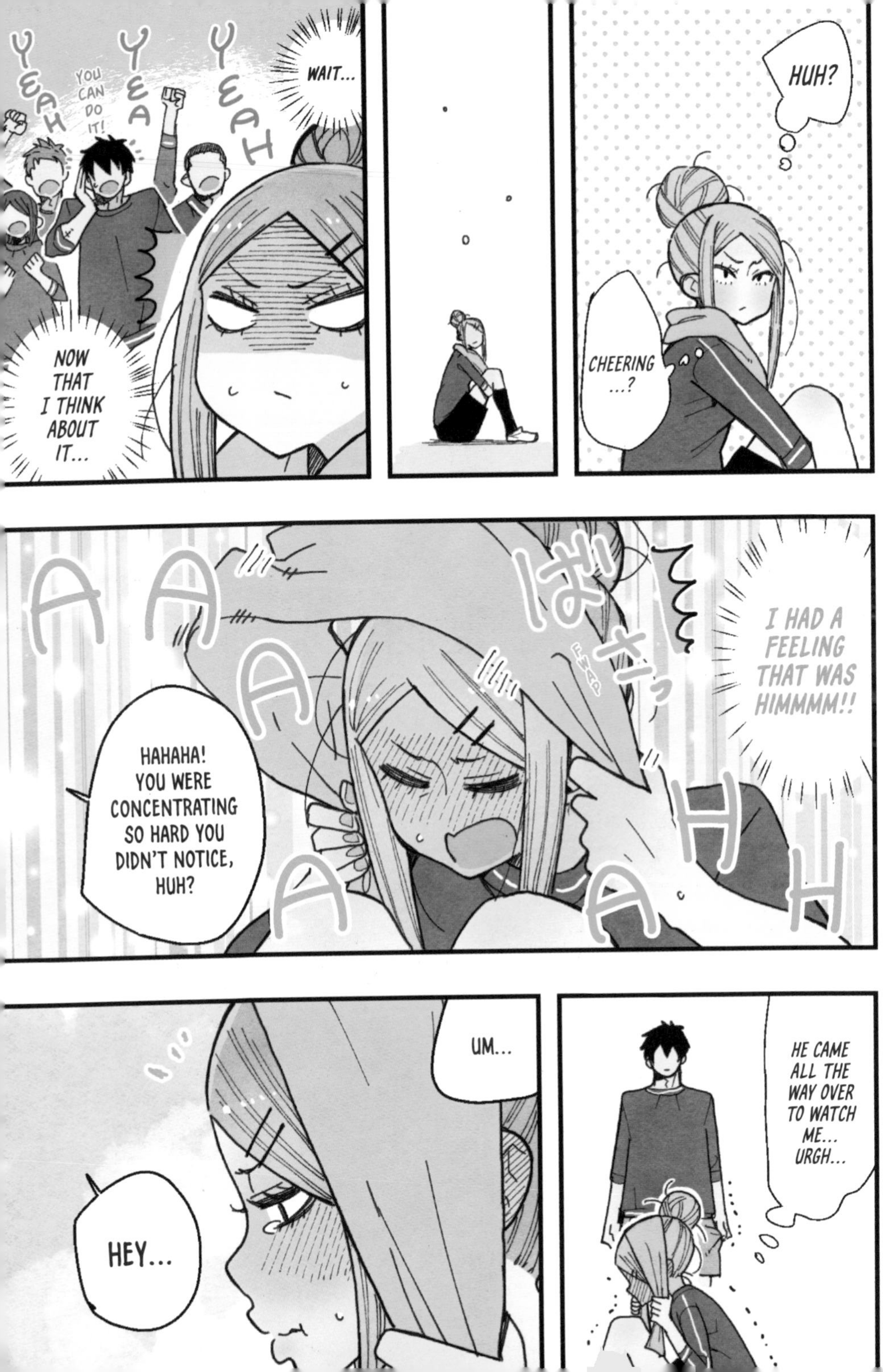
HUH?
CHEERING ...?
WAIT...
YEAH
YEAH
YOU CAN DO IT!
YEAH
NOW THAT I THINK ABOUT IT...
I HAD A FEELING THAT WAS HIMMMM!!
ぱさっ
FWAP
AAAAAAHHH
HAHAHA! YOU WERE CONCENTRATING SO HARD YOU DIDN'T NOTICE, HUH?
HE CAME ALL THE WAY OVER TO WATCH ME... URGH...
UM...
HEY...

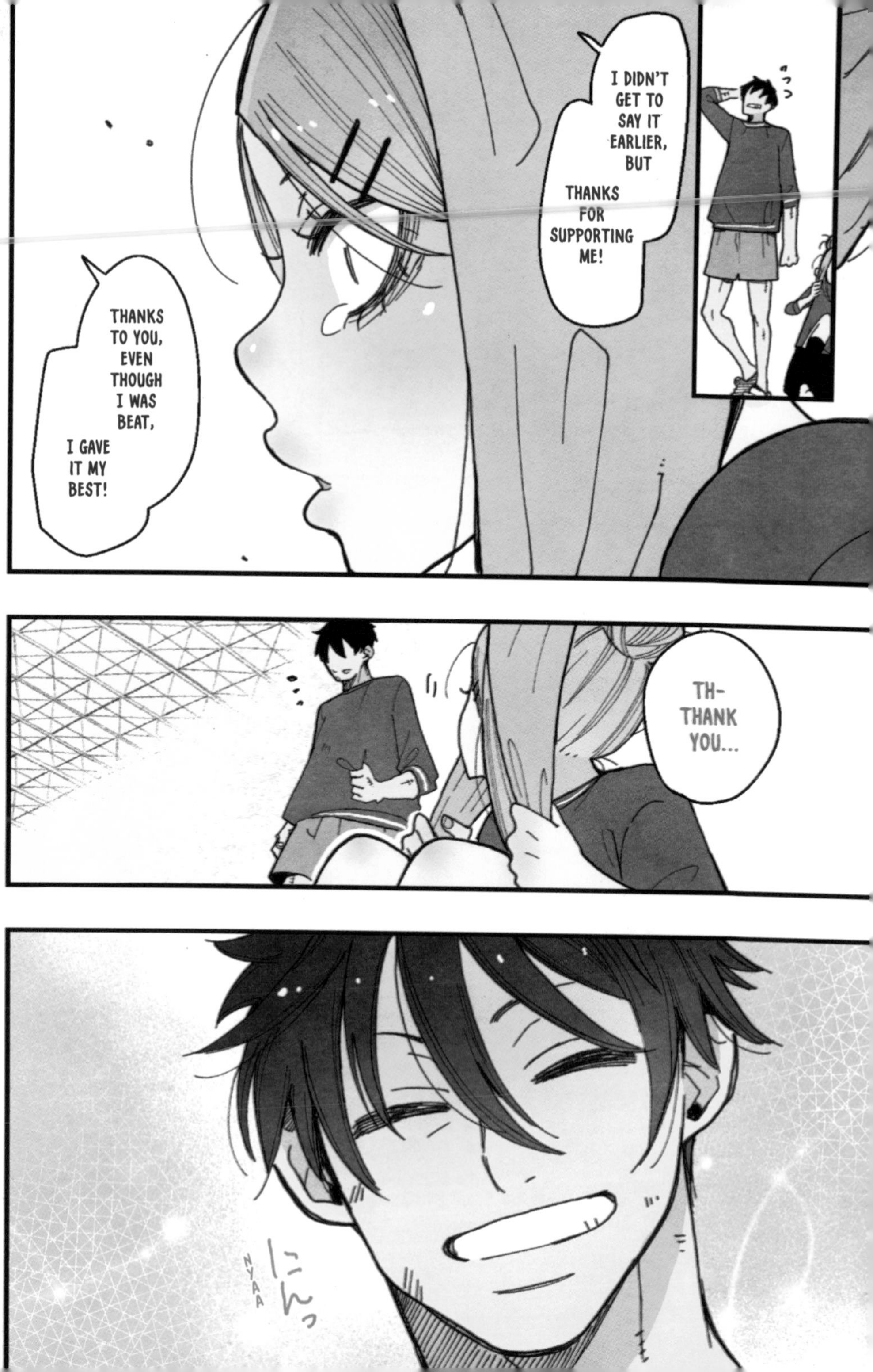
I DIDN'T GET TO SAY IT EARLIER, BUT
THANKS FOR SUPPORTING ME!
THANKS TO YOU, EVEN THOUGH I WAS BEAT,
I GAVE IT MY BEST!
TH-THANK YOU...
にんっ
NYAA

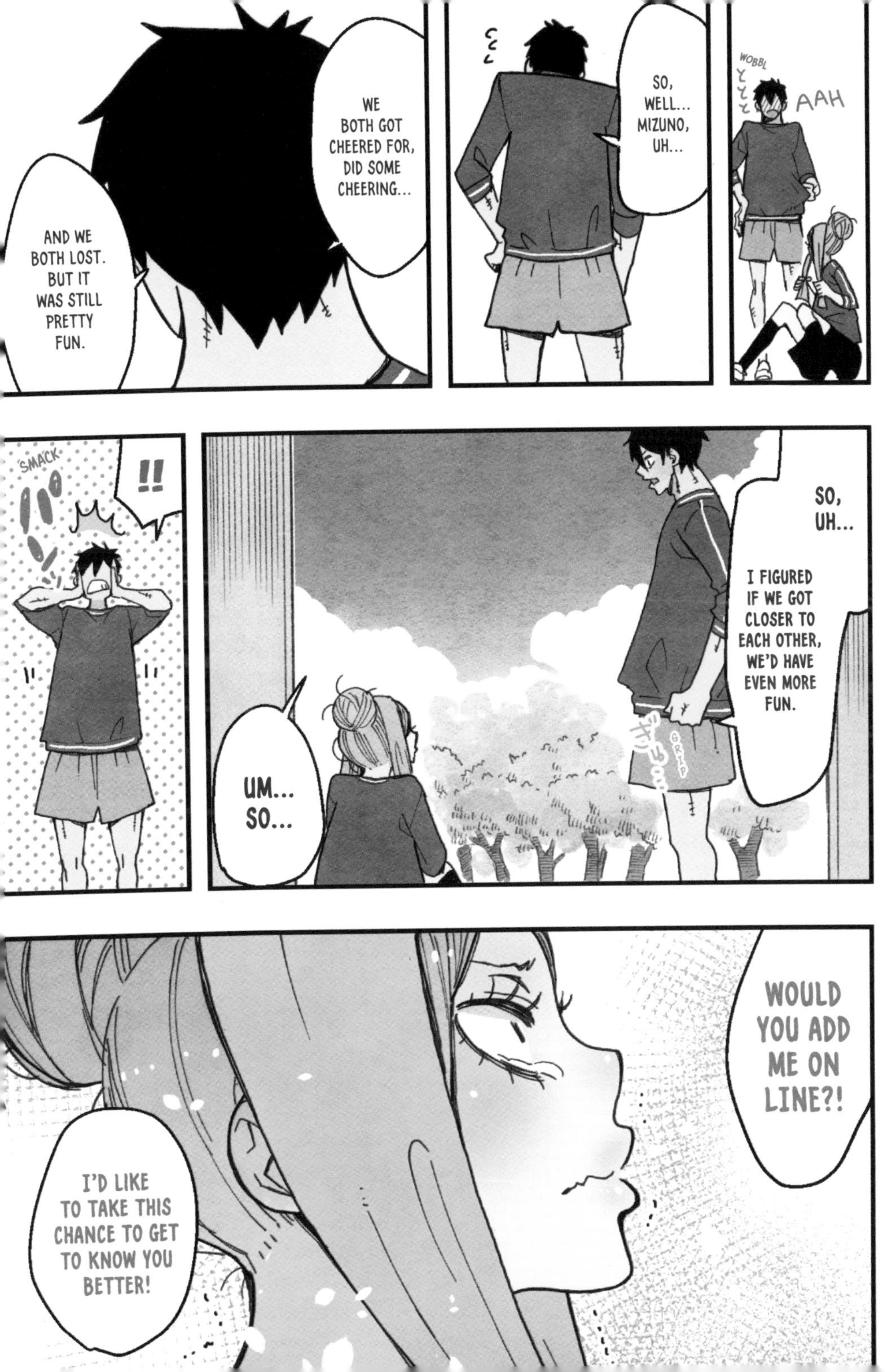
WE BOTH GOT CHEERED FOR, DID SOME CHEERING...
AND WE BOTH LOST. BUT IT WAS STILL PRETTY FUN.
SO, WELL... MIZUNO, UH...
WOBBL
AAH
SMACK
!!
UM... SO...
SO, UH...
I FIGURED IF WE GOT CLOSER TO EACH OTHER, WE'D HAVE EVEN MORE FUN.
GRIP
I'D LIKE TO TAKE THIS CHANCE TO GET TO KNOW YOU BETTER!
WOULD YOU ADD ME ON LINE?!

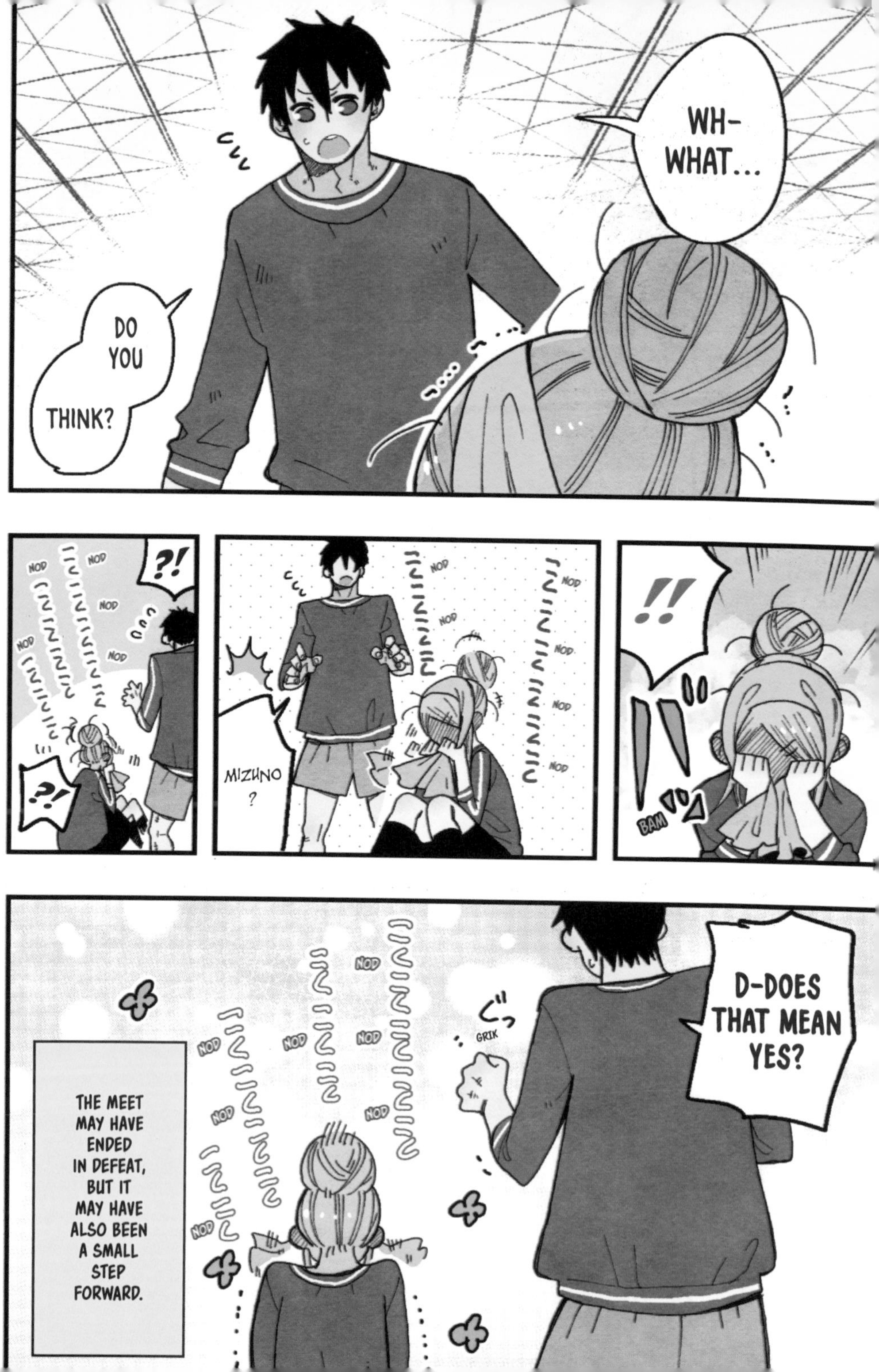
WH- WHAT...
DO YOU THINK?
!!
BAM
NOD NOD NOD NOD NOD
MIZUNO ?
?!
NOD NOD NOD NOD NOD
?!
D-DOES THAT MEAN YES?
GRIK
NOD NOD NOD NOD NOD NOD
THE MEET MAY HAVE ENDED IN DEFEAT, BUT IT MAY HAVE ALSO BEEN A SMALL STEP FORWARD.

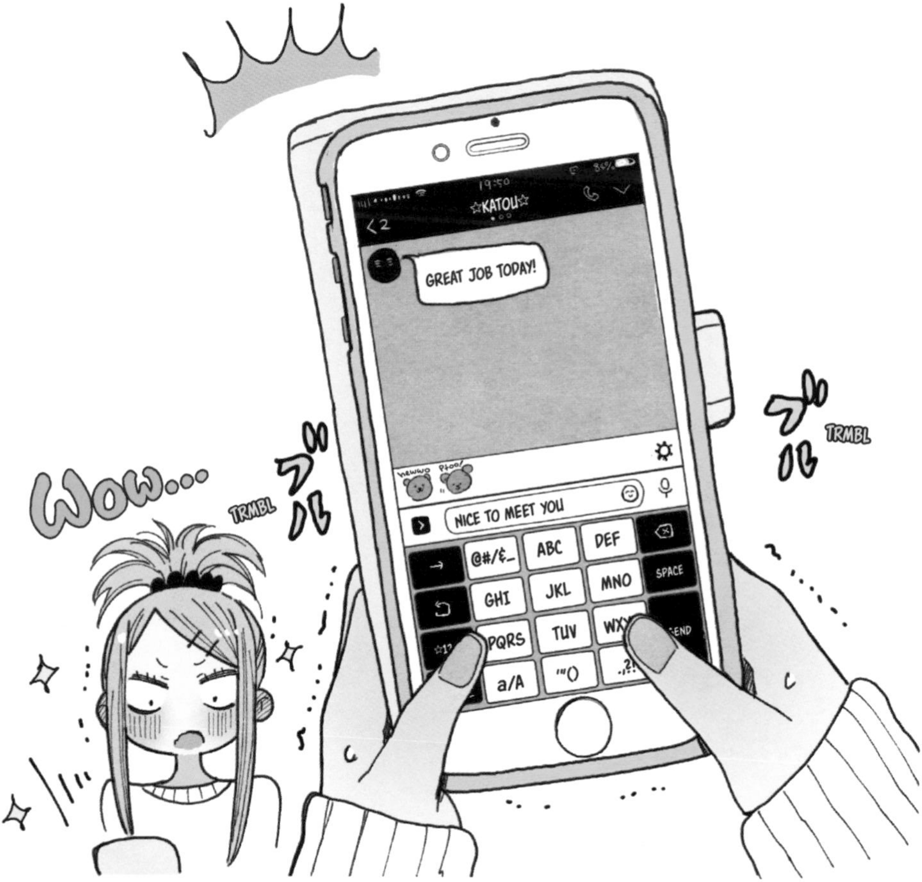

☆KATOU☆
GREAT JOB TODAY!
NICE TO MEET YOU
TRMBL
TRMBL
Wow...

THE GIRL
WITH THE
SANPAKU
EYES

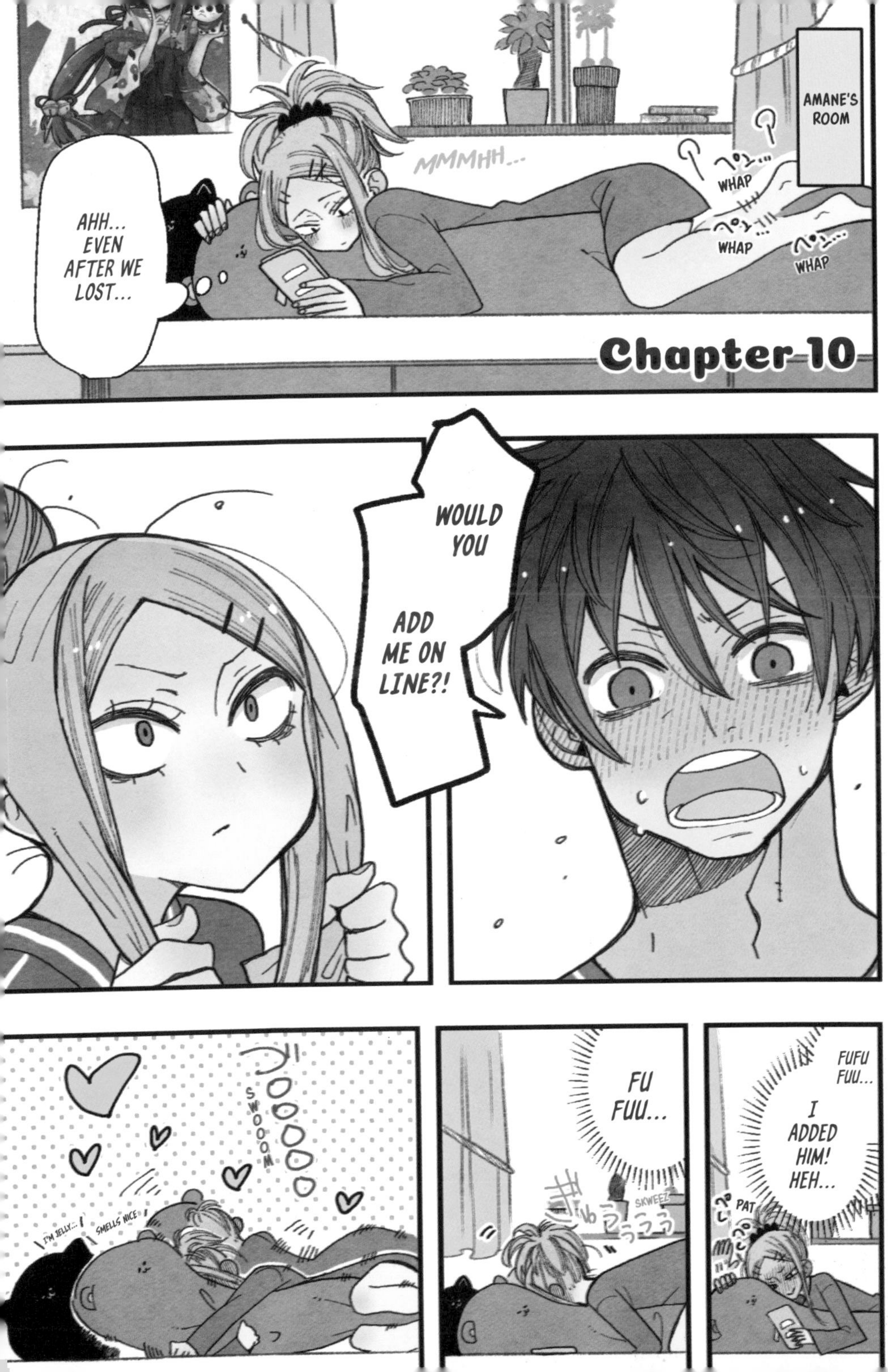
AMANE'S ROOM
WHAP
WHAP
WHAP
MMMHH...
AHH... EVEN AFTER WE LOST...
Chapter 10
WOULD YOU
ADD ME ON LINE?!
FUFU FUU...
I ADDED HIM! HEH...
PAT
FU FUU...
SKWEEZ
SWOOOM
SMELLS NICE
I'M JELLY...!

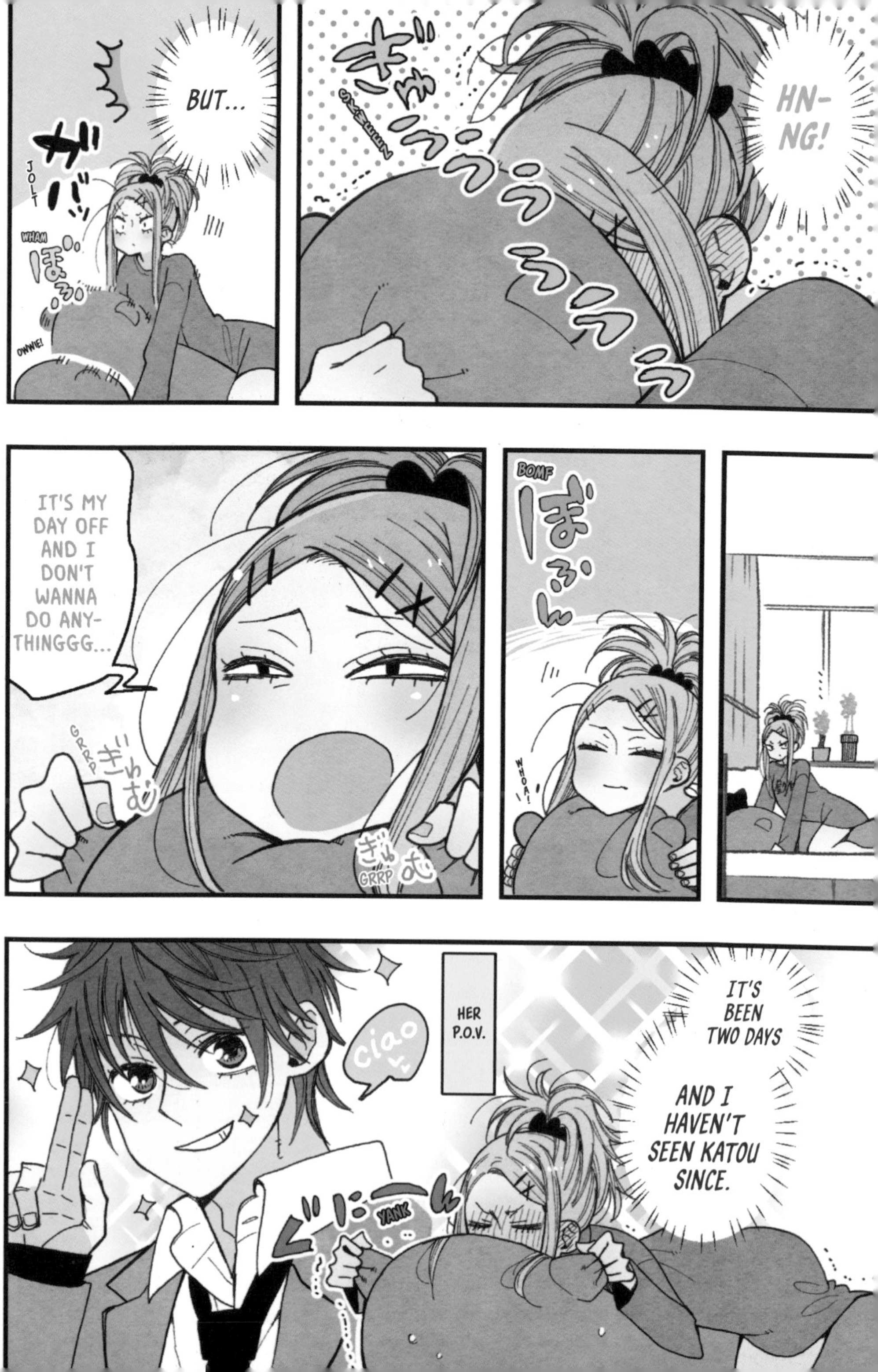
HN-NG!
BUT...
JOLT
WHAM
OWWIE!
BOMF
WHOA!
IT'S MY DAY OFF AND I DON'T WANNA DO ANYTHINGGG...
GRRP
GRRP
IT'S BEEN TWO DAYS
AND I HAVEN'T SEEN KATOU SINCE.
HER P.O.V.
ciao
YANK

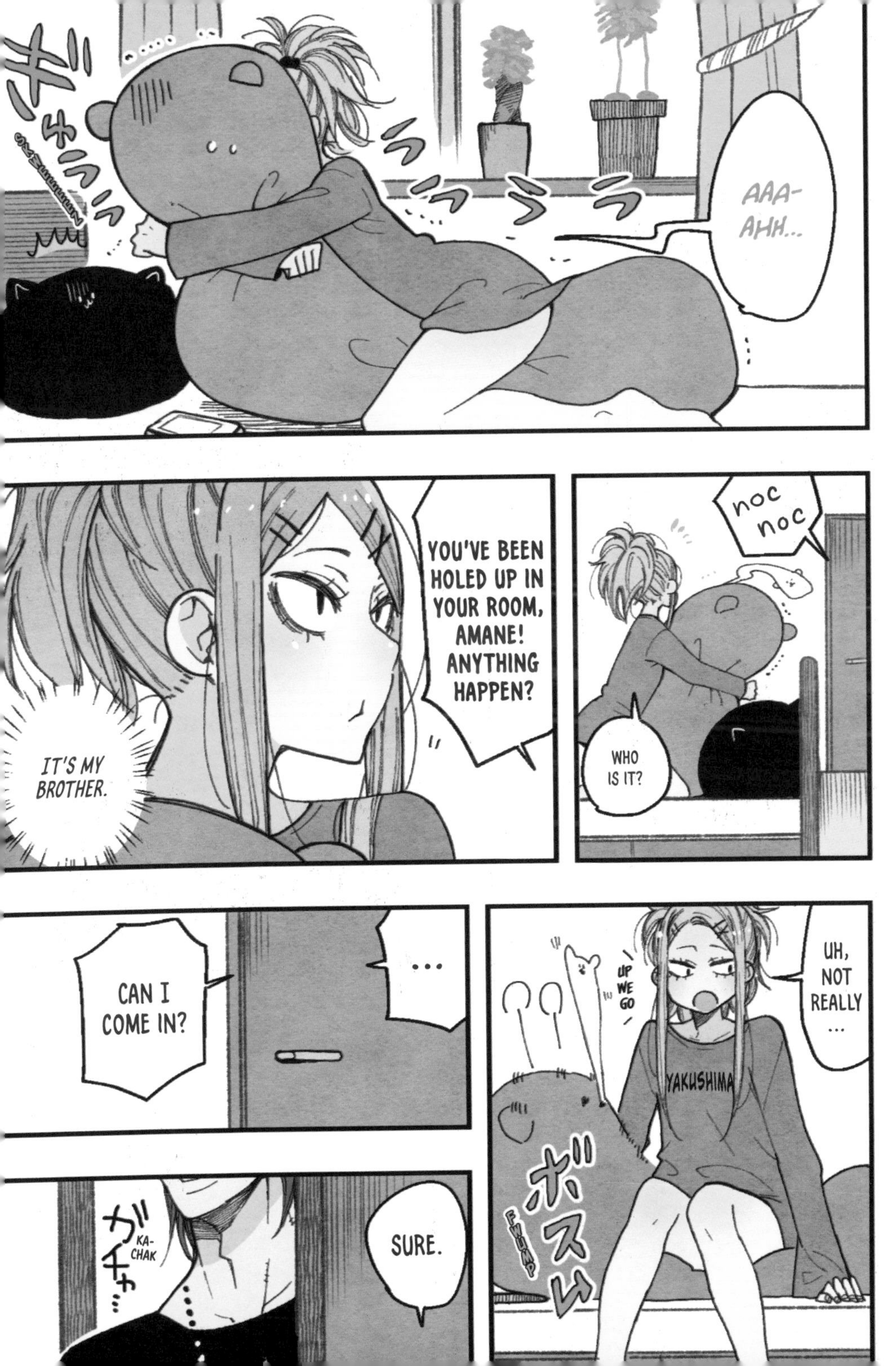
.....
AAA-AHH...
noc noc
WHO IS IT?
YOU'VE BEEN HOLED UP IN YOUR ROOM, AMANE! ANYTHING HAPPEN?
IT'S MY BROTHER.
UH, NOT REALLY ...
UP WE GO
YAKUSHIMA
FWUMP
...
CAN I COME IN?
SURE.
KA-CHAK

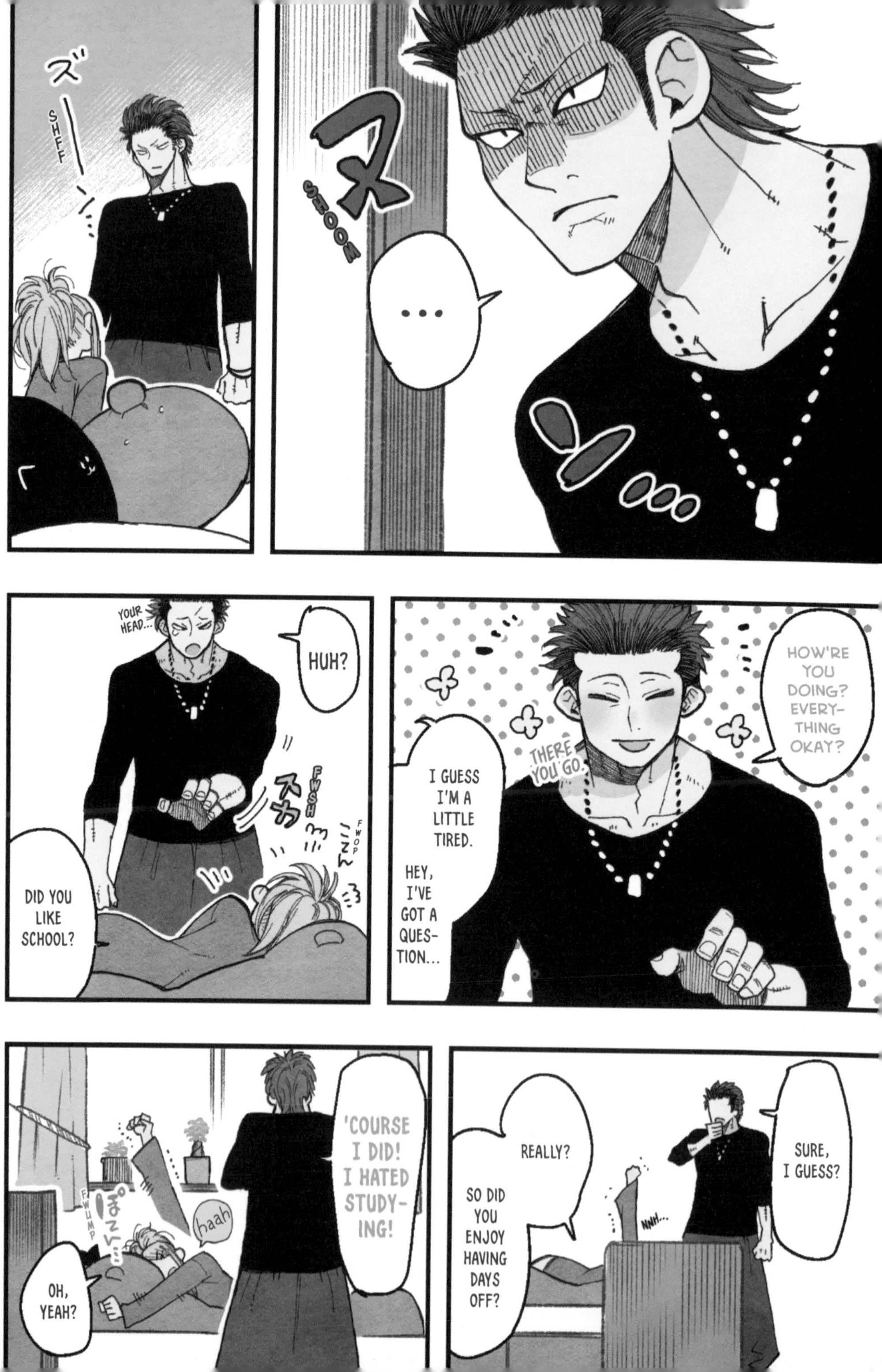
ヌ
SHOOM
...
ズー
SHFF
HOW'RE YOU DOING? EVERYTHING OKAY?
THERE YOU GO.
I GUESS I'M A LITTLE TIRED.
HEY, I'VE GOT A QUESTION...
YOUR HEAD...
HUH?
FWSH
FWOP
DID YOU LIKE SCHOOL?
SURE, I GUESS?
REALLY?
NNH...
SO DID YOU ENJOY HAVING DAYS OFF?
'COURSE I DID! I HATED STUDYING!
haah
FWUMP
OH, YEAH?

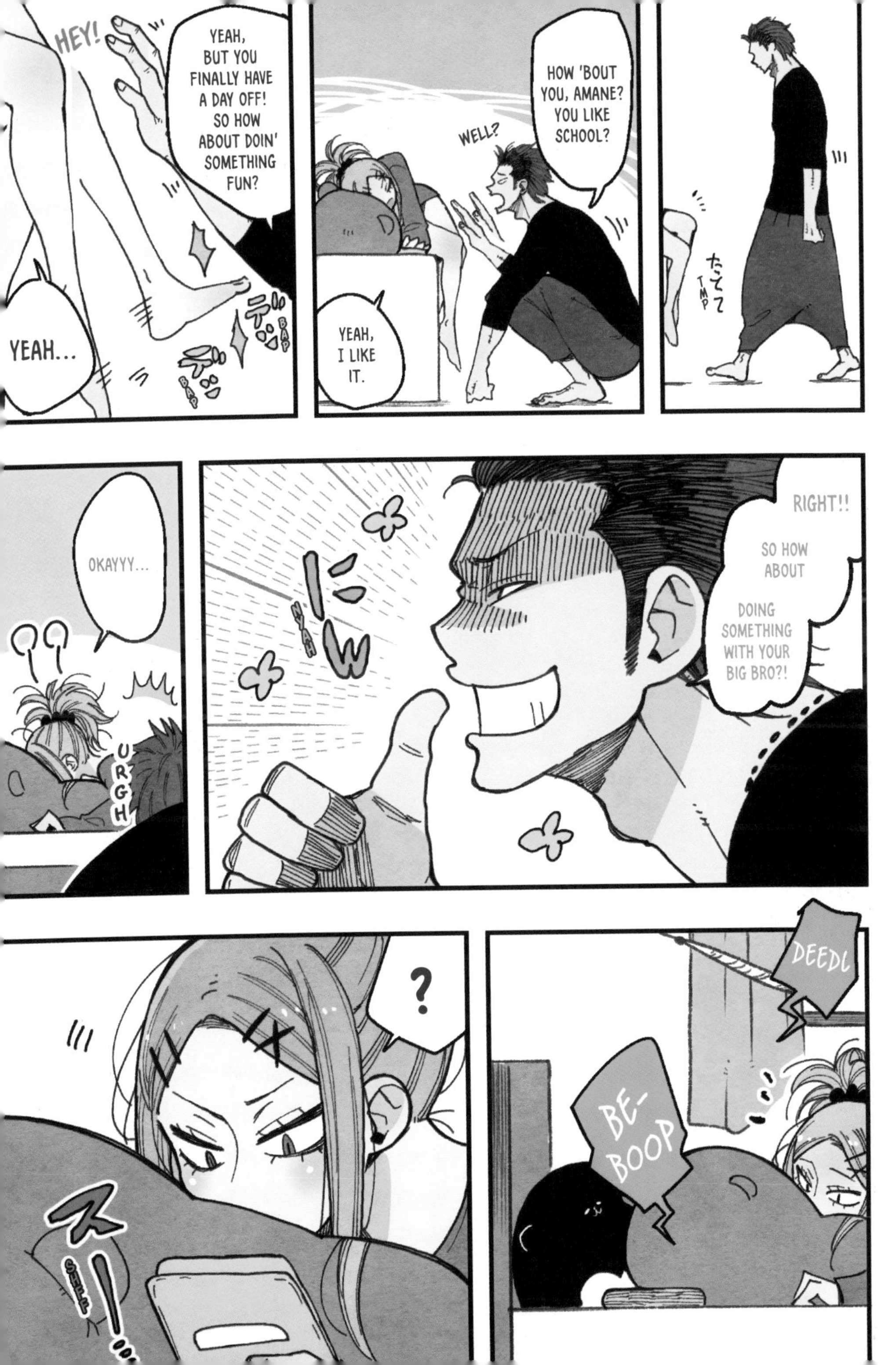
たてて
TMP
WELL?
HOW 'BOUT YOU, AMANE? YOU LIKE SCHOOL?
YEAH, I LIKE IT.
HEY!
YEAH, BUT YOU FINALLY HAVE A DAY OFF! SO HOW ABOUT DOIN' SOMETHING FUN?
BAP
BAP
YEAH...
RIGHT!!
SO HOW ABOUT DOING SOMETHING WITH YOUR BIG BRO?!
NYAH
OKAYYY...
URGH
DEEDL
BE-BOOP
?

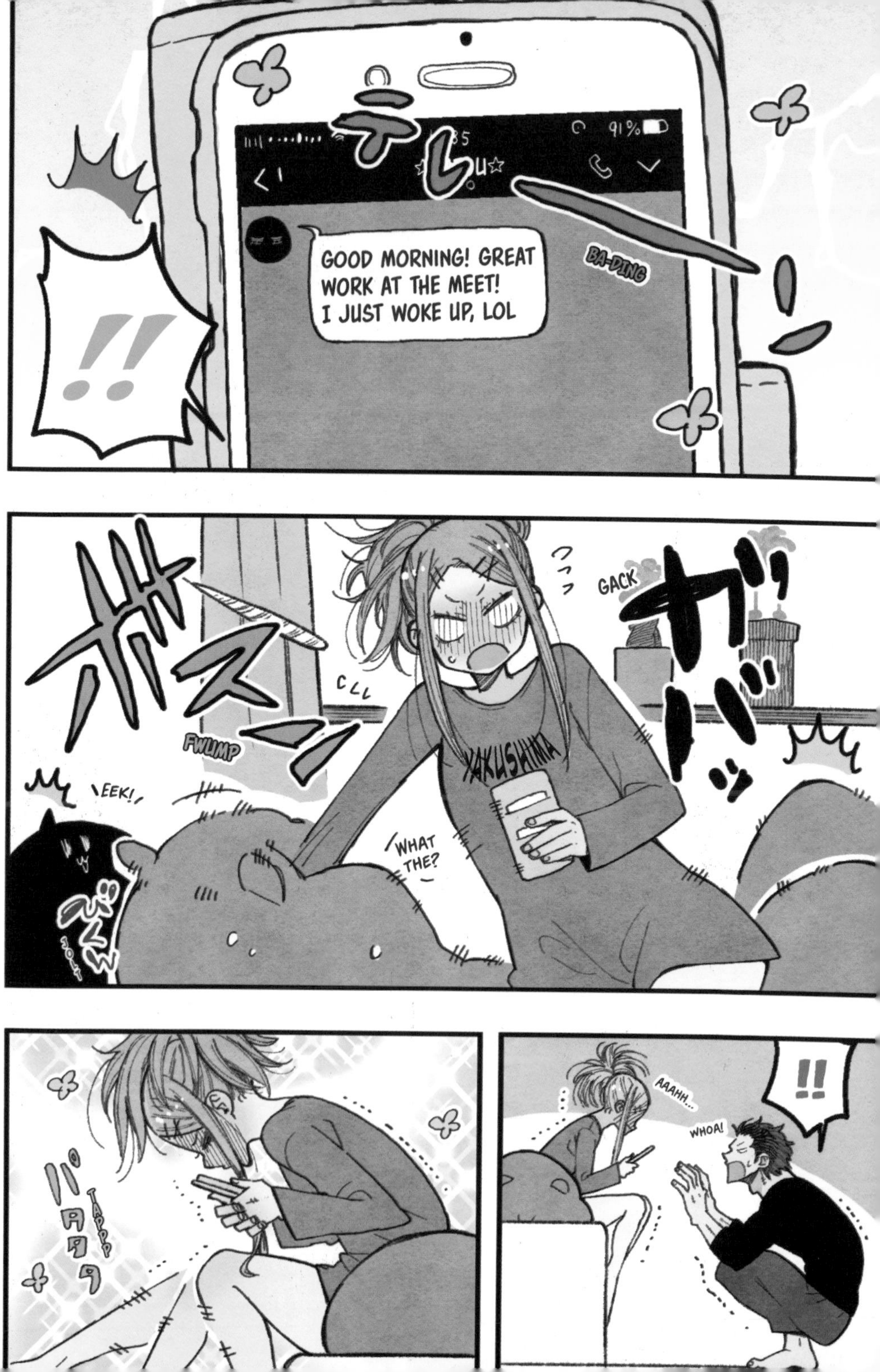

!!
GOOD MORNING! GREAT WORK AT THE MEET! I JUST WOKE UP, LOL
BA-DING
GACK
WHAT THE?
YAKUSHIMA
FWUMP
EEK!
JOLT
!!
WHOA!
AAAHH...
TAPPP

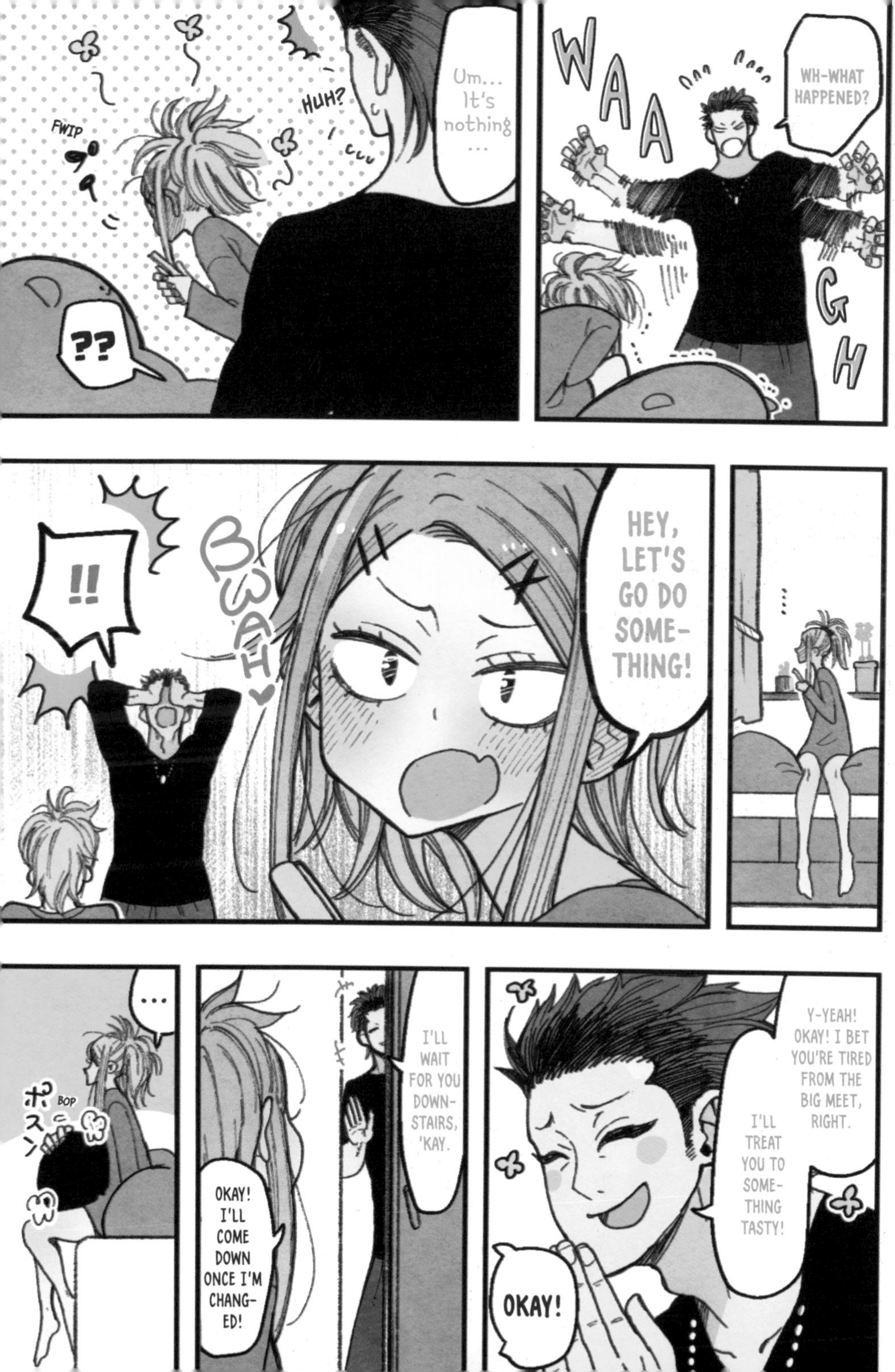
WH-WHAT HAPPENED?
WAAAGH
Um... It's nothing...
HUH?
FWIP
??
....
HEY, LET'S GO DO SOME-THING!
BWAH
!!
Y-YEAH! OKAY! I BET YOU'RE TIRED FROM THE BIG MEET, RIGHT.
I'LL TREAT YOU TO SOME-THING TASTY!
OKAY!
I'LL WAIT FOR YOU DOWN-STAIRS, 'KAY.
OKAY! I'LL COME DOWN ONCE I'M CHANG-ED!
...
ポスン
BOP

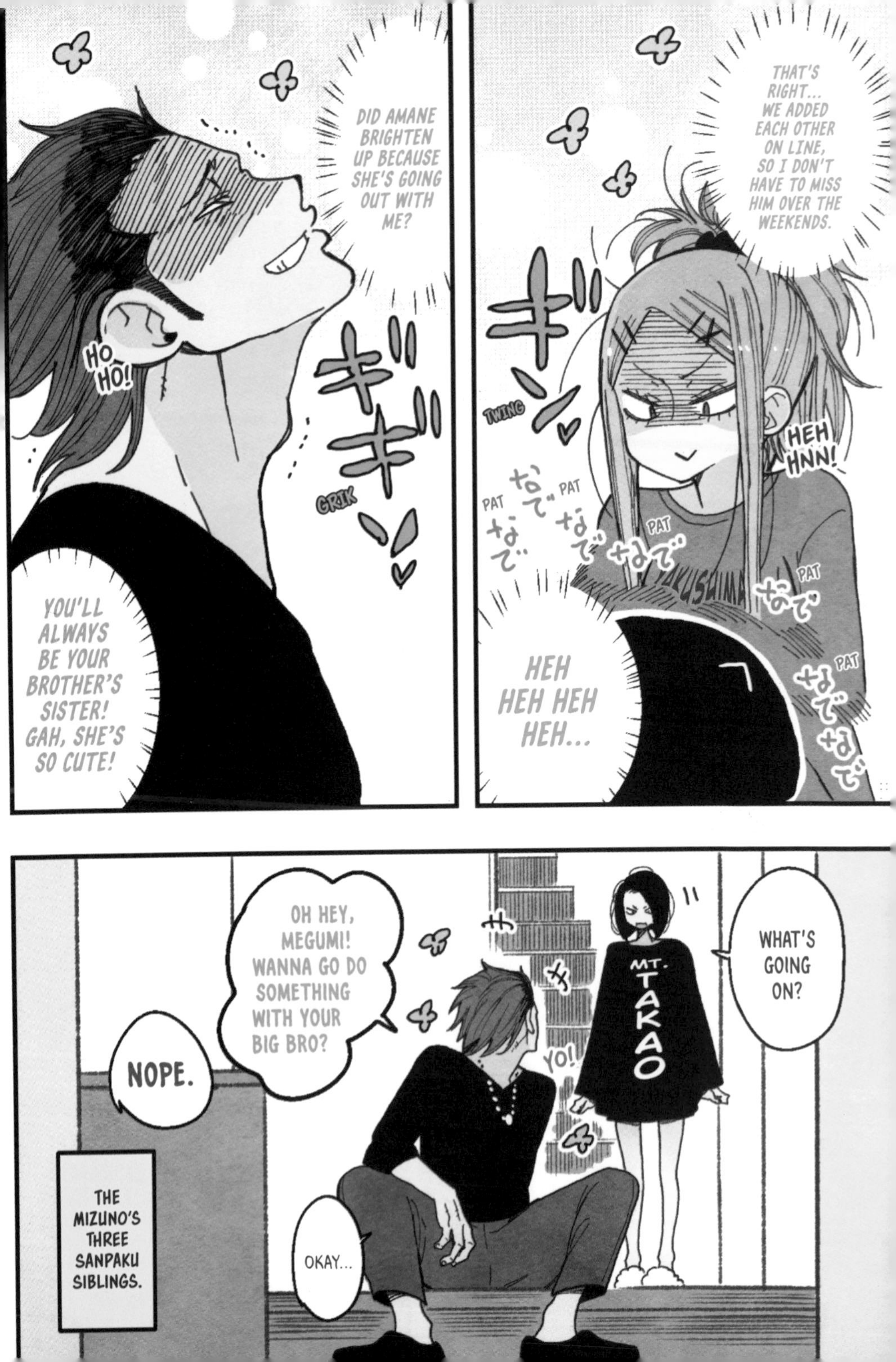
THAT'S RIGHT... WE ADDED EACH OTHER ON LINE, SO I DON'T HAVE TO MISS HIM OVER THE WEEKENDS.
TWING
HEH HNN!
PAT PAT PAT PAT PAT
HEH HEH HEH HEH...
DID AMANE BRIGHTEN UP BECAUSE SHE'S GOING OUT WITH ME?
HO HO!
GRIK
YOU'LL ALWAYS BE YOUR BROTHER'S SISTER! GAH, SHE'S SO CUTE!
WHAT'S GOING ON?
MT. TAKAO
YO!
OH HEY, MEGUMI! WANNA GO DO SOMETHING WITH YOUR BIG BRO?
NOPE.
OKAY...
THE MIZUNO'S THREE SANPAKU SIBLINGS.

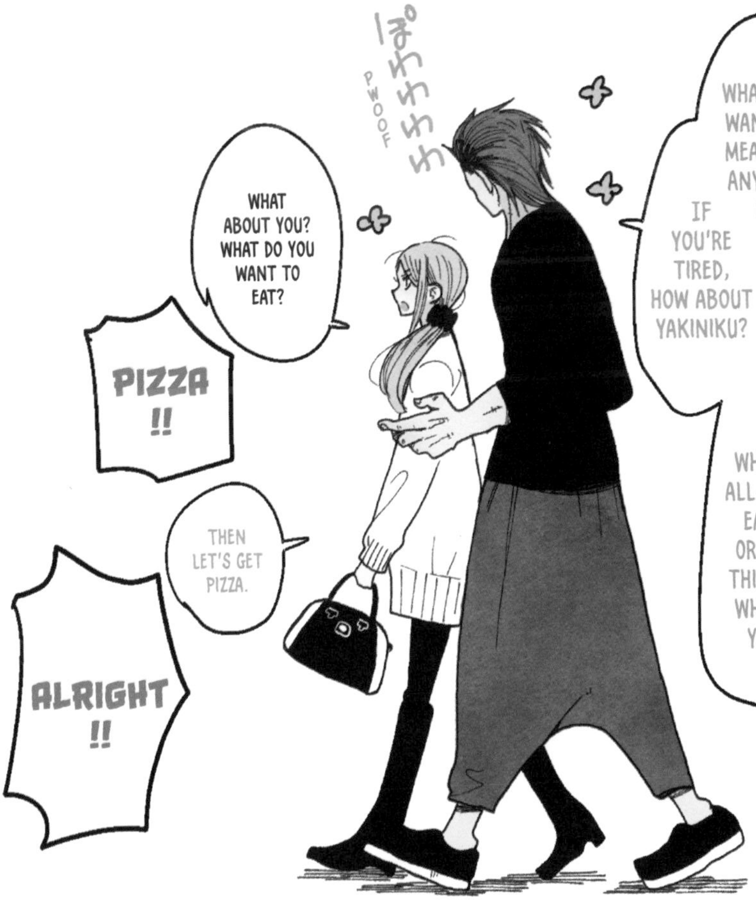
WHAT DO YOU WANNA EAT? MEAT? FISH? ANYTHING'S FINE!
IF YOU'RE TIRED, HOW ABOUT YAKINIKU?
WHAT ABOUT ALL-YOU-CAN-EAT PIZZA? OR A SUPER-THICK STEAK? WHAT WOULD YOU LIKE?
ぽわわわわ
PWOOF
WHAT ABOUT YOU? WHAT DO YOU WANT TO EAT?
PIZZA!!
THEN LET'S GET PIZZA.
ALRIGHT!!

THE GiRL
WiTH THE
SANPAKU
EYES

Side Story 1

Talking to the Girl with Sanpaku Eyes

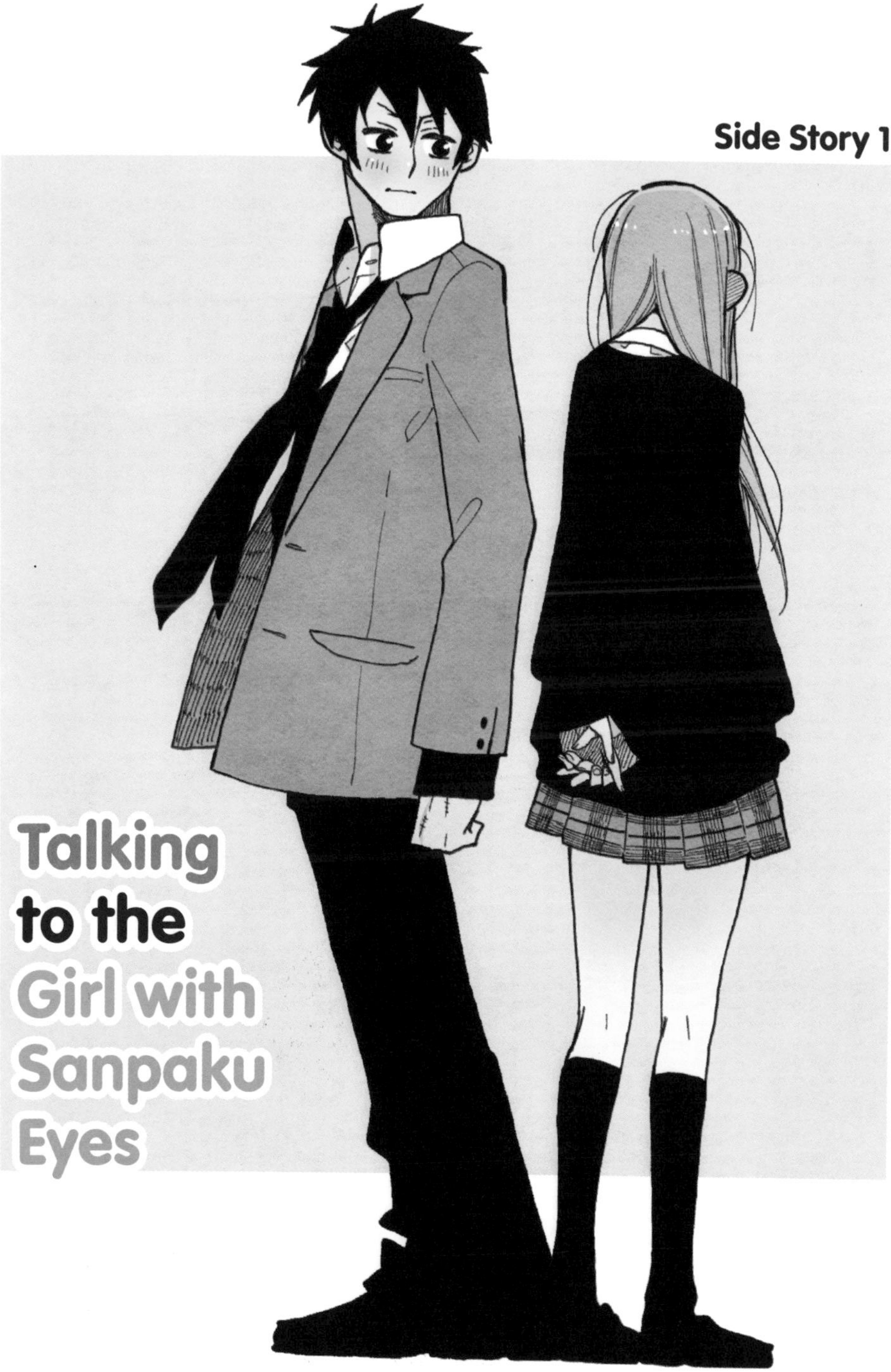

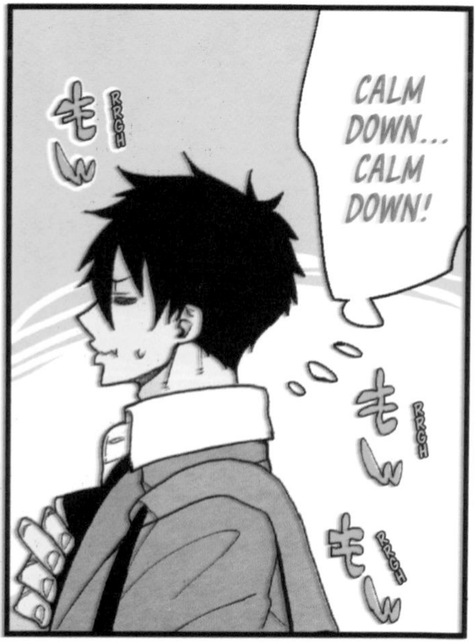
CALM DOWN... CALM DOWN!
もん RRGH
もん RRGH
もん RRGH

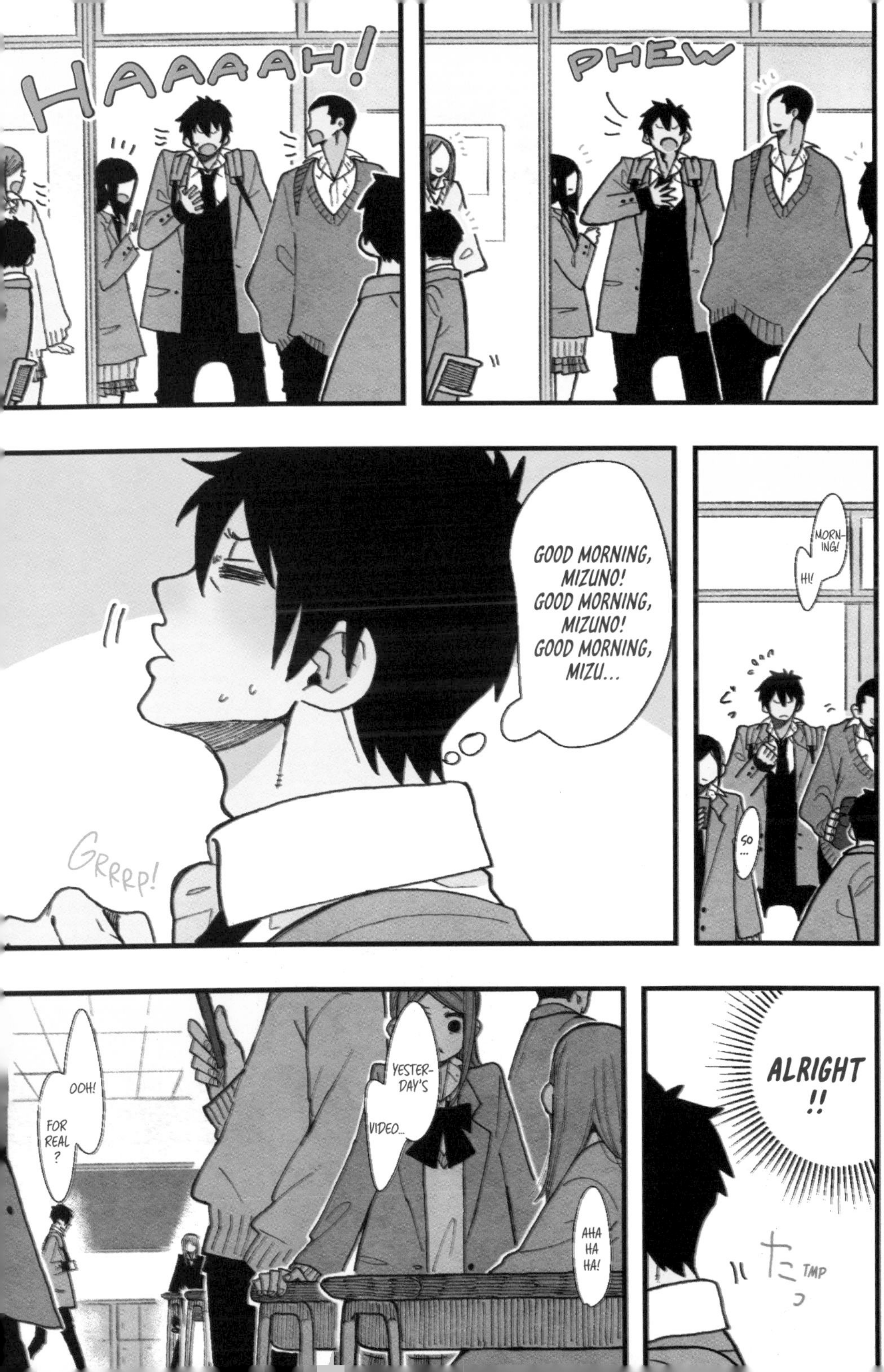
PHEW
HAAAAH!
MORNING!
HI!
SO...
GOOD MORNING, MIZUNO! GOOD MORNING, MIZUNO! GOOD MORNING, MIZU...
GRRRP!
ALRIGHT!!
TMP
YESTER-DAY'S
VIDEO...
AHA HA HA!
OOH!
FOR REAL?

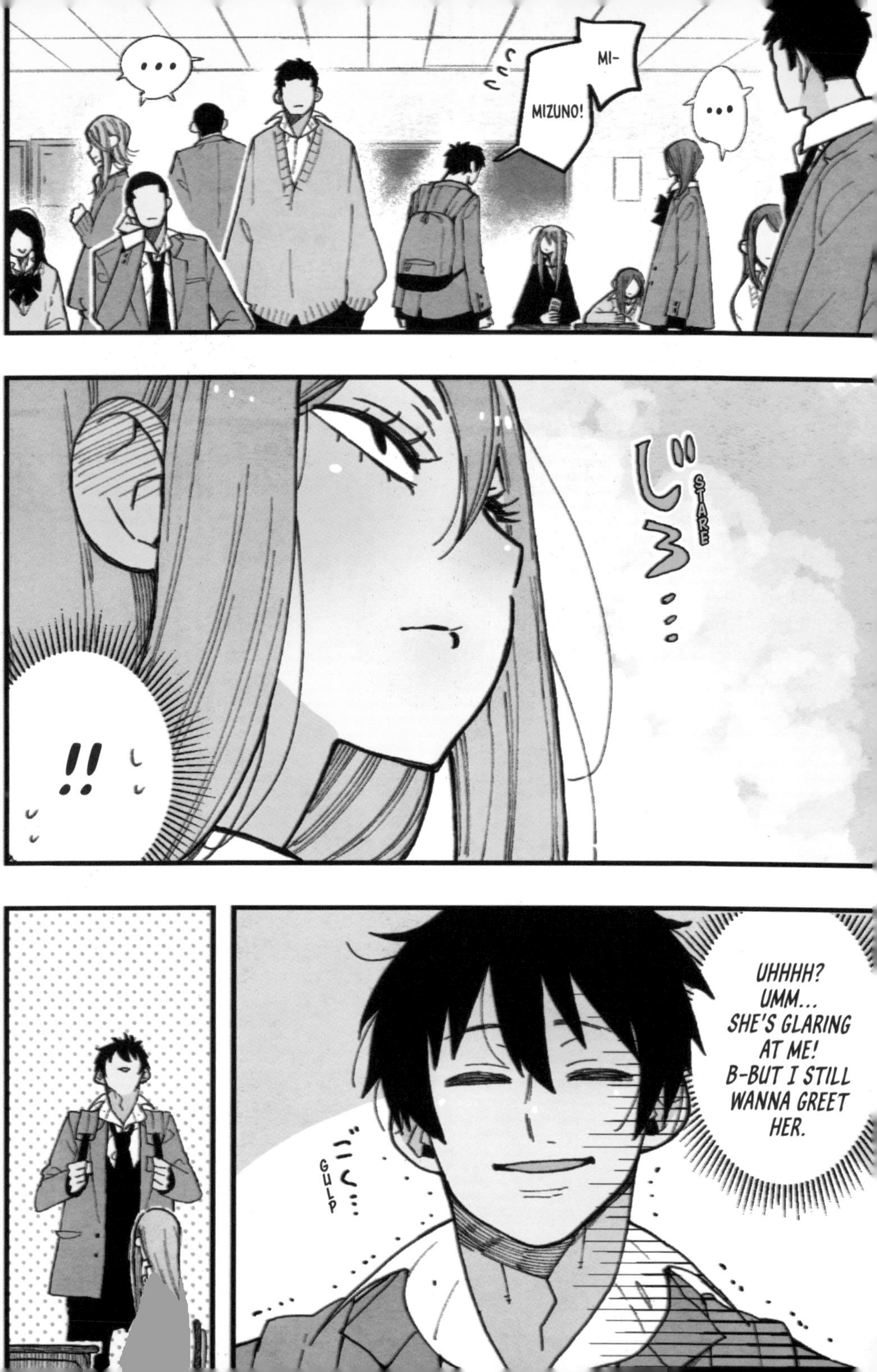
...
MI-
MIZUNO!
...
じろ
STARE
!!
UHHHH? UMM... SHE'S GLARING AT ME! B-BUT I STILL WANNA GREET HER.
ごく
GULP

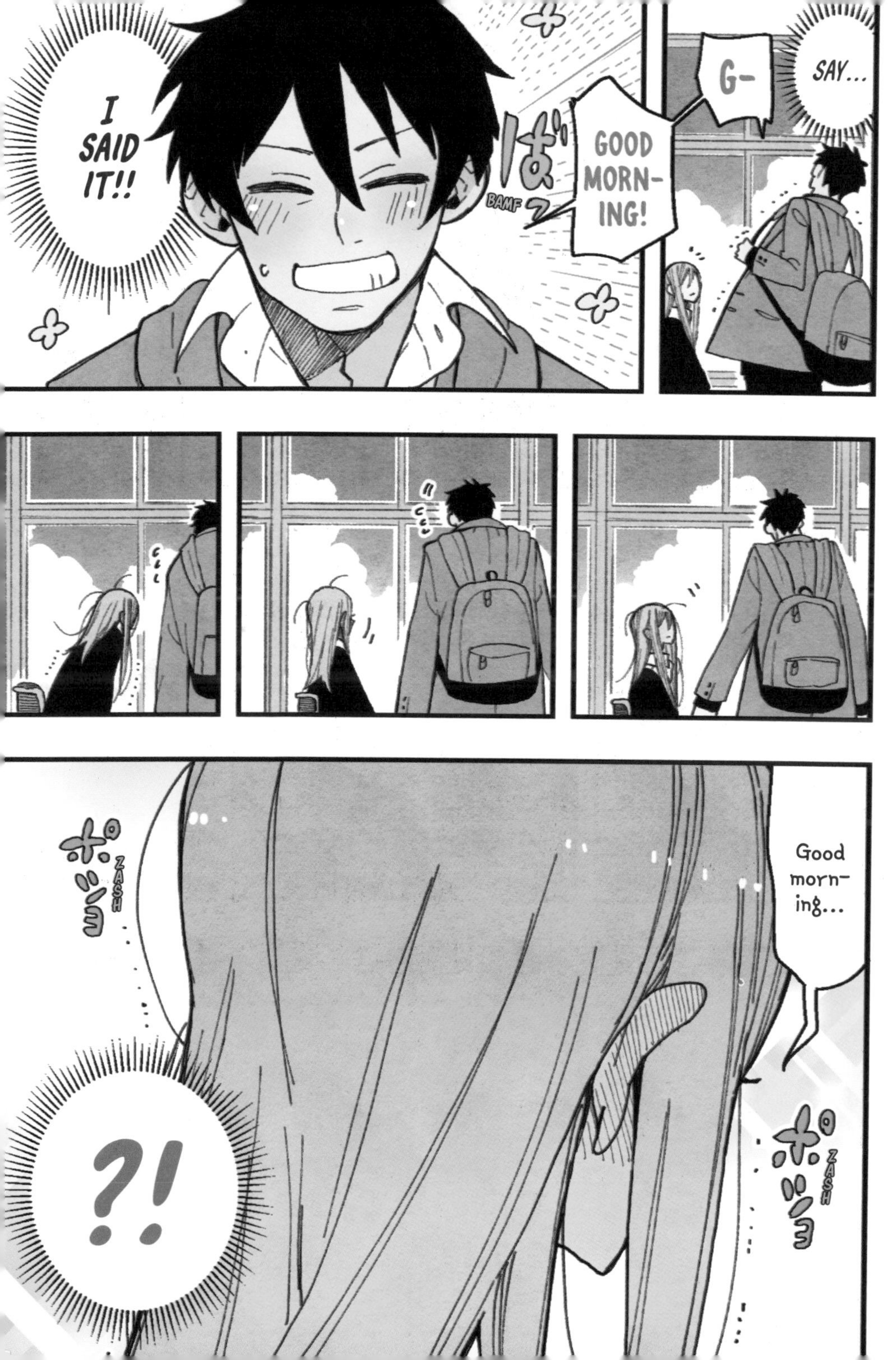
SAY...
G-
GOOD MORNING!
BAMF
I SAID IT!!
Good morning...
ZASH
?!
ZASH

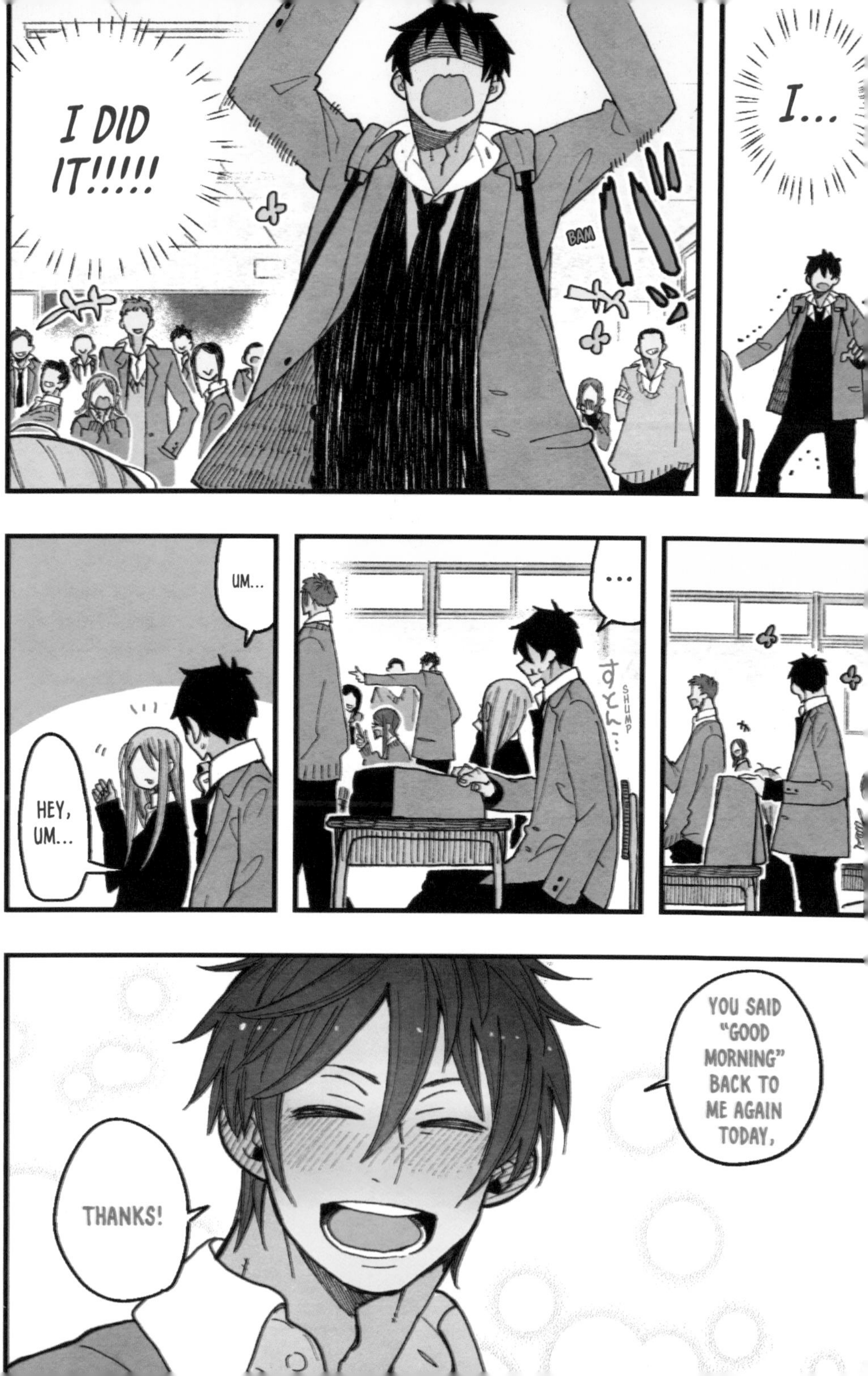
I...
I DID IT!!!!!
BAM
...
すとん…
SHUMP
UM...
HEY, UM...
YOU SAID "GOOD MORNING" BACK TO ME AGAIN TODAY,
THANKS!

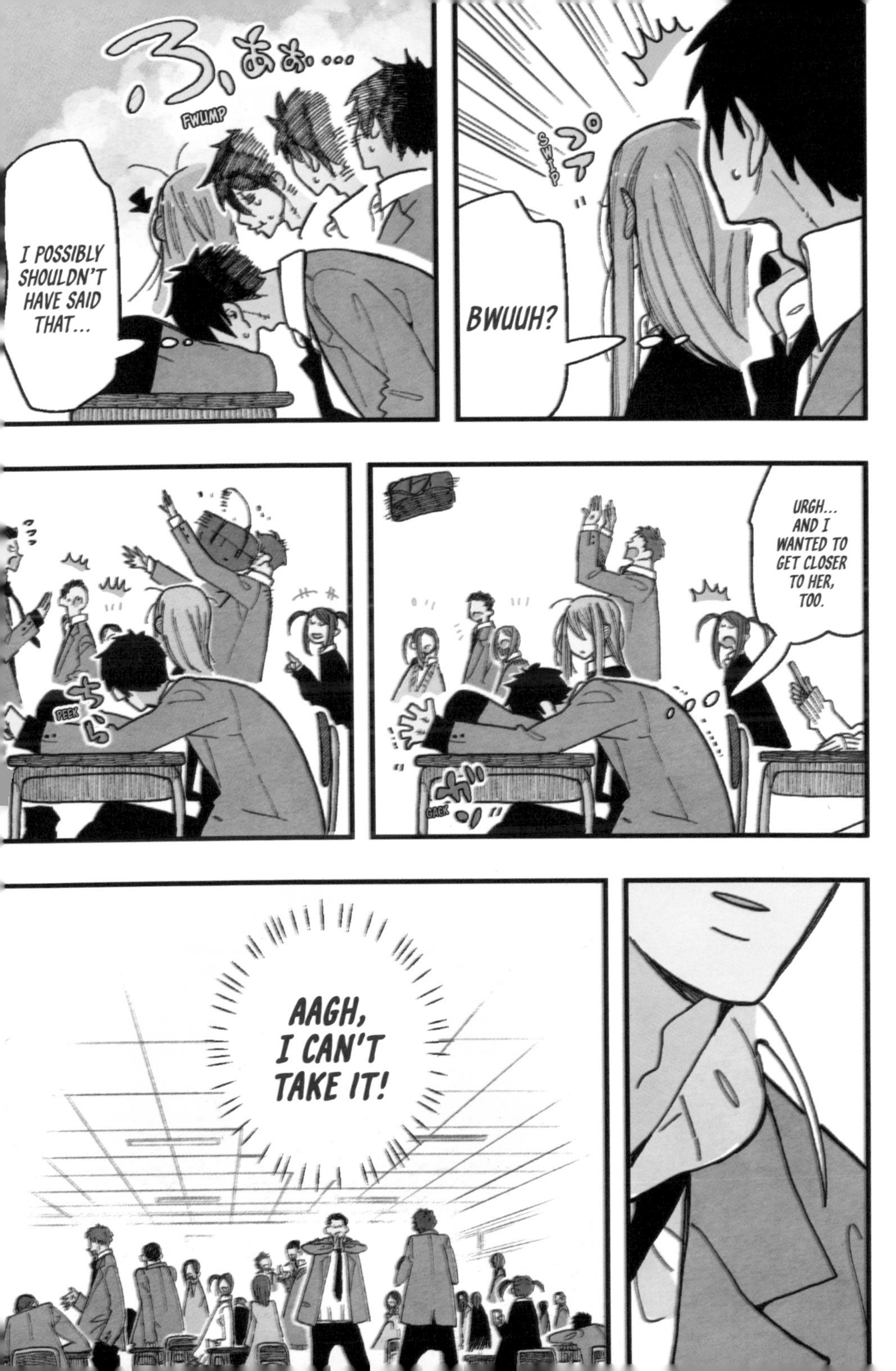
SWIP
BWUUH?
FWUMP
I POSSIBLY SHOULDN'T HAVE SAID THAT...
URGH... AND I WANTED TO GET CLOSER TO HER, TOO.
GACK
PEEK
AAGH, I CAN'T TAKE IT!

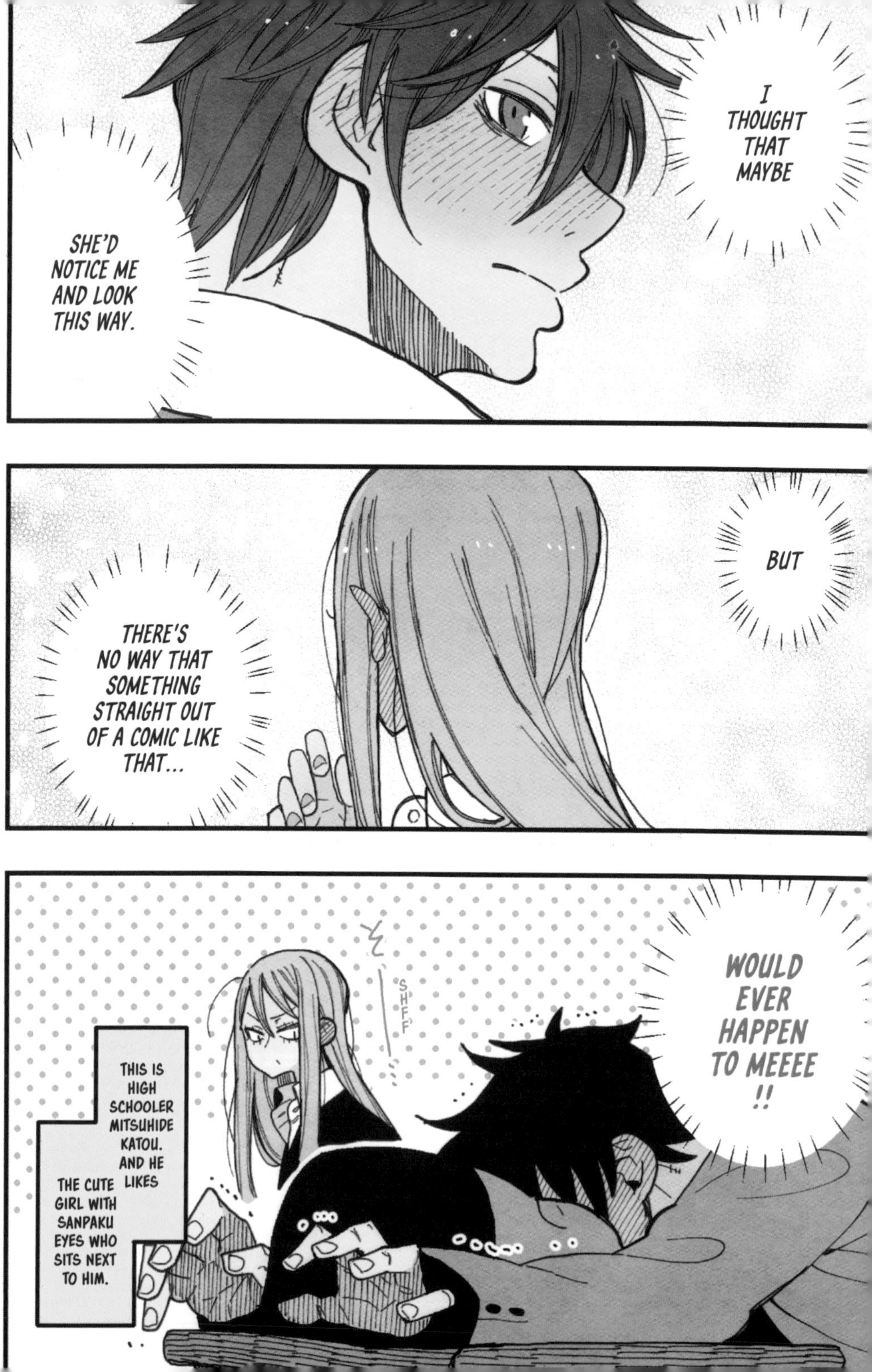
I THOUGHT THAT MAYBE
SHE'D NOTICE ME AND LOOK THIS WAY.
BUT
THERE'S NO WAY THAT SOMETHING STRAIGHT OUT OF A COMIC LIKE THAT...
WOULD EVER HAPPEN TO MEEEE!!
SHFF
THIS IS HIGH SCHOOLER MITSUHIDE KATOU. AND HE LIKES THE CUTE GIRL WITH SANPAKU EYES WHO SITS NEXT TO HIM.

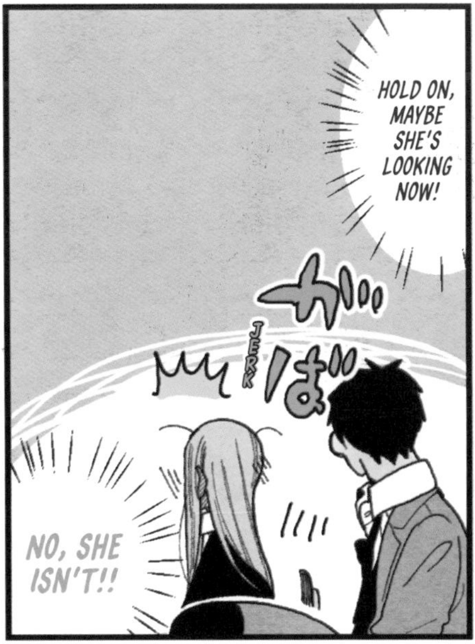
HOLD ON, MAYBE SHE'S LOOKING NOW!
JERK
NO, SHE ISN'T!!

Side Story 2

Protectors of the Girl with Sanpaku Eyes

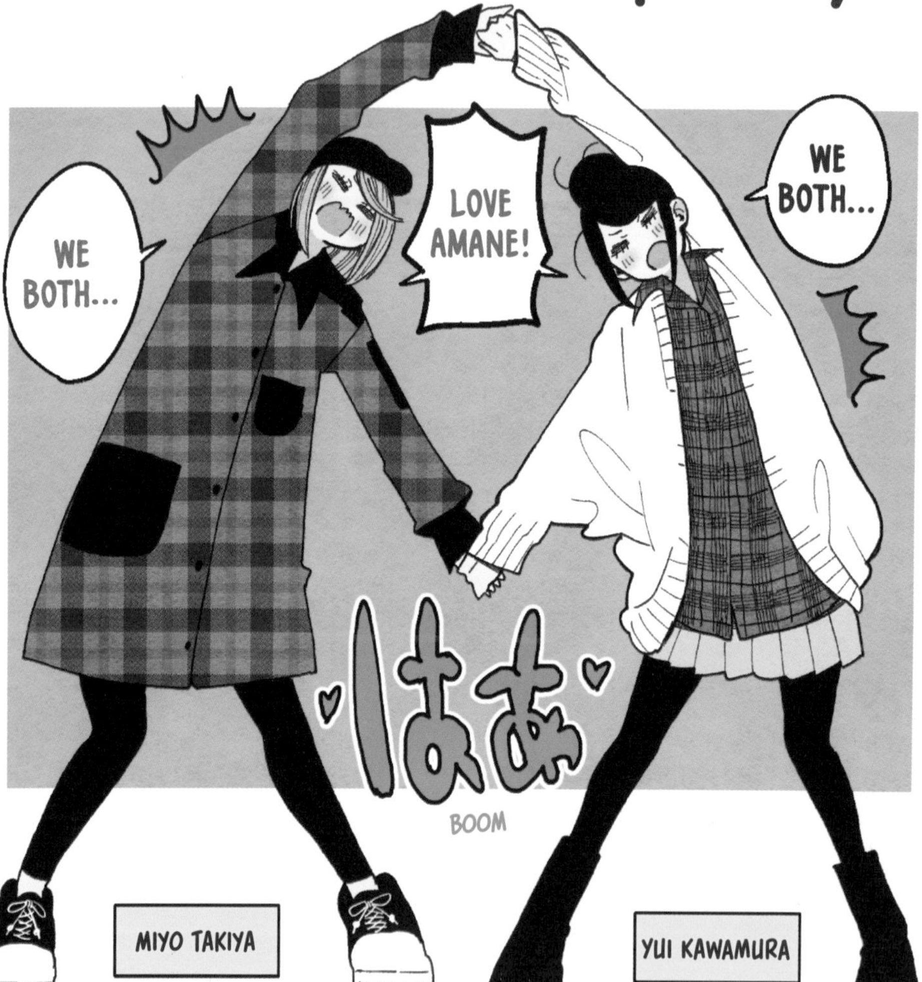
WE BOTH...
LOVE AMANE!
WE BOTH...
はぁ
BOOM
YUI KAWAMURA
MIYO TAKIYA

When You Aren't Here

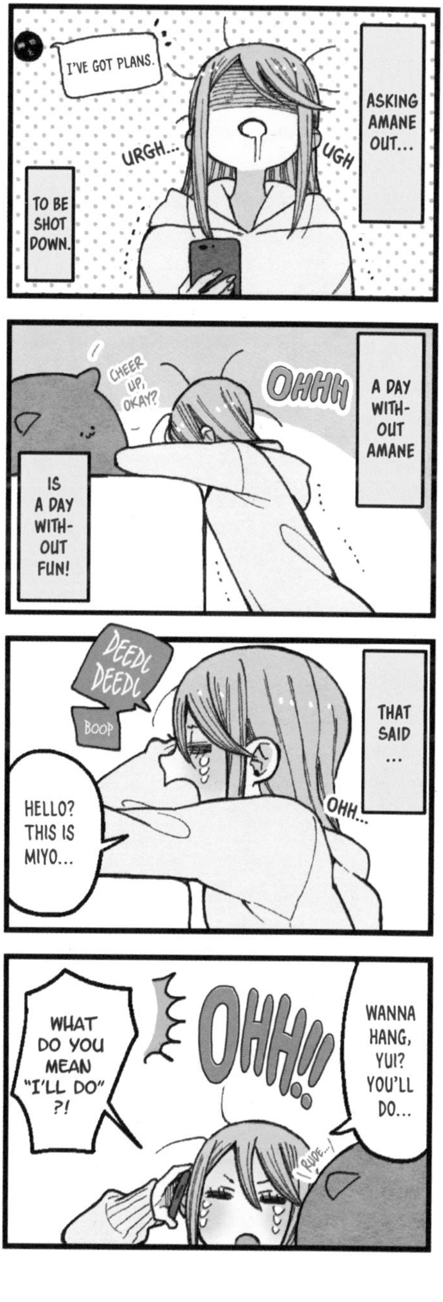
ASKING AMANE OUT...
I'VE GOT PLANS.
UGH
URGH...
TO BE SHOT DOWN.
A DAY WITH-OUT AMANE
OHHH
CHEER UP, OKAY?
IS A DAY WITH-OUT FUN!
THAT SAID ...
DEEDL DEEDL
BOOP
OHH...
HELLO? THIS IS MIYO...
WANNA HANG, YUI? YOU'LL DO...
RUDE...!
OHH!!
WHAT DO YOU MEAN "I'LL DO" ?!

Come Think About It

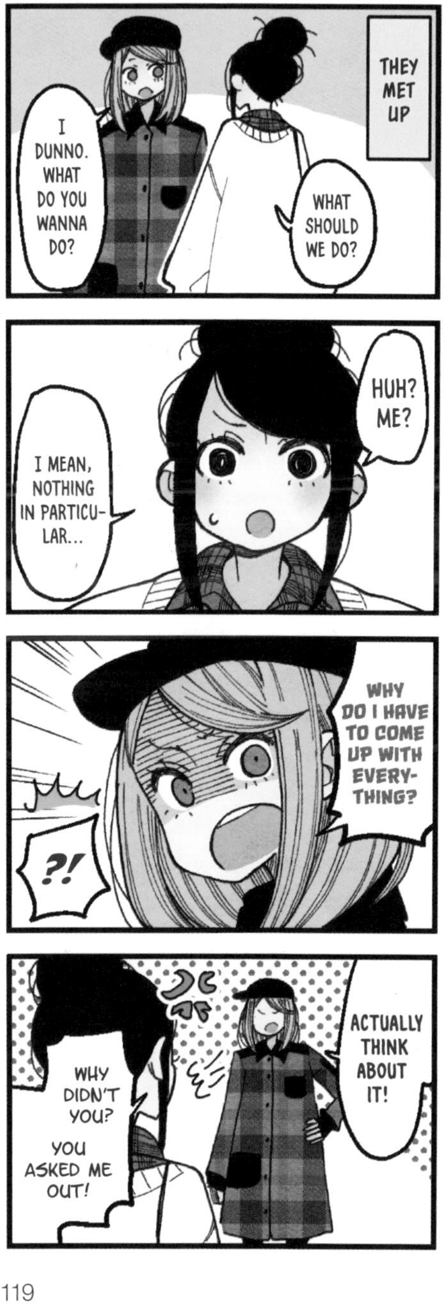
THEY MET UP
WHAT SHOULD WE DO?
I DUNNO. WHAT DO YOU WANNA DO?
HUH? ME?
I MEAN, NOTHING IN PARTICU-LAR...
WHY DO I HAVE TO COME UP WITH EVERY-THING?
?!
ACTUALLY THINK ABOUT IT!
WHY DIDN'T YOU?
YOU ASKED ME OUT!

Huh? Wait?!

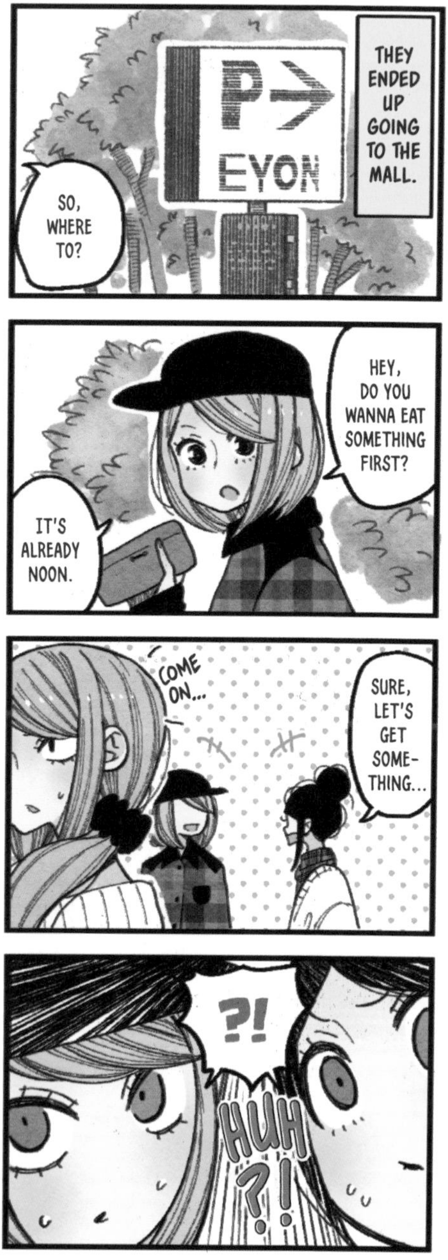
THEY ENDED UP GOING TO THE MALL.
P →
EYON
SO, WHERE TO?
HEY, DO YOU WANNA EAT SOMETHING FIRST?
IT'S ALREADY NOON.
SURE, LET'S GET SOME-THING...
COME ON...
?!
HUH?!

Getting Spotted

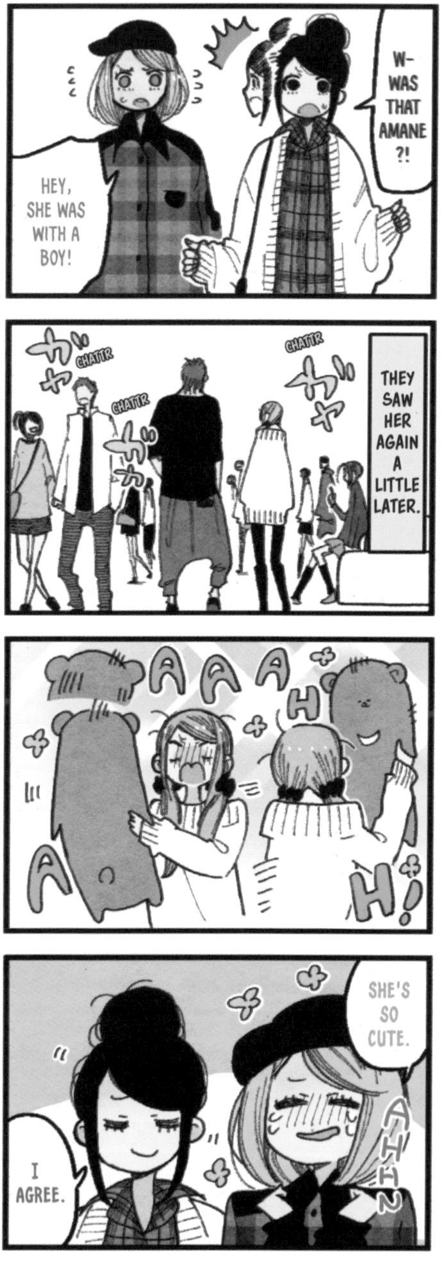
W-WAS THAT AMANE?!
HEY, SHE WAS WITH A BOY!
THEY SAW HER AGAIN A LITTLE LATER.
CHATTR
CHATTR
CHATTR
AAAAH!
SHE'S SO CUTE.
AHHHN
I AGREE.

Could He Be...

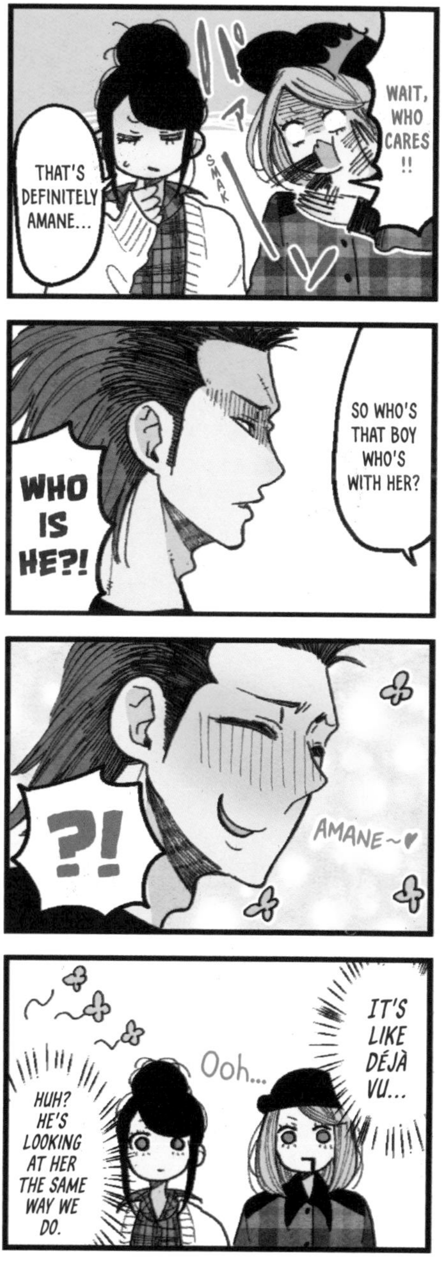

WAIT, WHO CARES!!
SMAK
THAT'S DEFINITELY AMANE...
SO WHO'S THAT BOY WHO'S WITH HER?
WHO IS HE?!
AMANE~♥
?!
IT'S LIKE DÉJÀ VU...
Ooh...
HUH? HE'S LOOKING AT HER THE SAME WAY WE DO.

There's No Way

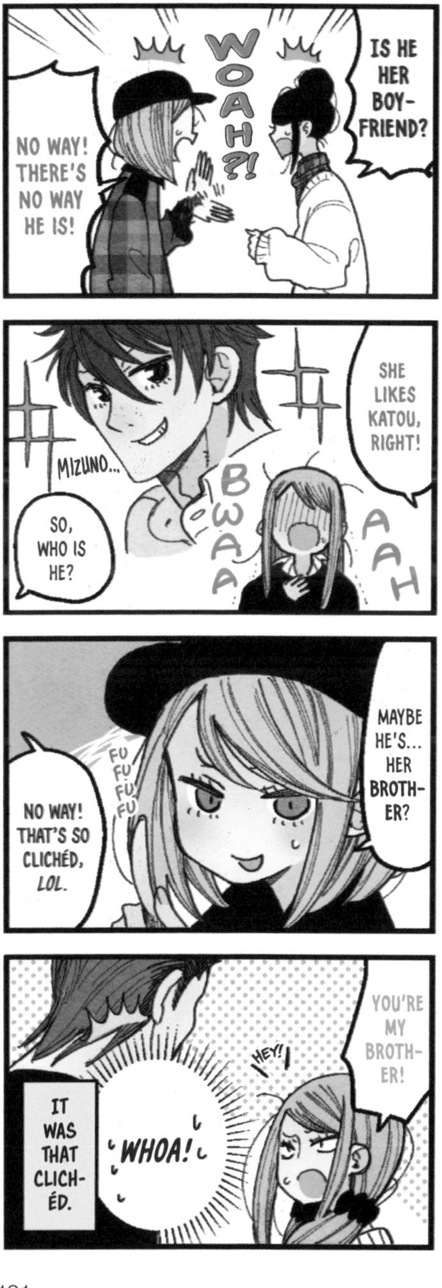

IS HE HER BOY-FRIEND?
WOAH?!
NO WAY! THERE'S NO WAY HE IS!
SHE LIKES KATOU, RIGHT!
AAH
BWAAA
MIZUNO...
SO, WHO IS HE?
MAYBE HE'S... HER BROTHER?
FU FU FU FU
NO WAY! THAT'S SO CLICHÉD, LOL.
YOU'RE MY BROTHER!
HEY!
WHOA!
IT WAS THAT CLICHÉD.

Discovered!

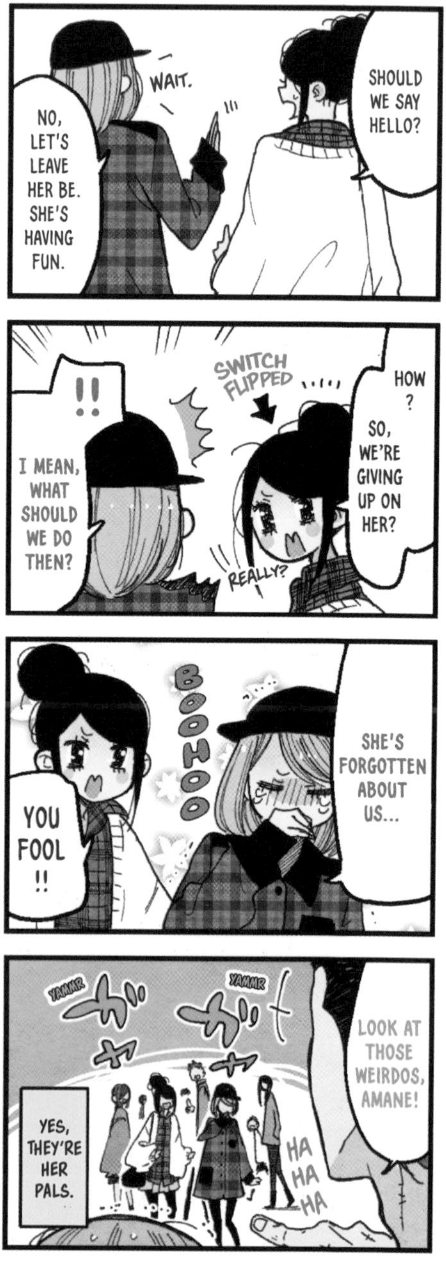
SHOULD WE SAY HELLO?
WAIT.
NO, LET'S LEAVE HER BE. SHE'S HAVING FUN.
HOW?
SO, WE'RE GIVING UP ON HER?
SWITCH FLIPPED
REALLY?
!!
I MEAN, WHAT SHOULD WE DO THEN?
SHE'S FORGOTTEN ABOUT US...
BOOHOO
YOU FOOL!!
LOOK AT THOSE WEIRDOS, AMANE!
YAMMR
YAMMR
HA HA HA
YES, THEY'RE HER PALS.

Dodging the Question!

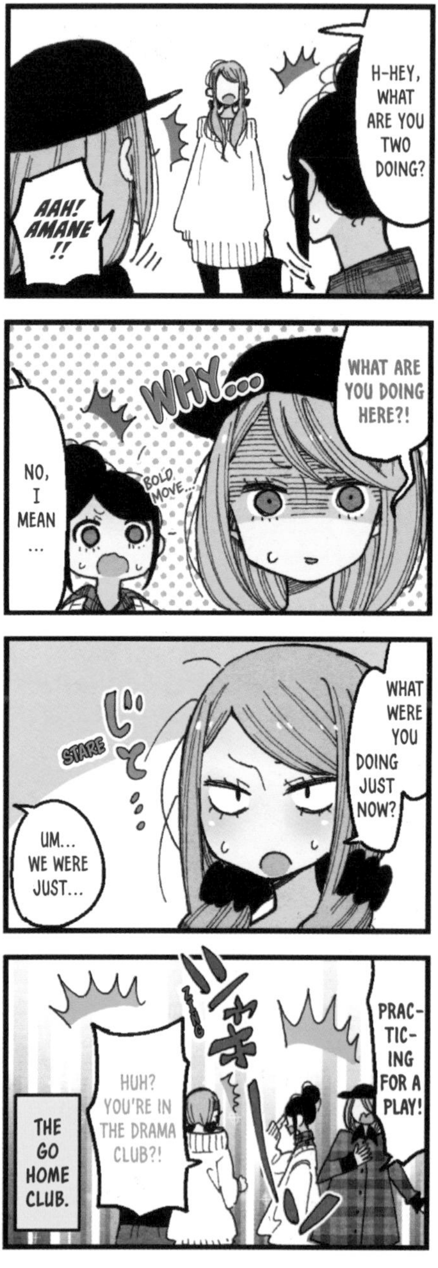
H-HEY, WHAT ARE YOU TWO DOING?
AAH! AMANE!!
WHAT ARE YOU DOING HERE?!
WHY...
BOLD MOVE...
NO, I MEAN ...
WHAT WERE YOU DOING JUST NOW?
STARE
UM... WE WERE JUST...
PRAC-TIC-ING FOR A PLAY!
HUH? YOU'RE IN THE DRAMA CLUB?!
THE GO HOME CLUB.

Please Don't Make a Fuss in the Mall

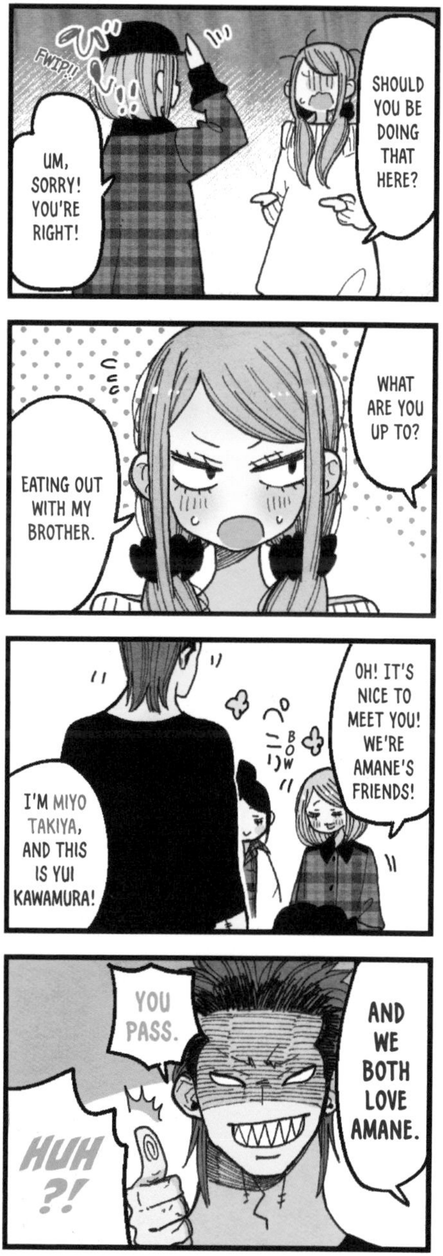

FWIP!!
SHOULD YOU BE DOING THAT HERE?
UM, SORRY! YOU'RE RIGHT!
WHAT ARE YOU UP TO?
EATING OUT WITH MY BROTHER.
OH! IT'S NICE TO MEET YOU! WE'RE AMANE'S FRIENDS!
BOW
I'M MIYO TAKIYA, AND THIS IS YUI KAWAMURA!
AND WE BOTH LOVE AMANE.
YOU PASS.
HUH ?!

Birth of the Love Squad

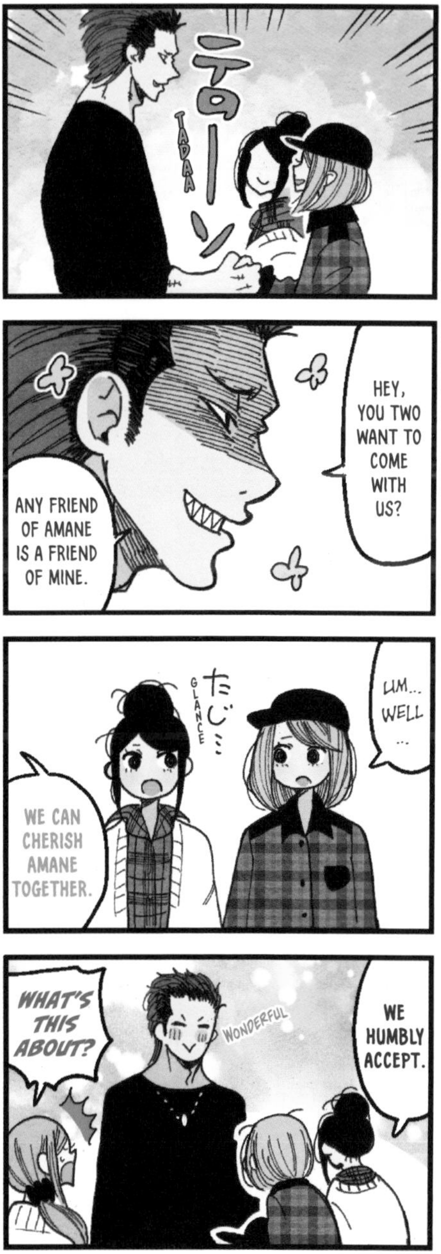

TADAA
HEY, YOU TWO WANT TO COME WITH US?
ANY FRIEND OF AMANE IS A FRIEND OF MINE.
UM... WELL...
GLANCE
WE CAN CHERISH AMANE TOGETHER.
WE HUMBLY ACCEPT.
WONDERFUL
WHAT'S THIS ABOUT?

Brother Dearest?!

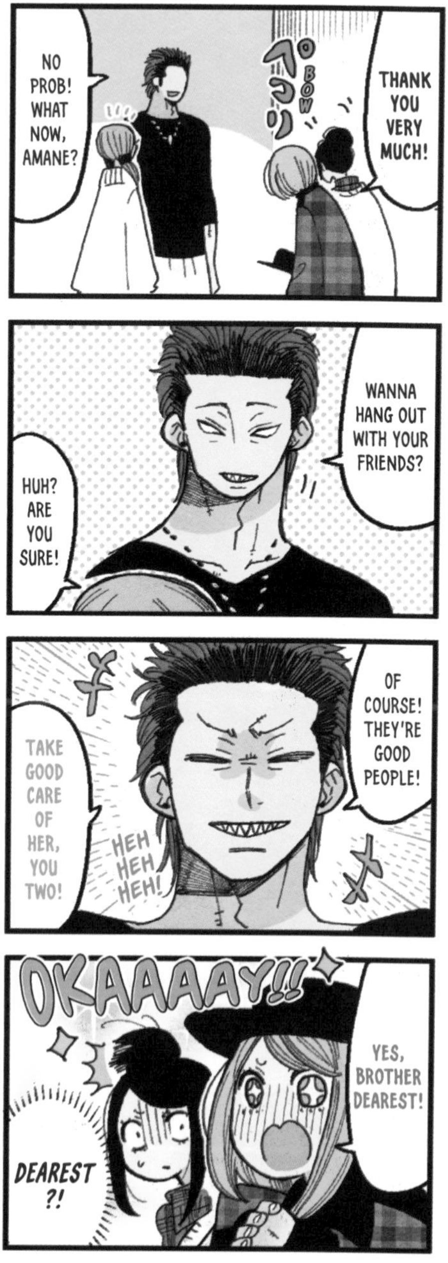
THANK YOU VERY MUCH!
BOW
NO PROB! WHAT NOW, AMANE?
WANNA HANG OUT WITH YOUR FRIENDS?
HUH? ARE YOU SURE!
OF COURSE! THEY'RE GOOD PEOPLE!
TAKE GOOD CARE OF HER, YOU TWO!
HEH HEH HEH!
OKAAAAY!!
YES, BROTHER DEAREST!
DEAREST ?!

(Brother with the) Sanpaku Eyes

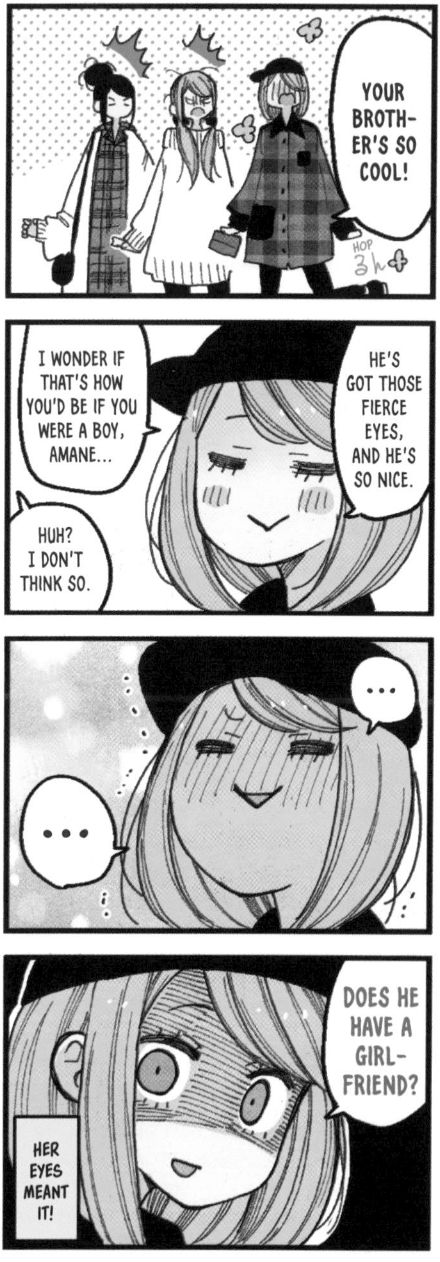
YOUR BROTHER'S SO COOL!
HOP
HE'S GOT THOSE FIERCE EYES, AND HE'S SO NICE.
I WONDER IF THAT'S HOW YOU'D BE IF YOU WERE A BOY, AMANE...
HUH? I DON'T THINK SO.
...
...
DOES HE HAVE A GIRLFRIEND?
HER EYES MEANT IT!

Predator

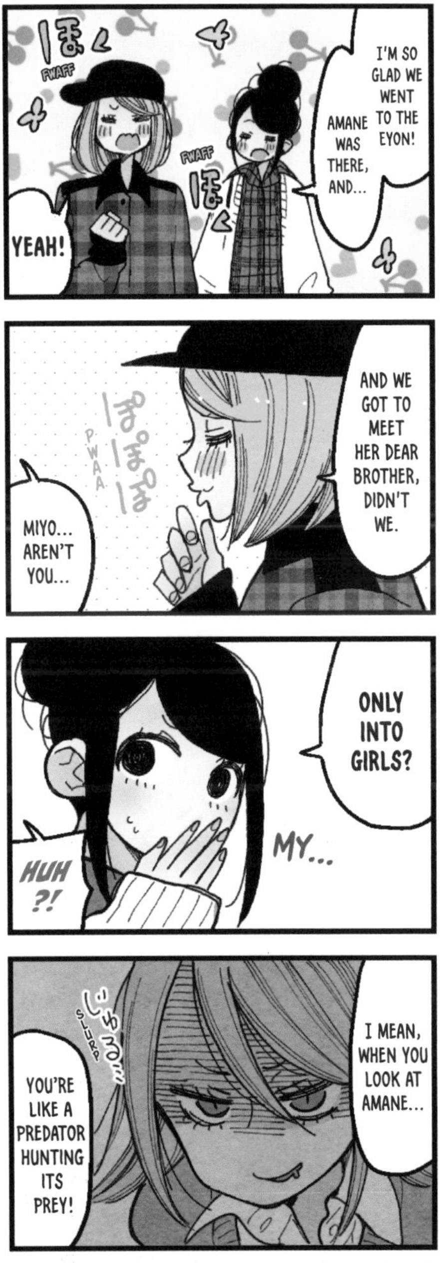
I'M SO GLAD WE WENT TO THE EYON!
AMANE WAS THERE, AND...
FWAFF
FWAFF
YEAH!
AND WE GOT TO MEET HER DEAR BROTHER, DIDN'T WE.
P-WAA
MIYO... AREN'T YOU...
ONLY INTO GIRLS?
MY...
HUH?!
I MEAN, WHEN YOU LOOK AT AMANE...
SLURP
YOU'RE LIKE A PREDATOR HUNTING ITS PREY!

She is Serious!!

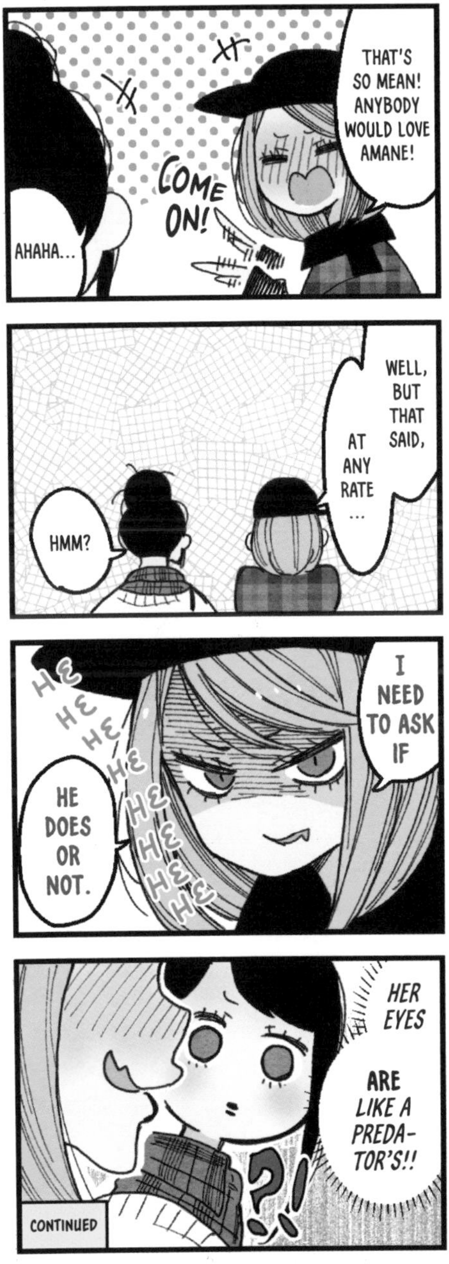
THAT'S SO MEAN! ANYBODY WOULD LOVE AMANE!
COME ON!
AHAHA...
WELL, BUT THAT SAID,
AT ANY RATE...
HMM?
I NEED TO ASK IF
HE HE HE HE HE HE HE HE HE
HE DOES OR NOT.
HER EYES
ARE LIKE A PREDATOR'S!!
CONTINUED

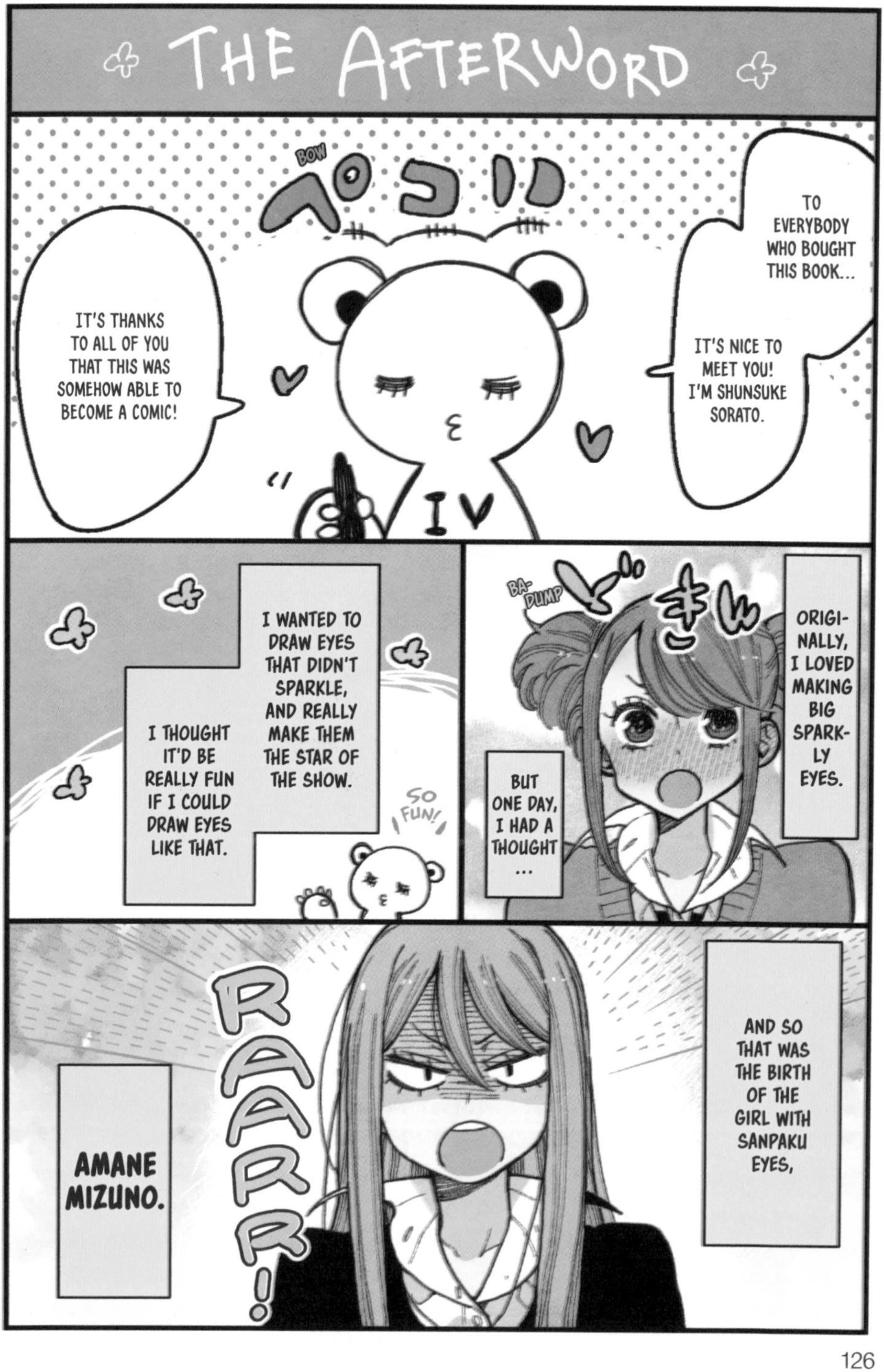
THE AFTERWORD
TO EVERYBODY WHO BOUGHT THIS BOOK...
IT'S NICE TO MEET YOU! I'M SHUNSUKE SORATO.
BOW
IT'S THANKS TO ALL OF YOU THAT THIS WAS SOMEHOW ABLE TO BECOME A COMIC!
ORIGI-NALLY, I LOVED MAKING BIG SPARK-LY EYES.
BA-DUMP
BUT ONE DAY, I HAD A THOUGHT...
I WANTED TO DRAW EYES THAT DIDN'T SPARKLE, AND REALLY MAKE THEM THE STAR OF THE SHOW.
I THOUGHT IT'D BE REALLY FUN IF I COULD DRAW EYES LIKE THAT.
SO FUN!
AND SO THAT WAS THE BIRTH OF THE GIRL WITH SANPAKU EYES,
RAARR!
AMANE MIZUNO.

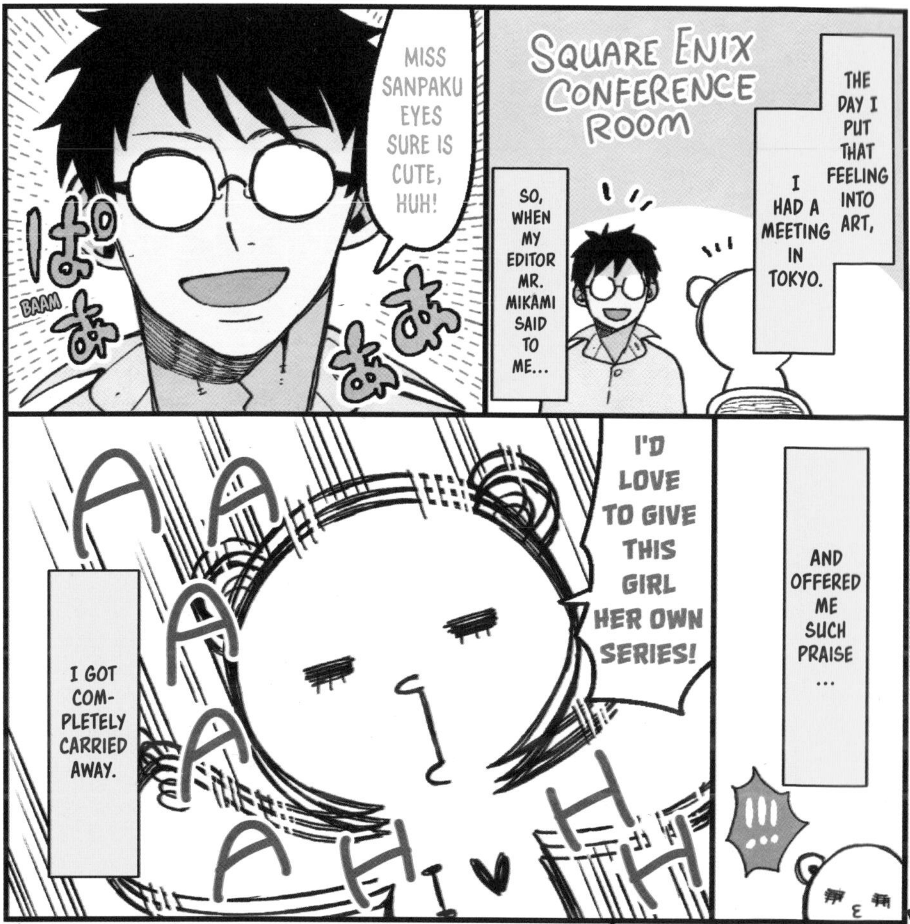
SQUARE ENIX CONFERENCE ROOM
THE DAY I PUT THAT FEELING INTO ART,
I HAD A MEETING IN TOKYO.
SO, WHEN MY EDITOR MR. MIKAMI SAID TO ME...
MISS SANPAKU EYES SURE IS CUTE, HUH!
BAAM
AND OFFERED ME SUCH PRAISE...
!!!
I'D LOVE TO GIVE THIS GIRL HER OWN SERIES!
AAAAAAHHH
I GOT COMPLETELY CARRIED AWAY.

^SO UNCOOL! (EDITOR)

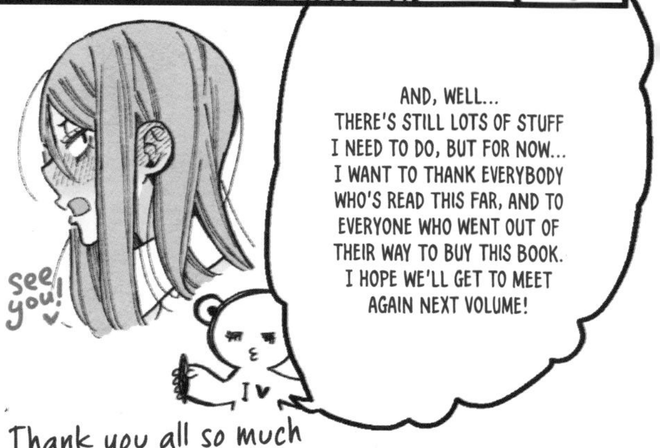
AND, WELL...
THERE'S STILL LOTS OF STUFF I NEED TO DO, BUT FOR NOW... I WANT TO THANK EVERYBODY WHO'S READ THIS FAR, AND TO EVERYONE WHO WENT OUT OF THEIR WAY TO BUY THIS BOOK. I HOPE WE'LL GET TO MEET AGAIN NEXT VOLUME!
see you!

SEND YOUR LETTERS OF ENCOURAGEMENT TO SORATO!

FAN LETTER ADDRESS

SQUARE ENIX
GANGAN PIXIV EDITORIAL DEPT.
C/O SHUNSUKE SORATO
6-27-30 SHINJUKU
SHINJUKU EAST SIDE SQUARE 2F
SHINJUKU, TOKYO 160-8430
JAPAN

WE CAN'T WAIT FOR YOUR LETTERS!

Thank you all so much for the health and happiness that you've brought me.

そらと
SORATO

Volume 1

Translator: David Goldberg
Proofreading: Patrick Sutton
Production: Glen Isip
Nicole Dochych

SANPAKUGAN-CHAN WA TSUTAETAI. volume 1
©2020 Shunsuke Sorato/SQUARE ENIX CO., LTD.
First published in Japan in 2018 by SQUARE ENIX CO., LTD. Tokyo
English translation rights arranged with SQUARE ENIX CO., LTD. and
DENPA, LLC. through Tuttle-Mori Agency, Inc.
Published in English by DENPA, LLC., Portland, Oregon 2020

Originally published in Japanese as *Sanpakugan-chan wa Tsutaetai*.
by SQUARE ENIX CO., LTD. 2018
The Girl with the Sanpaku Eyes vol. 1 originally serialized in
GANGAN Pixiv Oct. 2018 - Feb 2019 by SQUARE ENIX CO., LTD.

This is a work of fiction.

ISBN-13: 978-1-63442-958-0
Library of Congress Control Number: 2020940856
Printed in the USA

Third Edition published March 2022.

Denpa, LLC.
625 NW 17th Ave
Portland, OR 97209
www.denpa.pub